# FROM PAGE TO PLACE

# From Page to Place

## *American Literary Tourism and the Afterlives of Authors*

Edited by
JENNIFER HARRIS
and
HILARY IRIS LOWE

University of Massachusetts Press
*Amherst and Boston*

Printed in the United States of America

ISBN 978-1-62534-233-1 (paper); 232-4 (cloth)

Designed by Jack Harrison
Set in Adobe Garamond Pro with Monotype Bell display
Printed and bound by The Maple-Vail Book Manufacturing Group

Cover design by Jack Harrison
Cover art: John Muir National Historic Site, photograph by Hilary Iris Lowe.

Library of Congress Cataloging-in-Publication Data
Names: Harris, Jennifer, 1971– editor. | Lowe, Hilary Iris.
Title: From page to place : American literary tourism and the afterlives of authors / edited by Jennifer Harris and Hilary Iris Lowe.
Description: Amherst : University of Massachusetts Press, 2017. | Includes bibliographical references and index.
Identifiers: LCCN 2016041703| ISBN 9781625342331 (pbk. : alk. paper) | ISBN 9781625342324 (hardcover : alk. paper)
Subjects: LCSH: Literary landmarks—United States. | Authors, American—Home and haunts—United States. | United States—Intellectual life.
Classification: LCC PS141 .F76 2017 | DDC 810.9—dc23
LC record available at https://lccn.loc.gov/2016041703

British Library Cataloguing-in-Publication Data
A catalog record for this book is available from the British Library.

# *Contents*

# *Acknowledgments*

It is impossible to thank all of those who should be acknowledged along the path that each contributor took to his or her contribution here. As editors, we feel an excess of gratitude toward our contributors, who traveled with us on this long journey. We came together as a result of Jennifer Harris's work to organize a panel on American literary tourism for the Northeast Modern Language Association in 2011, sponsored by the Canadian Association for American Studies. The response to her call for papers was so enthusiastic (as was a response to an earlier panel at the American Studies Association in 2007) that we had already decided to put together a collection before we ever met in person. That NeMLA panel introduced us to two early contributors to this collection, Mara Scanlon and Susann Bishop.

We count ourselves incredibly lucky to have found Brian Halley as our supportive editor at the University of Massachusetts Press. Carol Betsch and Karen Fisk at the press also deserve warm and enthusiastic recognition. Andrew Lopez has been our indexer and is a fellow literary tourist.

Since we began work on *From Page to Place,* we have each changed jobs, moved, expanded our families, and called upon the generous resources of a number of institutions and individuals along the way. We are indebted to numerous colleagues. Among them at Temple University are Douglass Greenfield, David Watt, Laura Levitt, and Kate Henry, who were willing to talk about literary tourism and literary material culture for hours; at the University of Kansas, Cheryl Lester, Karl Janssen, and Susan K. Harris were longtime champions; at Mount Allison University, Janine Rogers and Peter Brown were particularly supportive. We also benefited from the grace and insights of Charles Baraw in ways for which we are forever grateful.

There is a long list of literary institutions discussed here whose docents, curators, volunteers, and archivists have contributed to our thinking as we put together this collection. Many thanks are due to the staff and former staff at Edith Wharton's home The Mount, the Harriet Beecher Stowe Center, the Mark Twain House and Museum, the Emily Dickinson Museum, the House of the Seven Gables, the Longfellow House–Washington's Headquarters National Historic Site, the Elmira College Center for Mark Twain Studies, the Constitution Island Association, the Rosenbach Museum and Library, the Joseph Lloyd Manor, the Henry Lloyd Manor House, Washington Irving's Sunnyside, the Walden Pond State Reservation, the Concord Museum, Thoreau Farm, the Walt Whitman House, the Library of Congress, the Laura Ingalls Wilder Historic Home and Museum, and more. Debts are always owed to the librarians and interlibrary loan staff whose ability to track materials enriched many a piece in this collection.

In addition to personal debts, we must acknowledge financial ones. Jennifer Harris benefited from the SSHRC Aid to Small University grant program, as well as Mount Allison University's CultureWorks.

We would be terribly remiss not to thank our families, who have suffered years of literary tourism torment and travel all in good spirits. Daniel Vogel and Seth Bruggeman are the best tourists we know, and they've looked favorably at our initiation of that next generation of critical literary tourists: Emil, Juniata, and Teleene.

# FROM PAGE TO PLACE

# *Introduction*

JENNIFER HARRIS and
HILARY IRIS LOWE

There's nothing particularly American about literary tourism. People have been doing it for at least five centuries: haunting the house of Petrarch; tracing the journeys of Pablo Neruda; sketching, photographing, and now Instagramming the homes of Edgar Allan Poe. Yet as Americans have practiced literary tourism, it is undeniably and defiantly American, reflecting the emotional, philosophical, intellectual, anti-intellectual, and national themes, anxieties, and desires of their cultural moments. While what America reads—as reflected by school curriculum, best-seller lists, and canonical formations—may give us a certain insight into understanding Americans' relationships with reading and literature, where people travel, or what sites are memorialized, is even more revealing. After all, if it was simply a matter of reading words on pages, why would there be competing claims for Mark Twain's birth site? Who would travel to Piru, California, to see sites associated with Helen Hunt Jackson's *Ramona*? Would anyone care about the fate of an old house on Constitution Island, where the Warner sisters lived in isolation, or a nondescript brownstone row house in New York, the Harlem Renaissance residence of Langston Hughes? Would discovering Zora Neale Hurston's grave be the subject of a groundbreaking feminist essay?[1] Considering these sites and residences as they function as tourist destinations—even unofficial ones—has the potential to tell us a great deal about how Americans think about their own literary history and their relation to it.

The essays in this volume assert that there is much to be learned from the study of American literary tourism. In particular, through a variety of methodological approaches, the contributors draw back the curtain on different sites and spaces as a means of critically interrogating the origins, evolution, operations, and future of American literary tourism and its sites, from the well-known Walden Pond to the endangered home of Susan Warner on Constitution Island, New York. We demonstrate that the study of American literary tourism provides a window on American cultural production, whether personal, regional, or national, or some combination thereof. These productions can be singular efforts or collaborative ones between the author, preservationist, curator, docent, reader, and tourist. Complicating this is the fact that every site is in some way implicated in the relationship between profit and nonprofit, preservation and entertainment, verisimilitude and fantasy, and competing narratives of history. Therefore it is not surprising that meaning at such sites may not be stable, the sites themselves functioning alternately or simultaneously as markers of community, memorials, conduits, exemplars, and training grounds in ways authors themselves surely never imagined. Writing of birthplace monuments in the United States, historian Seth C. Bruggeman suggests they often "tell us much more about the people who sponsor them than the people, places, and events they commemorate."[2]

Likewise, sites of literary tourism have the ability to both celebrate literary figures and tell us about the kinds of narratives that have historically been valued in the United States, and by whom. For just as each site has its own history, tied to a particular time period, region, author or authors, and specific works, each of these factors influences the types of people who are most likely to visit a site. These visitors remind us that books are not static or dead. Together we can see, if not through the kind of detailed engagement that we have collected here then through continued popular interest, that literature is alive. Moreover, its deployment or interpretation is not simply the purview of literary scholars. Indeed, as long as books are brought to life through the process of reading, readers will inevitably stake their claims and desires in ways not necessarily anticipated by authors or bounded by the text itself. In this way, American literary tourism is in part a study of the afterlives of authors and books, their meaning, circulation, symbolism, and value, far beyond the page. Ultimately these afterlives are what undergird each and every American literary tourism site.

Obviously, contemporary American literary tourists are not operating in isolation, or even contained by their own shores and borders. In some cases they are participating in contemporary international movements, as when children queue up at Platform 9¾ at King's Cross railway station, re-creating Harry Potter's travels to Hogwarts, or when adults sign up for the *Angels and Demons* treasure hunt tour of Rome, marking Dan Brown's novel. Each is an effort to inhabit the world of an engrossing or beloved book. In other cases, tourists make deliberate pilgrimages to the sites affiliated with authors themselves: a visit to the grave of Oscar Wilde (conveniently located in the famous Père Lachaise Cemetery in Paris, alongside Balzac, Proust, and others); a tromp around the Lake District of Wordsworth and Coleridge; a hike along Thomas Hardy Way; or a quick wade into Thoreau's Walden Pond. At the opposite end of the pilgrimage spectrum, no doubt many an American tourist who loathed Shakespeare in high school has found himself or herself at the Bard's birthplace, turning over a souvenir at shops with names like Much Ado about Toys, or Falstaff's Antiques. What we learn from these international encounters is that literary tourism is not always bounded by the national. In *The Literary Tourist,* Nicola J. Watson attributes the "readerly impulse to locate author and text within real places [to] the extended nineteenth century's love affair with biography and with realist fiction."[3]

It seems apparent, however, that this is not the sole motivation: the desire to travel to literary sites might also be rooted in popular culture, voyeurism, a sense of cultural obligation, a reverence for history, an impulse toward nostalgia, or a genuinely felt connection with an author or her characters. It should come as no surprise that there might be a desire to then materialize that experience through visiting related sites. Moreover, people have long used literature as a means of escape or of discovering worlds outside their own. With the rise of inexpensive travel, the literary escape can now become a physical one, as more readers have the means to become tourists. Such visits can take radically varied shapes over time, from a reverential early nineteenth-century trip to Westminster Abbey's Poets' Corner, to a drunken nightclub tour through 1920s Harlem following a reading of Carl Van Vechten, to a sentimental visit to the landscape of one's most treasured childhood book.[4] And with the advent of the Internet, as Mara Scanlon reminds us in her contribution to this volume, we might not even leave our sofas, relying on a wireless connection and to get us to the literary destinations we crave.

Admittedly, authors and texts often inspire vastly different audiences. To return to the context of the United States, the majority of those Americans who buy a ticket for a tour of Mark Twain's Hartford, Connecticut, house don't walk two minutes across the lawn to the home of Harriet Beecher Stowe next door, and it would be surprising if visitors to either regularly ask for directions to the site of the home of their neighbor and contemporary, author Charles Dudley Warner. Despite their willingness to travel to scattered sites associated with *Little House on the Prairie,* as documented in this volume by Michelle McClellan, it seems unlikely that most card-carrying members of the Laura Ingalls Wilder Fan Club (known as Bonnetheads) have been to the Florida home of Ernest Hemingway. Those who plan trips to the Alex Haley Museum and Interpretive Center, which foregrounds Haley's novel *Roots,* probably have little interest in attending Minnesota's Deep Valley Homecoming, a nostalgic celebration of Maud Hart Lovelace's

*Betsy-Tacy* children's books. And, as contributor Rebecca Rego Barry demonstrates, few if any of these people are clamoring for access to Constitution Island, where Susan Warner penned the nineteenth-century best seller *The Wide, Wide World.* Even if there is overlap between sites, there is no guarantee that literary tourists witness or interpret the sites or activities in the same way. If America's reading habits differ to some degree according to age, race, gender, and class, it makes sense that tourism based on that reading—not to mention any interpretation of the sites or associated events—would reflect similar divergences and commonalities. According to cultural critics and scholars John Urry and Jonas Larsen: "There are many ways of gazing within tourism, and tourists look at 'difference' differently. This is in part because tourist gazes are structured according to class, gender, ethnicity and age."[5] As Jennifer Harris notes in her chapter on the enslaved African American writer Jupiter Hammon, there is still much work to be done at sites that default to a white Euro-American perspective, in terms of both curatorial work and the way the subjects are interpreted.

Just as the identity of the author and his or her subject matter is integral to the site's tourism potential, so is the associated geography and history. Notably, different literary settings and landscapes shape visitors' expectations of experience in profoundly divergent ways. Pilgrims to Henry David Thoreau's Walden Pond enter that space through the text, just as visitors to Poe's Baltimore house interpret the site though their awareness of his life. It is impossible to visit Booker T. Washington's birthplace without reflecting on his rise "up from slavery"—and the lives of those who lacked that opportunity. And then there are readers whose understandings of texts and the sites related to them are shaped by their own diverse experiences, worldviews, and values. There are literary scholars seeking insight into their scholarly subject; religious home-schooling families who embrace Wilder and Lovelace and plan educational trips with their children; those who were once dubbed hippies who still look to Thoreau for guidance; and book clubbers who take an afternoon tour of Philadelphia's Woodlands after reading Elizabeth Gilbert's best-selling novel *The Signature of All Things* to find the nineteenth-century models for its setting. As Klara-Stephanie Szlezák observes in this volume, literary tourists reflect deeply individuated, and sometimes social, connections to and uses of texts that likely differ in crucially important ways from those of the ticket buyers in line next to them. There are as many kinds of literary tourists as there are sites, books, and interpretations. In some ways, the physical practice of literary tourism is one of the only constants in our attempts to understand relationships between readers, authors, and the places that commemorate writers and their works.

Though Americans are often tourists on the world stage, it is clear that when Americans understand themselves as literary tourists within their own borders—or, in the case of international sites associated with sometime expatriates like Hemingway, as visitors to sites inhabited by Americans—there is usually something more involved than mere entertainment or a connection to a single author or his work. Even as cultural tourism abroad might attract those who are simply taking advantage of local opportunities during a vacation, for Americans, American literary tourism isn't generally perceived as lighthearted "fun" in the same way a visit to a local cultural festival might be.[6] In their study of how Americans use history, Roy Rosenzweig and David Thelan find "many people . . . make quite deliberate trips—even pilgrimages—to specific sites and museums in order to honor a particular history, to instill patriotism in their children, to understand current problems, or to retreat from the present by visiting the past."[7] While all literary tourism might be seen as a way of staking a claim to an author or her work, national literary tourism adds the layer of a shared heritage to this intellectual, cultural, or emotional ownership, and—in some cases—is a patriotic exercise of the American narrative itself. After all, many tourists have likely not read much of the work of those celebrated authors. In such cases, theirs is not just an assertion of ownership over a writer or her work; it is perhaps the act of staking a claim to where the tourist and writer both fit within the broader national narratives of inclusion. These narratives unite them, tying them to the same place, ideals, and sentiments—to that imagined community that simultaneously excludes and knits together a people.[8]

Granted, there are also far more mundane reasons for literary tourism. To paraphrase a comment made to one of the authors by an architect touring the Hartford home of Mark Twain, "I wanted to see how he did the billiards room; I've got a client who's a Twain fan who's interested." Ignoring that the billiards room was actually Twain's writing space, the client nevertheless articulated a connection with the author and what he stands for in the American imaginary. A visitor to the House of the Seven Gables confessed to buying a ticket for the tour simply because it was one of the more famous tourist attractions in Salem, and his family had "already seen all the witch sites." It seems doubtful that his sense of patriotism was fueled by either the persecution of those deemed witches or the tight squeeze up the "secret" staircase of the gabled house. The tension between tourism as entertainment and tourism as preservation or high culture is clear. Some literary tourism sites are self-consciously a matter of entertainment rather than preservation. Tourists flock to the sites associated with L. Frank Baum's *Wonderful Wizard of Oz,* or the fictional Tom Sawyer and Anne of Green Gables, as well as the theme park experience of "The Wizarding World of Harry Potter" at Universal Studios in Orlando, Florida.[9] Capitalizing on the power of associative connections, these sites attempt to meet the desire to bring a work to life, whether through visiting the fictional Ramona's wedding site, or witnessing a fence-painting competition during a "Tom Sawyer Days" festival. The belief that experiencing the actual environment, or—in the instances just mentioned—completely fabricated environments, might facilitate an intimate connection with literature ignores the reality that all experiences of literacy tourism, even when historic preservation is involved, are inevitably mediated by the managers and designers of these sites. After all, even Walden Pond has a parking lot.

In some cases mediation is desirable; tourists want to see Alcott's desk looking as if she were in the midst of composing their favorite work or an intimate epistle. The accumulation of clutter in Twain's study conveys a verisimilitude, even if it is a carefully calculated reproduction based on period photos. Indeed, almost all sites that coincide with the place where an adult author worked and wrote attempt to preserve the fiction that the author has just popped out for a spot of tea, a cigar, or a stroll, and will soon return to his desk. Such stagings play into what Robert Thompson, in a discussion of historic homes, describes as a belief that "art and personality and greatness is created in physical space. If we can see those physical spaces and the context in which things were happening, those can give us important insights into people when they were at their peak."[10]

In this volume Caroline Hellman documents how such beliefs undergirded the decision at The Mount, the home of Edith Wharton, to raise a considerable sum for the acquisition of Wharton's library. The home is more complete, Hellman argues, because of this purchase, and by extension, our understanding of Wharton is enhanced by seeing her books—exuding both material and symbolic value—in place. The cultural historian Harald Hendrix makes an even more explicit argument for the relevance of authors' homes, symbolic and physical: "Writers' houses have meaning, even beyond their obvious documentary value as elements in the author's biography. They are a medium of expression and of remembrance. Planning, building and decorating a house provides a writer the opportunity not only to materialize his architectural fantasies and fictions, but also to experiment with a mode of expression fundamentally different from his own."[11] Authors themselves are not immune to the belief that spaces might be integral to their art. Ellen Glasgow wrote of the Richmond, Virginia, home where she composed all but one of her books: "The many tragedies of my life, and a fair measure at least of the happiness, have come to me in this house. The fibers of my personality are interwoven, I feel, with some indestructible element of the place; and this element is superior to time and chance, as well as to the material substance of brick and mortar."[12]

Such statements are marketing gold; certainly most published guides to authors' homes are premised upon the connection between domestic spaces and artistic production. The question is: Does it matter if these insights Thompson describes are false, a conglomeration of preservation, celebrity, nostalgia, historic interpretation, and sentimentality? If it is true, as Urry and Larsen have put it, that "much of what is appreciated [by tourists] is not directly experienced reality but representations, particularly through the medium of photography. . . . And even when the object fails to live up to its representation, it is the latter which will stay in people's minds, as what they have really 'seen,' "[13] then in the case of literary tourism, is the experience of the site secondary to the perception that one has gained a deepened connection to a literary work or its author? To put it another way, is what the traveler really seeks insight into the author or his works, or is it something else? Perhaps it is a *Wizard of Oz*–type search for affirmation and home, or a deepening of our already existing beliefs in what was there all along—whether those beliefs stem from our personal connections or preexisting narratives of how to respond appropriately to a cultural site or artifact.

Perhaps that affirmation is precisely what some cultural tourists seek. Recent literary tourists—schooled in postmodern reflections on mediated experience—have tackled this question in their published accounts with varying conclusions. Many of our contributors respond to Anne Trubek's book *A Skeptic's Guide to Writers' Houses.* Trubek, like scores of others who note a dip in visitorship to historic sites across the country, dares to ask: Do we really need another literary house museum?[14] It seems our answer is a somewhat qualified yes. The insights gathered from our attempts to unpack the places and practices of literary tourism tell us a great deal about how carefully constructed and maintained places themselves construct connections between reader-citizens and the past. For instance, the children's author Wendy McClure documents her travels to *Little House on the Prairie* sites (alongside experiments with recipes and sunbonnets) in a book for adults, *The Wilder Life: My Adventures in the Lost World of "Little House on the Prairie,"* and acknowledges that in the end, her obsession with Laura Ingalls Wilder was about something else—a way to ground herself in something meaningful and escapist and real all at once, following her mother's death.[15] This does not make her engagement with the works or the sites associated with them any less rewarding or profound for McClure; if anything, it enriches her experience by giving it additional resonance. Readers' relationships—like McClure's—to both fictional characters and their authors have a long history.

## *The Origins of Literary Tourism*

Literary tourism, alongside cultural tourism and heritage tourism, has its roots in the once popular phenomenon of the Grand Tour.[16] Undertaken primarily by privileged young British men from the mid-seventeenth century through the early nineteenth century, it was intended to provide polish, breadth, and culture beyond what might be acquired at university. Replacing the medieval religious pilgrimage with the educational tour, by the eighteenth century it was "synonymous with artistic concerns."[17] The length of the Grand Tour could be anywhere from six months to several years, and while the itinerary might vary, there was a general script, which usually included Paris and the principal Italian cities.[18] The pretense to education, and the refinement of one's taste, theoretically elevated the Grand Tour participant above the supposedly crass thrill seeker—even if there was more overlap than participants might wish to acknowledge. Jennifer Craik, a scholar of cultural tourism, differentiates between tourists for whom cultural experience is the primary motivation for travel and those for whom it is secondary (meaning they access cultural resources because these are convenient). For those undertaking the Grand Tour it might be certainly be both; they might acquire the distinction of the experience as a means to an end, even if less interested in visiting sites of art and culture.[19] Many travelers found themselves visiting literary sites and writing about them in letters and diaries and occasionally in memoirs and guidebooks. These published and unpublished accounts served not only as attestations to their own taste and worldliness but also, significantly, as interpretive road maps for other would-be travelers. In *The Tourist Gaze 3.0,* Urry and Larsen write: "Gazing at particular sights is conditioned by personal experiences and memories and framed by rules and styles as well as by circulating images and texts of this and other places. Such 'frames' are critical resources, techniques, cultural lenses that potentially enable tourists to see the physical forms and material spaces before their eyes as 'interesting, good, or beautiful.' They are not the property of mere sight. And without these lenses the beautiful order found in nature or the built world would be very different."[20]

In this way, appropriate responses are often modeled even before visitors encounter tourist sites.[21] Moreover, in the case of the Grand Tour, those positioned as experts were not necessarily local informants or cultural guides, but rather arbiters of taste from the home country. By the time North Americans entered into the tradition of the Grand Tour in the late eighteenth and the long nineteenth centuries, the contours of connoisseurship had been mapped and remapped by over a hundred years of travel writings which appeared in book form, periodicals, and elsewhere. The Grand Tour was by this time manifest physically in the museums of Britain and the architecture and decoration of the homes of its aristocracy. American tourists often embraced British values and ways of seeing both Europe and Britain itself, taking up an established itinerary of nationalist cultural and literary tourism.[22]

Not surprisingly, nineteenth-century Americans became active consumers of British literary tourism, participating in and sometimes leading the veneration of England's literary heritage.[23] Yet the first literary tourists on United States soil may have predated the American embrace of British cultural norms, motivated instead by their own emotional engagement with the earliest American novels. It seems likely that American literary tourism really began with visits to the graves associated with the tragic heroines of best-selling late eighteenth-century seduction novels like Susanna Rowson's *Charlotte Temple* (1794) and Hannah Webster Foster's *The Coquette* (1797). While Charlotte Temple's Manhattan grave is patently a fiction—as was the novel—the Danvers, Massachusetts, grave of Elizabeth Whitman (Eliza Wharton's nonfictional correlative from *The Coquette*) was decidedly real. The well-known eighteenth-century Connecticut scandal inspired Foster, and then her readers. Individuals who felt moved by the novel traveled to Whitman's grave well into the nineteenth century, slowly chipping away pieces of the tombstone as souvenirs until only the last line of the inscription remained: "and the tears of strangers watered her grave."[24] These early iterations of literary tourism—if we recognize them as such—may have been motivated by a belief in the veracity of the text, or at the very least a *desire* to believe that such texts were true. In this formulation, the craft or innovation of the author was of less concern to the reader than the emotional response the text initiated.

Reflecting the new nation's disregard for its own writers of fiction, the authors of these early novels cannot claim the same renown as their heroines: their graves did not appear in nineteenth-century travel guides; their houses were not destinations; and the wave of historic preservation that swept the nation in the late nineteenth century missed them entirely.[25] Perhaps a better question, then, is when did Americans become self-conscious literary tourists, touring for the sake of encountering American authors, as opposed to undertaking travel as a conduit to connections with sympathetic heroines? When did American authors become celebrities? In chapter 10, "The Allure of American Authors' Homes: Surveying Nineteenth- and Twentieth-Century Literary Guides," Susann Bishop considers the proliferation of American tourist guides in the nineteenth century, locating such an impetus in the travel writings of authors themselves. In chapter 2, "'Step forth and again take up its magic pen': The Author's House as Informal Memorial," on the home of Washington Irving, Erin Hazard demonstrates how the experiences of American authors as literary tourists in Britain transformed them into self-conscious subjects and creators of literary tourism on their native soil, cultivating and curating their own environs. American literary tourism thus emerged with the professionalization of the American literary marketplace and the economic viability of the profession of author.

This move to professionalization was part and parcel of how American authors participated in the wider national currents of the nineteenth century by embracing the desire to represent United States literary production as a worthy subject of consumption and national celebration. Too much has been written about nineteenth-century American anxieties over authorship, authority, and the New World—most of it anticipated or inspired by Hawthorne—to recount here. But it is worth noting that by the mid-nineteenth century, authors and publishers were actively engaged in promoting United States literary production as a sign of a national arrival on an international stage.[26] If international recognition was elusive, celebrating indigenous literary celebrity was an exercise in patriotism. Some American authors, facing stiff competition from British writers, understood that self-promotion was necessary to economic survival and promoted themselves accordingly, such as nineteenth-century author and editor Nathaniel Parker Willis, who actively marketed himself through the mode of his day: *cartes de visite*. As Erin Hazard charts in her chapter, savvy authors were not averse to exploiting an interest in their homes and lifestyles. Thus for each author complaining of gawkers, there was a Willis or an Irving actively encouraging them (perhaps while simultaneously complaining). Writes Hazard, "Under Irving's direction, Sunnyside became a fantastic historicist environment, akin to Sir Walter Scott's Abbotsford." Willis, like Irving, linked the aesthetic experience of his carefully landscaped "naturalistic" grounds and his Gothic Revival home in the Hudson Valley with the values he promoted. In short, by his own suggestion, to fully appreciate Willis the author, one must become a literary tourist—even if it is only a vicarious trip via the page.[27] Harriet Beecher Stowe may have gone one step further, not only actively promoting her Florida home in her post–Civil War writing, but also, it is rumored, getting "a cut of the profits from steamship tours" that traveled past her family residence, and perhaps even charging passengers who embarked at the Stowe wharf "25 cents to enter their gardens."[28]

By the late nineteenth century, literary tourism was part of American literary culture. The proliferation of guidebooks meant that authors might expect—even if they did not always welcome—such visitors. Tourists could purchase postcards featuring the homes of authors from local shops; newspapers might describe sites unknown to their readers in the hopes of generating new interest and revenue. Nonliterary magazines and journals also regularly ran pieces describing the various homes and studies of American authors. Even those who had never cracked a book by Hawthorne might find themselves conversant with the settings and features of his various homes and knowledgeable about how such spaces shaped his writing habits. In this way, average American readers were transformed into literary tourists with their knowledge of literary culture gained from such encounters. Well into the twentieth century, Americans might be quite familiar with Henry Wadsworth Longfellow's house in Cambridge because images of it were so widely reproduced, much the way many of us today recognize Elvis Presley's home, Graceland, whether we have visited there or not.

Late nineteenth- and early twentieth-century United States literary tourism benefited from shifts in national tourism more broadly: as the European Grand Tour faded in popularity, travelers turned to indigenous scenes and sites, wooed in part by the expansion and increased affordability of railway travel and the railways' extensive marketing campaigns encouraging national tourism. These sites might be part of the fad for romantic tourism to sublime vistas, but increasingly, by the beginning of the twentieth century, readers were also turning to urban locales.[29] The mantra "See America First," intended to keep tourist dollars at home, capitalized on economic and cultural nationalism. Sites associated with authors provided ideal opportunities for national leisure tourism. Most Americans who had the means to engage in literary tourism were close enough to at least one site, and it might provide a destination for those who did not possess the financial capital to travel farther afield. Those living in New England, with its longer history of professional authorship and density of storied sites, had even more opportunities for day or weekend trips to visit locations of historical or cultural importance. Who exactly these late nineteenth- and early twentieth-century literary tourists were is a matter of speculation. Personal writings and ephemera provide some clues to the identities of select middle- and upper-class travelers, but the vast majority of early tourists left few traces, and we must contend with scant evidence aside from the rare guest register. Even then, registers rarely account for why a tourist travels and never account for enthusiasts who might have viewed a private house from the roadside.

We do know who the ideal tourist was according to the industry. The historian Marguerite S. Shaffer argues that in presenting tourism as a patriotic duty, the era's promoters were encouraging "white, native-born middle- and upper-class Americans to re-affirm their American-ness by following the footsteps of American history and seeing the nation firsthand." This might be a chicken-and-egg phenomenon, as promoters no doubt targeted those most likely to have the financial and educational capital to fund such adventures by playing to their desires, beliefs, and anxieties. Nonetheless, Shaffer argues that in the process, promoters "invented and mapped an idealized American history and tradition."[30] Such marketing also appealed to those for whom the cost of overseas travel was prohibitive, but who wanted to prove and perhaps test their cultural worth. Letters and diaries attest to the place of literature within this national travel narrative. As a late nineteenth-century contributor to a cycling magazine wrote: "The next morning, Sunday, we were awheel bright and early, steering for Cambridge, where we saw Longfellow's home and Washington's headquarters, the 'old elm tree' under whose wide-spreading branches Washington took command of the army; then we passed Lowell's home and Harvard College, then through Massachusetts avenue and across the long bridge into Boston."[31] More romantically, an 1892 book for young readers described "the later home of Hawthorne, a little out from the village. . . . [B]ehind the house a low, sloping ridge of land glories in its historical fame as a ridge from which the patriotic farmer soldiers poured down their fire upon the retreating Britishers."[32] The authors were within living memory; the Revolution less so. Still, situating authors within this lineage demonstrated not just their belonging in national narratives of pride, patriotism, and progress, but in some cases their invention of these very narratives.

Promoting patriotism through encounters with national history and culture was not the only function ascribed to authors' homes. Indeed, house museums in particular were seen as serving an additional purpose, namely, introducing new immigrants to American life, values, and practices. Thus curators of house museums sometimes also attempted to indoctrinate new Americans in the national narrative, instilling a sense of reverence for the American past and American achievements. William J. Murtagh calls this preservation for acculturation a kind of "secular pietism," and it was evident in the activities of the late nineteenth-century preservationist societies that sprang up across the country with the intent of saving sites associated with American history, culture, and identity not only for future generations but also as a means of defining what constitutes America.[33] Nowhere was this more evident than at the house believed to have inspired Hawthorne's *House of the Seven Gables,* which functioned simultaneously as a funding source for a settlement house largely serving Polish immigrants *and* as a tourist attraction.[34] Also revealing is Orchard House, the Concord home of Louisa May Alcott and her family. Local old-line residents were concerned about "the wave of alien inundation" the turn-of-the-century town was experiencing and the threat this posed to the character of Concord's historic community. Preserving Orchard House as a landmark was both a matter of shoring up essential historical ruins and trying to turn the tide of immigrant assimilation.[35] Murtagh argues, "Patriotism fueled the energies of nineteenth-century preservationists to the exclusion of any of the other interests—education, aesthetics, the environment, or more recently, economics—which have motivated later individuals."[36] Many sites, like Harriet Beecher Stowe's Hartford house, were similarly born of both xenophobia and patriotism, as its founder, Katherine Seymour Day, believed Stowe's legacy of activism and gentility deserved emulation and appreciation.[37] That said, just because Day believed that Stowe was worthy of celebrating did not mean Day was interested in emulating Stowe by taking on contemporary black causes; if anything Day seems to have been more invested in using Stowe's house to enforce the status quo and ensure adherence to values of a previous generation than in continuing Stowe's legacy of activism.[38]

What these examples demonstrate is that preservation of authors' homes and sites is not a coherent or unified enterprise, in step with the formation of the American literary canon or the ascription of literary value by an academic or cultural elite, or a direct reflection of trends in book sales. In reality, the preservation of literary sites is far more random. Contributors to this volume show how the value and fate of sites might be variously determined by a relative, an inspired individual, a needy community, or a tourism board. As Stephanie Kraft observed in 1979: "The question of whose house is preserved seems to have more to do with writers' relationships to their localities than with the long-range consensus as to the quality of what they achieved. Otherwise, why would the homes of James Whitcomb Riley be house museums and not the childhood home of T. S. Eliot?"[39] Moreover, the meaning or value attributed to these sites might shift over time as their audiences change, contract, or expand. Writing of Thoreau sites, volume contributor Klara-Stephanie Szlezák shows that "there are distinct strands of Thoreau tourism, including both traditional and more innovative approaches, disintegrated over time and now catering to the demands of different audiences." As Tami Christopher observes, "History alters because the market for history changes. Society's needs for history change over time, and historic sites adjust to meet these societal needs."[40] Perhaps ironically, the Stowe House today continues to celebrate Stowe's legacy of activism by including voices Katherine Seymour Day would have found less desirable, even if she supported their causes. Likewise, as Longfellow's extreme popularity has wavered recently, so has the name of the federal historic site devoted to him. Since 2011 the site has officially been Longfellow House–Washington's Headquarters National Historical Site to reflect the fact that, indeed, George Washington slept here.[41] American literary sites are hardly stable archives of literary and biographical meaning-making, and those featured in this collection show how our perceptions of literary celebrity, biography, and worth are, in part, shaped over time by our collective memories of the places where our writers have lived.

## *Our Contributions*

In this volume our contributors demand that we remember that sites of literary tourism are the shared property of local historians, volunteers, readers, and especially visitors. Together they raise a new set of questions, in particular, how do caretakers and travelers conceive of these sites and their literary ties? What curatorial, touristic, and literary practices do these sites deliberately or inadvertently stage, invite, or inspire? Are authors, their homes, or written work represented in ways that simplify or complicate our understanding of their lives? Do their literary works themselves contest such places? Do visitors and readers conduct counter-readings of literary texts at sites of literary tourism? The answers to these questions are as diverse as the sites themselves, and those who travel to them—or, in some cases, imagine themselves traveling to them. After all, unlike some other forms of special interest tourism, literary tourism most often begins in the mind, in the reciprocal encounter with a novel, author, or cultural artifact, and the relationships an individual develops or feels she should develop. In this way, literary tourism can be an assertion of cultural belonging and taste (following Bourdieu), or it can be a deeply personal pilgrimage. Both might signal one's imagined difference from the masses, even while they signal one's belonging in a larger national project.

This collection demonstrates the multiple histories, experiences, and uses of such sites and the ephemera associated with them. From Mara Scanlon's account of her students' moving experience of Whitman sites, to the devoted fans of *Little House on the Prairie* discussed by Michelle McClellan, Hilary Iris Lowe's investigation of the use of Mark Twain's Elmira home as a writers' retreat, and Rebecca Rego Barry's argument for the preservation of the Warner sisters' home as a way of understanding their sense of deprivation and isolation, this volume implicitly accepts that these sites can have meaning for those who visit them—even if that meaning is at times at odds with their historical function, educational programming, or curatorial practices. Relatedly, our contributors all value the ways in which imaginative reading practices might inform the experience of tourism—even to its potential detriment, as Jennifer Harris argues, demonstrating that authors, texts, or histories that invite ambivalence might also pose problems for both curators and audiences.

It would be impossible for a single volume to address every aspect of American literary tourism noted in this introduction, or to cover the pantheon of American literature. Absences here are significant: writers of color throughout the history of American literature have been little celebrated by literary tourists or preservationists. For instance, there are as yet no historic sites open to the public that celebrate Langston Hughes, Ralph Ellison, Jessie Redmon Fauset, or Countee Cullen, though slowly, historical markers are starting to dot the landscapes where these Harlem Renaissance writers grew up, lived as adults, and wrote. Our collection in many ways reflects the economic, gender, race, and cultural realties under which literary tourist sites are developed and maintained by popular interest in literary figures and their works. Shelley Fisher Fishkin's guide to American literary landmarks, *Writing America* (2015), sets out a path through which we might all imagine a more inclusive literary itinerary. We hope this volume helps us all understand why the opening of literary sites not only adds to the literary historical cannon but also provides national and local avenues for critically understanding the work and daily lives of all American writers and their role in shaping the past and present.

Thus this collection stands as an introduction to all these issues, signposting directions, concerns, and possibilities, without seeking to reduce American literary tourism to a single narrative. Our approach is very much informed by print culture studies and book history, which consider the intersections of history, authorship, and reader experience. While such an orientation might diverge from approaches of tourism studies scholars who often foreground the marketing surveys and the data of social sciences, it is very much in keeping with the disciplinary orientation of the scholars who populate this volume, and many of the practices of literary tourism they document, but which cannot always be easily quantified.

Organizing the collection chronologically, as best as possible, by the date of authors' births, we begin with perhaps the least-known and less-celebrated author, Jupiter Hammon. In co-editor Jennifer Harris's chapter, "The Eighteenth-Century Author No One Knows and Other Problems: Promoting Jupiter Hammon on Long Island," Harris examines the difficulties of marketing an enslaved author in tandem with the homes in which he resided. As a potential figure for literary tourism, Hammon presents problems on multiple fronts—not least because both he and the houses he lived in were the legal property of the Lloyd families. In addressing Hammon and comparing him with other early African American authors, this chapter attends to the specificity of African American literary tourism, as well as the emerging interest in tourism that uncovers and explicates the places and history of slavery in the United States.

Moving from the admittedly obscure Hammon to some of the most historically popular American authors—Washington Irving, Henry David Thoreau, Nathaniel Hawthorne, and Louisa May Alcott—Erin Hazard investigates the factors that led to the emergence of American literary tourism and facilitated its growth. Her chapter, "'Step forth and again take up its magic pen': The Author's House as Informal Memorial," uncovers how early nineteenth-century American authors and their heirs, guided by their own experiences of British literary tourism, began to self-consciously understand and even construct their homes in ways that suggest they saw them as important destinations.

Building on the literary legacy of Henry David Thoreau, Klara-Stephanie Szlezák takes on one of the most iconic figures of American literary tourism in "Keeping (the Spirit of) Thoreau Alive in Concord: Reflections on Diversity and Innovation in American Literary Tourism." Chronicling the expansion of Thoreau tourism from related sites to a larger milieu in Concord, Szlezák argues that Thoreau's shifting meaning has created a variety of iterations of tourism, which cater to a wide variety of audiences. In examining these iterations, we can chart Thoreau's reputation, reception, and cultural cachet in American culture more broadly.

Rebecca Rego Barry takes us into the home of two women writers, Susan and Anna Warner, who truly lived in the isolation that Thoreau may have sought at Walden Pond. Although Susan Warner was a wildly popular bestselling author in the middle of the nineteenth century, she and her sister have been largely forgotten by today's literary tourists. In "The Wide, Wide World beyond a Tiny, Deserted Island: At Home with Susan and Anna Warner," Barry foregrounds the Warner sisters' life on Constitution Island, demonstrating how their remote locale influenced and drove their writings. Simultaneously Barry charts the evolution of the place as a historic site, documenting current threats to its existence and debates about the future of its contents. That the Warners are less well known today is essential to the debates about the potential fate of the historic site.

Signaling how literary tourism continues to evolve with new forms of media, Mara Scanlon introduces us to the virtual world with " 'Afoot with my vision': Whitmania and Tourism in the Digital Age." Scanlon's chapter emerges from a college course she taught titled "Digital Whitman," which explored Walt Whitman through a range of online resources. Scanlon first led her students through the digital archives before guiding them through the physical sites and repositories associated with Whitman. In comparing the experience of digital literary tourism to the confrontation with actual artifacts, and their effect on both herself and her students, Scanlon compellingly assesses the meaningful nature of each.

Along with Walt Whitman, Mark Twain is perhaps one of the most recognizable American literary figures. Each has not one but multiple historic sites devoted to his life and work. Volume co-editor Hilary Iris Lowe, author of *Mark Twain's Homes and Literary Tourism,* returns to Twain in "Commemorating Writers' Workplaces: The Case of Mark Twain's Study and Quarry

Farm." From the one-hundred-square-foot gazebo-style study now on the green at Elmira College's campus to the writing table enshrined at the Henry Ford Museum, Lowe uncovers how and where Samuel Clemens's workplaces have been preserved. She finds that Twain's workplaces, especially at his longtime summer retreat, Quarry Farm, have been surprisingly mobile and adaptable, and today they serve tourists, scholars, and writers alike.

Mobility is likewise a feature in Caroline Hellman's contribution, " 'Shut not your doors to me, proud libraries!': The Repatriation of Edith Wharton's Library.' " Characterizing the 2005 purchase of Edith Wharton's library by The Mount as a "repatriation," Hellman considers how the books' "homecoming" enriches the site in ways that the relics we often find in house museums—a kettle, a sewing kit, a dresser—cannot. Addressing both the emotional resonance of the books for the layperson who might visit, as well as their value to Wharton scholars, Hellman demonstrates what the books bring to The Mount aesthetically, emotionally, and academically.

Michelle McClellan in "Making a Little House: Literary Tourism at Rocky Ridge Farm" takes on sites that are perhaps some of the best known—or at least their screen representations are—and considers why. In particular, McClellan addresses how Laura Ingalls Wilder's "Little House" sites became a marketable brand, one self-consciously manufactured in response to the nostalgia the "Little House" books and, later, television series inspired in American readers and viewers. At the same time, McClellan considers the brand as displayed at Little House sites and its relation to Wilder's own life and adult home, as well as the way in which the celebration of the Little House ideal depends on the prioritizing of certain narratives, ultimately obscuring others.

From an investigation of specific literary figures and sites, the collection moves to contributions that consider advances in literary tourism facilitated by evolving media. In "Author Homes in Coffee Table Books: Half-Reading, Literary Décor, and the Good Life," Ben De Bruyn directs our attention to contemporary coffee table books that feature literary homes, their authority, and the almost fetishistic quality they embody. In particular, De Bruyn theorizes about contemporary relations between readers and tourism and how they mediate the tension between highbrow and lowbrow practices.

We conclude the collection with Susann Bishop's assessment of the practical outcome of our collective interest in literary tourism in "The Allure of American Authors' Homes: Surveying Nineteenth- and Twentieth-Century Literary Guides." Here Bishop, herself a guide specializing in literary tours, introduces the origins and history of the literary tour guide between 1853 and 1940. Considering how these guides functioned both as products for publishers and as advertisements for their wares, Bishop explores what such books tell us about literary culture, readers, and writers themselves. As an avid collector of such guides, Bishop provides a richly textured essay on the subject.

Each of these chapters takes us into the "where" of literary America. While they don't necessarily paint the perfect map for a literary tourist in the United States, they ponder why these places exist and what important work they do. What is it that Edith Wharton's house (and library) can tell us about her work and times that *The Age of Innocence* cannot? What can we learn about Jupiter Hammon the man and the poet from the physical places where he was enslaved? Why do we need sites devoted to Twain when his best books never lack for readers? Should sites devoted to long-forgotten—or, for that matter, never remembered—literary figures be discarded? Where do literary celebrity and reputation end and historical importance begin?

The conversations begun in these chapters promise a rich future for the study of American literary tourism more broadly. This collection is our attempt to bring the United States and its sites and practices into a broader conversation about literary tourism, cultural tourism, and more. Let us take up the tour.

## NOTES

1. Hilary Iris Lowe, *Mark Twain's Homes and Literary Tourism* (Columbia: University of Missouri Press, 2012); Dydia DeLyser, *Ramona Memories: Tourism and the Shaping of Southern California* (Minneapolis: University of Minnesota Press, 2005); for the Warner House, see Rebecca Rego Barry's essay in this volume; Alice Walker, "In Search of Zora Neale Hurston," *Ms.*, March 1975, 74–79, 85–89.
2. Seth C. Bruggeman, introduction to *Born in the U.S.A.: Birth, Commemoration, and American Public Memory*, ed. Seth C. Bruggeman (Amherst: University of Massachusetts Press, 2012), 16.
3. Nicola J. Watson, *The Literary Tourist* (Houndmills: Palgrave Macmillan, 2006), 201.
4. For more about Westminster Abbey, see ibid., 23–32. As of yet, no significant study has been undertaken linking the interrelation of literature and tourism in Harlem, though the groundwork has been laid. Namely, Shane Vogel discuses literary writings about the Harlem cabaret, Chad Heap addresses Harlem slum tourism, and Justin Edwards treats the literature as travel writing. Shane Vogel, *The Scene of Harlem Cabaret: Race, Sexuality, Performance* (Chicago: University of Chicago Press, 2009); Chad Heap, *Slumming: Sexual and Racial Encounters in American Nightlife, 1885–1940* (Chicago: University of Chicago Press, 2010); Justin Edwards, *Exotic Journeys: Exploring the Erotics of U.S. Travel Literature, 1840–1930* (Hanover: University Press of New England, 2001).
5. John Urry and Jonas Larsen, *The Tourist Gaze 3.0* (London: Sage, 2011). The Nielsen Company publishes annual reports on United States consumer trends broken down by ethnicity, which include trends in tourism. See www.nielsen.com; "PCA Expects an Increase in Travel and Leisure Needs among Asian Americans and Asians Abroad," www.plancagency.com.
6. Jennifer Craik distinguishes those for whom cultural tourism is a primary goal, defining these individuals as part of a special interest group. Alternatively, there are those who

engage in it because it is convenient. Jennifer Craik, "The Culture of Tourism," in *Touring Cultures: Transformations of Travel and Theory*, ed. Chris Rojek and John Urry (London: Routledge, 1997), 113–36.

7. Roy Rosenzweig and David Thelan, *The Presence of the Past: Popular Uses of History in American Life* (New York: Columbia University Press, 1998), 264. The authors also write that such visits "sparked an associative process of recalling and reminiscing about the past that connected [visitors] to their own history" (32).
8. Benedict Anderson, *Imagined Communities: Reflections on the Origin and Spread of Nationalism* (New York: Verso, 2006). Though Anderson does not directly implicate literary tourism in the spread of nationalism, it is clear that he and others believe that works of literature can work in defining nations (26, 92).
9. Twain sites abound, as do many other sites that fabricate literary destinations out of whole cloth, like those in Kansas associated with Dorothy, including the Oz Museum and Dorothy's house and Munchkin Land at the Seward County Historical Society, and many, many others.
10. Robert Thompson quoted in Alan Greenblatt, "While Graceland Booms, Other Historic Homes Rot," NPR, www.npr.org.
11. Harald Hendrix, "Writers' Houses as Media of Expression and Remembrance: From Self-Fashioning to Cultural Memory," in *Writers' Houses and the Making of Memory*, ed. Harald Hendrix (New York: Routledge Taylor and Francis, 2008), 1.
12. Ellen Glasgow, *The Woman Within: An Autobiography* (1954; repr., Charlottesville: University of Virginia Press, 1994), 26.
13. Urry and Larsen, *The Tourist Gaze 3.0*, 101.
14. Anne Trubek, *A Skeptic's Guide to Writers' Houses* (Philadelphia: University of Pennsylvania Press, 2010), 4.
15. Wendy McClure, *The Wilder Life: My Adventures in the Lost World of "Little House on the Prairie"* (New York: Riverhead, 2011).
16. Norman Douglas, Ngaire Douglas, and Ros Derrett, eds., *Special Interest Tourism: Contexts and Cases* (Brisbane: John Wiley, 2001), xviii.
17. Edward Chaney, *The Evolution of the Grand Tour: Anglo-Italian Cultural Relations since the Renaissance* (London: Frank Cass, 1998), 203.
18. Jeremy Black, *The British and the Grand Tour* (London: Croom Helm, 1985), 4.
19. Craik, "The Culture of Tourism," 35.
20. Urry and Larsen, *The Tourist Gaze 3.0*, 2.
21. Tony Bennett has explored this phenomenon at length in *The Birth of the Museum: History, Theory, Politics* (New York: Routledge, 1995).
22. Watson, *The Literary Tourist*, 9.
23. Paul Westover, "How America 'Inherited' Literary Tourism," in *Literary Tourism and Nineteenth-Century Culture*, ed. Nicola J. Watson (Houndmills: Palgrave Macmillan, 2009), 184–95.
24. Cathy Davidson, *Revolution and the Word: The Rise of the Novel in America* (New York: Oxford University Press, 1986); C. J. Hughes, "Buried in the Churchyard: A Good Story, at Least," *New York Times*, December 12, 2008; Hannah Webster Foster, *The Coquette and The Boarding School*, ed. Jennifer Harris and Bryan Waterman (New York: W. W. Norton, 2013).
25. Although women authors' homes did not early show up in literary itineraries, they have a place among the literary guidebooks that Susann Bishop explores in the last chapter in this volume. Of special interest might be the 1903 volume of largely republished sketches from the *New York Times Saturday Review of Books*, featuring at least twenty-seven women authors. Francis Whiting Halsey, ed., *Women Authors of Our Day in Their Homes* (New York: James Pott and Company, 1903).
26. For the rise of professional authorship, see William Charvat, *The Profession of Authorship in America, 1800–1870* (1968; repr., New York: Columbia University Press, 1992). The

anxiety of authorship is treated by Stephen Railton in *Authorship and Audience: Literary Performance in the American Renaissance* (Princeton: Princeton University Press, 1991). Nina Baym addresses iterations of literary nationalism in *Novels, Readers, and Reviewers: Responses to Fiction in Antebellum America* (Ithaca: Cornell University Press, 1984).

27. Willis is better remembered today as the brother of the far more famous Fanny Fern (as well as the unwitting employer of Harriet Jacobs). For more on Willis, see Adam Sweeting, *Reading Houses and Building Books: Andrew Jackson Downing and the Architecture of Popular Antebellum Literature, 1835–1855* (Hanover: University Press of New England, 1996); and Thomas N. Baker, *Sentiment and Celebrity: Nathaniel Parker Willis and the Trials of Literary Fame* (New York: Oxford University Press, 1999).
28. Diane Roberts, "Harriet Beecher Stowe and Florida Tourism," in Watson, *Literary Tourism and Nineteenth-Century Culture,* 207.
29. Catherine Cocks, *Doing the Town: The Rise of Urban Tourism in the United States, 1850–1915* (Berkeley: University of California Press, 2001), 5–7. The United Kingdom has long been ahead of the United States in promoting cultural tourism.
30. Marguerite S. Shaffer, *See America First: Tourism and National Identity, 1880–1940* (Washington, D.C.: Smithsonian Institution, 2001), 4.
31. Willard Deane, "A Bicycle Tour," *Good Roads* 24 (July–December 1896): 548–49.
32. Maria Louise Pratt and Anna Temple Lovering, *Stories of Massachusetts* (Boston: Educational Publishing Company, 1892), 136.
33. William J. Murtagh, *Keeping Time: The History and Theory of Preservation in America,* 3rd ed. (Hoboken: John Wiley and Sons, 2006), xvii.
34. Tami Christopher, "The House of the Seven Gables: A House Museum's Adaptation to Changing Societal Expectations since 1910," in *Defining Memory: Local Museums and Constructions of History in America's Changing Communities,* ed. Amy K. Levin (New York: Alta Mira, 2007), 63–76.
35. Patricia West, *Domesticating History: The Political Origins of America's House Museums* (Washington, D.C.: Smithsonian Institution, 1999), 51–52.
36. Murtagh, *Keeping Time,* xvii.
37. James Lindgren, among others, has made the argument that xenophobia and patriotism played large roles in the preservation ethics of American in his two tomes on the history of preservation in the United States. See James Lindgren, *Preserving the Old Dominion: Historic Preservation and Virginia Traditionalism* (Charlottesville: University of Virginia Press, 1993), and *Preserving Historic New England: Preservation, Progressivism, and the Remaking of Memory* (New York: Oxford University Press, 1995).
38. Jennifer Harris, "Katherine Seymour Day: Preserving the Legacy of Harriet Beecher Stowe," 129th Modern Language Association Annual Convention, Chicago, 2014.
39. Stephanie Kraft, *No Castles on Main Street: American Authors and Their Homes* (Chicago: Rand McNally, 1979), 13.
40. Christopher, "The House of the Seven Gables," 64.
41. Christopher Klein, "Open House to Mark the Name Change for Longfellow House," *Boston Globe,* February 21, 2011.

# 1

# *The Eighteenth-Century Author No One Knows and Other Problems*

## Promoting Jupiter Hammon on Long Island

JENNIFER HARRIS

*It might seem odd to start our collection on American literary tourism with an exploration of a recent addition to our collective literary historical itinerary. Since the 1970s the Joseph Lloyd House and Henry Lloyd Manor House have been open to the public. But it wasn't until recently that the house museums have struggled to incorporate historical interpretation about Jupiter Hammon. Hammon, still relatively unknown to most Americans, even literary scholars, is one of the earliest identified African American poets. The Lloyd houses are where he and his family were enslaved, but also where he received an education and became a poet. Jennifer Harris positions Hammon—a complicated historical figure and poet who requires careful context—as a key to these sites' current survival and growth. Her chapter sets our scene for what is at stake for literary tourism and public literary history.*

For many people, the 2013 announcement of the discovery of a previously unknown poem by Jupiter Hammon was their first introduction to the author. Cedrick May and Julie McCown's uncovering of the poem "An Essay on Slavery" has made possible a mini-renaissance of sorts for Hammon: his name is newly circulated in media and discussed in classrooms, while scholars of early American and African American literature are revisiting his previously known works with fresh perspective. Often overlooked by scholars in the past, when Hammon has been remembered it is most often for his 1778 poem "An Address to Miss Phillis Wheatley," a moment that one might argue marks the birth of an African American literary community.[1]

But if scholars have not reliably foregrounded Hammon in recent years, there are two places where he has been experiencing a quiet resurgence. Joseph Lloyd Manor and Henry Lloyd Manor House in Lloyd Harbor, Long Island, are sites where Hammon was born and enslaved. Preserved since 1968 as a historic house museum, Joseph Lloyd Manor is run by the Society for the Preservation of Long Island Antiquities (SPLIA), while the Henry Lloyd Manor House is owned by the separate and more regional Lloyd Harbor Historical Society (LHHS). Joseph Lloyd Manor and Henry Lloyd Manor House face the same difficulties many historic house museums have encountered following the economic downturn beginning in 2008: the depletion of financial resources, government cutbacks, reduced endowments, the increasing cost of the upkeep of aging buildings, and declining attendance. In recent years, local school boards have canceled funds for class trips (fig. 1.1).[2] According to a 2014 article in the *Boston Globe,* there are more than fifteen thousand house museums in the United States struggling for survival; the Lloyd houses are part of an oversaturated market.[3]

Nevertheless, drawing on Hammon's newfound literary capital has the potential to broaden the sites' appeal and assert their ongoing relevance. That said, SPLIA and LHHS face two primary problems in capitalizing on this potential. The first is that very few people know who Jupiter Hammon is, despite the efforts of these societies to promote Hammon since the acquisition of the related sites.[4] The second problem—one faced by many houses with histories of slavery—is that representing enslavement can be difficult. On the one hand, it presents a quandary for organizations that often have a long-established narrative and mission statement in place celebrating the house and its early owners. On the other hand, it raises the issue of how to introduce slavery in a way that is educational, accessible, and yet not off-putting. Many United States historic houses and sites with significantly greater resources have struggled with these questions. In the northern states, where enslavement has been downplayed historically in favor of the liberatory narrative of the Underground Railroad, there are few house museums or historical sites that provide precedents to which SPLIA and LHHS might look. Introducing a third factor into the equation—an enslaved author of historic significance—complicates matters. As an early African American author, the first for whom an oeuvre exists, Hammon is a convenient "hook" for these historic sites. In highlighting his presence at the houses, both organizations are being responsible in recognizing the import of black historical figures and a black past, and savvy in attempting to expand their appeal and activities. In Hammon they are fortunate to have an individual who might enrich their interpretive presentations and activities. At the same time, trying to market Hammon as a dedicated attraction draws attention to (1) the

FIGURE 1.1. The Henry Lloyd Manor House, one of two homes where Jupiter Hammon was enslaved, offers educational programming. *Photo by Daniel Vogel.*

problems his personal narrative might pose for some, and (2) the difficulties of trying to craft a literary tourism site for an unknown author. But, I would argue, the uniqueness of Hammon might also facilitate a different path, one that these houses could build on to ensure their legacy.

Little about Hammon has been preserved, and he does not boast a celebrated dramatic narrative on a par with those of more famous early African Americans, such as Phillis Wheatley. What we do know is that Hammon was born into slavery on October 17, 1711, in Lloyd Neck, Long Island, to Rose and Obium Hammon.[5] It is believed Obium was literate, perhaps learning to read during his time in Boston, and local lore has it that Jupiter attended a small schoolhouse on the estate of Henry Lloyd in Queens Village, Long Island, alongside the Lloyd children.[6] While some have described Jupiter Hammon as a clerk to the Lloyds, this might be misleading in today's terms, though records indicate he carried money on their behalf. Hammon does note that he was "able to do almost any kind of business."[7] That Hammon was entrusted with performing business on behalf of the family in New York City suggests he possessed a familiarity with arithmetic, geography, and law, and Henry Lloyd owned volumes on these subjects, as well as history and philosophy, including works in French and Latin. Whether Hammon had access to them is unclear, but it is evident that his reading extended well beyond the Christian Bible.[8] Notes found in the accounts of others of Hammon's purchases between 1733 and 1797, ranging from a Bible to rum, suggest he had personal earnings to dispose of, and he admits: "My lot has been so much better than most slaves have had. . . . I have had more advantages and privileges than most of you, who are slaves, have ever known, and I believe more than many white people have enjoyed."[9]

Nonetheless, Hammon never achieved his freedom. Instead, he was inherited by three successive generations of the Lloyd family, and was last appraised in an inventory in 1792 at £16. Hammon's exact date of death is unknown, but scholars believe it occurred in 1805.[10] If one were to rely on the extensive Lloyd family records alone, Hammon—referred to as Jupiter in Lloyd letters and accounts—would seem no more nor less important than some others they held in slavery, distinguished primarily by his longevity.[11] Yet Hammon has been identified by scholars and historians as the first significant African American author. Five of Hammon's poems and three prose pieces have survived, all produced between 1760 and 1787. By comparison, only one piece by Lucy Terry (ca. 1730–1821), the first known African American poet, has survived—and that recorded from memory some years after her death—making Hammon the first author for whom we have an actual corpus of work.[12]

Although we know little about Hammon, the Lloyd family can be more easily traced and is the subject of three published books which draw on the family's extensive archives, now held at the New-York Historical Society.[13] The Lloyds took up residence on Long Island in the first decade of the eighteenth century, with Henry Lloyd overseeing the building of the house that now bears his name in 1711, the same year Hammon was born.[14] The Lloyd manor, populated by the Lloyd family and at least five enslaved individuals initially—probably more—was self-sufficient, capable of producing its own food, and boasted lucrative lumbering resources.[15] The property was not as isolated as it might seem: residing on the water, the family owned a sloop for transporting goods to the New York market.[16] As Leslie M. Harris writes, markets proved important meeting places for free and enslaved black New Yorkers in the seventeenth century.[17] Given Hammon's intercourse with the African Society of New York City, it is likely he repeatedly made the voyage himself, traveling with or on behalf of the Lloyds.

In 1763, with Henry Lloyd's death, Hammon became the property of Lloyd's son, Joseph Lloyd II, proprietor of the second historic house, who took Hammon with him to Hartford, Connecticut, during the Revolutionary War. Upon Joseph's suicide in 1780, Hammon became the property of John Lloyd II, Joseph's nephew.[18] The enslaved population in John Lloyd's household was listed as ten in the 1790 census, making it one of Long Island's largest slave-holding households. The nearby home of John Lloyd I contained five additional enslaved people.[19]

Of the two Lloyd houses, Joseph Lloyd Manor, dating from 1766, is the more prominent, having served in the twentieth century as a short-lived residence for both the aviator Charles Lindbergh and the musician Billy Joel. In 1968 it was bequeathed by Anna Matheson Wood to SPLIA, which describes it as "a handsome structure with fine interior woodwork by Connecticut craftsmen. Located in a spectacular setting overlooking Lloyd Harbor," noting that "the grounds contain a formal garden."[20] The restoration of the more modest Henry Lloyd Manor House, built in 1711, and the related George Weir Barn, both with ties to Hammon, have been the primary focus of the LHHS, a much smaller organization. In keeping with the reality of smaller house museums, especially those that are geographically isolated in some way, both Lloyd houses appear to be underutilized. While the Lloyds may have been prominent locally, they lack the broader historical import that would lead visitors to their admittedly out-of-the-way location, which is isolated from other tourist attractions. The houses are certainly museums with great local importance, which largely attract tourists who are already in the region. But they are not ordinarily primary destinations themselves.[21] Thus, turning to Hammon to boost interest would seem to be a strategic way to broaden their scope.

Unfortunately, as it stands, Jupiter Hammon lacks the kind of cultural capital that would make him a beacon for tourism. Unlike Thoreau or Hawthorne, he is not included in high school curriculums; he does not generate beloved or nostalgic associations with childhood as do Alcott and Wilder; he is not credited with fomenting social change, like Stowe. His writings, while occasionally anthologized, are less appealing to many contemporary readers when compared with the dramatic first-person narratives of African American writers such as Frederick Douglass or Harriet Jacobs. Visitors seeking a more intimate connection with an author or cause might be disappointed with Hammon's emphasis on spiritual rather than earthly equality. Those who privilege overt black activism are sure to be disappointed by Hammon's foregrounding of Christian salvation over black uprising. Certainly Hammon's evangelism doesn't just allow for but actively advances racial equality; he claims, "The same God will judge both us and them," and notes, "He will bring us all, rich and poor, white and black, to the judgment seat." Yet he also argues that slaves should be subservient to their masters. As Hammon writes, "Now whether it is right, and lawful, in the sight of God, for them to make slaves of us or not, I am certain that while we are slaves, it is our duty to obey our masters, in all their lawful commands, and mind them unless we are bid to do that which we know to be sin." He counsels that this should be done "cheerfully, and freely."[22]

This dual message characterizes Hammon's longest known work, "An Address to the Negroes of New York," delivered in 1786 to the first recorded meeting of the African Society of New York City, which urges his auditors, and later readers, to embrace a Christian God. "An Address" presents a problem: Hammon's definitive statement on slavery might be read by some contemporary readers as insufficiently radical on the subject, as endorsing white stereotypes about black competency, and as using the Christian Bible to counsel black subservience. In a long passage, but one worthy of consideration, Hammon writes:

> Now I acknowledge that liberty is a great thing, and worth seeking for, if we can get it honestly; and by our good conduct prevail on our masters to set us free: though for my own part I do not wish to be free, yet I should be glad if others, especially the young Negroes, were to be free; for many of us who have grown up slaves, and have always had masters to take care of us, should hardly know how to take care of ourselves, and it may be more for our own comfort to remain as we are. That liberty is a great thing we may know from our feelings, and we may likewise judge so from the conduct of the white people in the late war. How much money has been spent, and how many lives lost to defend their liberty! I must say that I have hoped that God would open their eyes, when they were so much engaged for liberty, to think of the state of the poor blacks, and to pity us.[23]

Praying for the conversion of whites, implicitly critiquing their self-interest and what he posits is willful blindness, Hammon asserts his own authority as a cultural critic and moral authority, an important move. Yet despite this pointed comment on white complacency, salvation remains his overarching theme. Implicit in such a focus is the comfort many enslaved blacks found in faith and the belief in, to quote the spiritual, a "better world a comin' "—even if it might be found only in the afterlife. There is no reason to suppose that Hammon was anything but genuine in his counsel to embrace God, and in his desire to offer solace to his black peers, enslaved or free.

To state that Hammon was genuine in his spiritual beliefs is not to undermine his awareness of the power of disseminating them in print. Given that the ways black people were primarily represented in the print culture of eighteenth-century America was either as property or as criminals, Hammon's assertion of Christian equality and faith is undeniably crucial.[24] While Blyden Jackson claims that Hammon was "no tribune for his people in the cause of liberation," in foregrounding black spiritual equality, Hammon is, according to the precepts of his time, "wag[ing] war against slavery in the biblical arena," and in a way that was revolutionary in the era.[25] Hammon asserts that blacks have the same capacity for humanity, morality, and reason as whites and urges his auditors to demonstrate the same, thus implicitly undermining the arguments for race-based slavery. These are also the qualities believed necessary at the time for good citizenship, and in urging both free and enslaved to practice them, he is asking everyone to participate in the project of demonstrating the worth of black peoples. It is an early articulation of the racial uplift precepts that would gain such currency post-emancipation. Nevertheless, reading Hammon's evangelism or instructions in good behavior as politically charged might seem to be a "hard sell" to those less comfortable with the literary tropes and religious conventions of the era. In this way, the recent discovery by May and McCown of the Hammon poem "An Essay on Slavery" is tremendously useful as it contains explicit condemnations of the "peculiar institution" instantly recognizable as such. The author characterizes the origins of slavery as "Dark and dismal," asking, "When shall we hear the joyfull sound / Echo the christian shore / Each humble voice with songs resound / That slavery is no more." Still, he counsels his audience, "When God doth please for to permit / That slavery should be / It is our duty to submit / Till Christ shall make us free."[26]

Therein lies part of the problem in selling Hammon as a figure of literary tourism: it is not merely that he is an unknown author, unlike Frederick Douglass, who currently appears on postcards, fridge magnets, and T-shirts, his iconic image a nineteenth-century equivalent of Malcolm X's. It is that Hammon's established biography is less saleable: he did not wrest his freedom from whites in a narrative of triumphant masculinity. He lived with his enslavers, planned to die with them, and at times even counseled submission to them—even as he counseled white slave owners to act compassionately. Perhaps this is why Hammon found himself in a pamphlet, intended to urge fellow blacks to embrace Christianity, also publicly disputing rumors he had petitioned against freedom.[27] If literary tourism is premised on the desire to enrich a connection with an author or his works, or pay him homage, Hammon's biography is currently insufficient to facilitate that initial connection. Ultimately Hammon lacks—at least by twenty-first-century standards—a sufficiently militant cachet or dramatic narrative that might garner particular audiences, and instead draws attention to the more complex relationship that sometimes emerged between those designated master and slave. It is the kind of complex relationship that slavery could engender, and yet still makes many uncomfortable. Finally, if part of the appeal of historic house museums in general is the nostalgia they can engender, foregrounding Hammon-as-slave has the potential to disrupt the pleasure many potential viewers seek at such sites, and demands a different kind of engagement.

Yet, given the dearth of literary sites associated with African American literary figures—or early African American figures at all—it would seem that, being among the few, Hammon's sites might generate more interest. Indeed, of the seventy-two additional dedicated tourist sites where authors lived, as identified by Anne Trubek in *A Skeptic's Guide to Writers' Houses,* only two are dedicated to African American writers: the Frederick Douglass National Historic Site in Washington, D.C., and the Paul Laurence Dunbar House in Dayton, Ohio. In keeping with her emphasis on the adult homes of writers, Trubek omits the museum at the Tennessee boyhood home of Alex Haley.[28] Crucially for our purposes, however, neither the Douglass nor the Dunbar site is affiliated with slavery, as the Hammon sites are. The Haley site, tied to his childhood in the 1920s and 1930s rather than to the subject matter of his best-known work, focuses on genealogy and Haley himself. Of all United States literary tourism sites, it is the Margaret Mitchell House and Museum in Atlanta that is most explicitly tied to slavery. Erected post-Reconstruction, the house nonetheless resonates with the associations of Mitchell's *Gone With the Wind,* a nostalgia-laden vision of plantation slavery. Materials and artifacts related to the novel are preserved in the house's collection and gift shop, and the house itself is a stop on the plantation house tour junket. In comparing Hammon and Mitchell, we can see that in the literary tourism industry, slavery sells best through a nostalgic focus on wealthy enslavers, not the disenfranchised enslaved.[29]

Though it is possible to market a white author who writes of slavery without explicitly addressing the institution, the same cannot be said for an enslaved black author. Marketing Hammon means somehow addressing slavery, historically a difficult task for tourist sites and museums. While there is a history of United States tourist sites explicitly centered on slavery, such as Somerset Place in North Carolina, considered "one of the country's most important sites for the interpretation of the slaves' experience," sites that began with other missions have been less quick to address the experience of enslavement.[30] Until recently, many sites suffered a kind of amnesia on the subject; while Colonial Williamsburg first introduced the topic in 1979, discussion was isolated to the slave quarters, spaces some have argued are sanitized and romanticized.[31] Docents at Monticello continued to refer to slave as "servants" into the 1980s, describing their activities in the passive voice; "meals 'were served' and furniture 'was built'" with no mention of the creators.[32] This still surpassed the awareness demonstrated at certain other sites. As James Oliver Horton writes, "In the mid-1990s, the permanent exhibition at Gettysburg National Battlefield . . . mentioned neither slavery nor slaves with regard to the war."[33] In some ways this is not surprising: these are all sites that implicitly celebrate a particular narrative of nationalism and are meant to further bind visitors to a particular vision of American progress. The commemoration of Civil War deaths suggests a redemptive vision of American history—the willingness to die in pursuit of a greater cause. By contrast, sites that specifically commemorate the experiences of those enslaved, such as the slave forts of Ghana, offer no redemption. Lacking agency, their subjects can only be remembered, honored, and mourned.[34]

In recent years some strides have been made in the representation of slavery at United States sites, but not without controversy or significant discomfort. Notably, the 1994 Colonial Williamsburg re-creation of a colonial slave auction received national attention. According to Horton:

> The staff at the African American Department [of Colonial Williamsburg] proposed the auction as a way to "teach the history of our mothers and grandmothers so that every one of you will never forget what happened to them." The statement and the re-creation of the auction drew strong reaction. At the end of the extremely moving reenactment of a family being broken apart through sale, the crowd of visitors grew silent and many wept. Clearly emotions were mixed. A black visitor and a white visitor jointly displayed a sign that read "Say no to racist shows." The Richmond chapter of the NAACP and the Southern Christian Leadership Conference attempted to interrupt the event, accusing the reenactment of "glorifying the horrors and humiliation of the evil of slavery" and calling it a trivialization of [our] African American heritage." One of the main concerns voiced by opponents of the reenactment was that it might be misinterpreted by visitors as entertainment.[35]

The site has yet to reproduce the event, though enactments of the stress and tension anticipating a slave auction have since been staged.[36] Whatever the outcome, it is clear that Williamsburg has attempted to confront a past other sites might attempt to repress. Sites in the North have not been immune to such historical amnesia, though it appears to be less a case of willful repression and more a case of genuine lack of awareness. The recently excavated African Burial Ground in New York has drawn attention to the operations of the "peculiar institution" in the North, as have the 2008 documentary *Traces of the Trade: A Story from the Deep North,* and the investigation by Brown University of its own relation to the transatlantic slave trade. None of these has been without controversy; each increases awareness of the North's role in the slave trade and demands a response from northern historical sites.[37]

As the Colonial Williamsburg reenactment attests, the question of how to stage, represent, or discuss slavery is a vexed one, yet it is one that Joseph Lloyd Manor advertises as part of its on-site educational programs for schoolchildren. While there are "Colonial Childhood" and "Colonial Craftsmen Program" units, suitable for grades two to four (children might learn to churn butter, write with quill pens, and "Discover artifacts made by colonial potters, carpenters, coopers, and blacksmiths"), there is also a unit titled "Slavery Program, designed for children in grades 5, 7, and 11." The unit is composed of three key elements. According to the literature, students will:

- Explore the African American experience in New York and Long Island by visiting the home of former slave owners.
- Role-play as the former slaves and owners of Lloyd Manor.
- Meet the first published African American poet, Jupiter Hammon, through a video reenactment and his writings.[38]

SPLIA is to be commended for introducing a unit on the topic, and drawing on a variety of historical writings and records in its research. As part of its educational outreach, SPLIA has made available resources for teachers to introduce in advance of visits, including a vocabulary list (from A is for Abolition to U is for Underground Railway), a fictional letter from an enslaved girl named Priscilla, a "Middle Passage" activity based on the writings of Olaudah Equiano, and another involving a bill of sale for a boy. The suggested post-visit activity asks students to construct a Venn diagram based on the question "Should I stay or should I go," foregrounding the tension between family ties and freedom for many enslaved peoples.[39]

Unfortunately, it is undeniable that the phrasing of the first bullet point ("Explore the African-American experience in New York and Long Island by visiting the home of former slave-owners") has the potential to be off-putting for teachers and parents attuned to the nuances of race. Reducing a posited African American experience to slavery is highly problematic. Likewise, suggesting that one learn about slavery through the home of slave owners reifies the owner's supremacy and further minimizes the lives and experiences of enslaved peoples themselves. Whether or not SPLIA ever actually staged the unit that featured student role play as the former slaves and owner, its inclusion might still make some shy away. Repeatedly schools have curtailed such exercises, citing reasons ranging from the inappropriate conduct of students and teachers to the discomfort of students and parents. African American parents in particular have been vocal in their condemnation of such activities.[40] Allan J. Singer writes: "While students may tolerate these reenactments and participate in them, it is not clear whether they can be done with either sufficient sensitivity or authenticity. White students end up thinking they have experienced and learned more about slavery than they have any right to believe, while Black students are left embarrassed or alienated by the attempted reenactments."[41] It is unclear how often SPLIA has run this particular component, if ever, but its presence on the group's website has the power to shape how people interpret the site and its activities.

Without previous experience of Joseph Lloyd Manor, parents and teachers might be understandably reluctant to arrange visits. As the example of Colonial Williamsburg demonstrates, no matter how thoughtful organizers are in the planning and execution of such events, members of the public cannot be expected to set aside their own experiences and understandings of history and its consequences.[42] Given that surveys show African Americans find first-person interpretations of slavery problematic, Joseph Lloyd Manor might be—however unintentionally—alienating potential visitors, even those interested in the site independent of the school program.[43] This is further complicated by the fact that statistically, African Americans judge schools and museums to be less trustworthy than white Americans do, instead privileging eyewitness accounts.[44]

While this is not to say that African Americans are or should be the primary audience for the Lloyd houses, it is clear that attending to the specifics of African American tourism should be crucial for sites wishing to foreground black history in some way. Black heritage tourism has a long history: twenty years before "cultural tourism" became a buzzword in the United States following the 1995 White House Conference on Tourism, Alex Haley's novel *Roots,* and the resulting television miniseries, spurred a wave of African American heritage tourism to various sites. Heritage tourism is a $30 billion a year industry in the United States; African Americans account for $10 billion of the tourism market overall. One study reported that in 2011, "44% of African-Americans surveyed visited a heritage site or museum and/or attended a cultural event during their last travel experience."[45] Where those numbers intersect is unclear, but it is obvious that they represent potential for sites like the Lloyd houses, even as the sites must contend with slavery.

At the same time, in competing for African American literary tourists, or literary tourists of any race with an interest in African American authors, the Lloyd sites must contend with other African American literary draws that have more cachet, such as the annual Zora Neale Hurston festival in Eatonville, Florida, initiated to raise funds for the Society to Preserve Eatonville. As an all-black town founded post-emancipation, Eatonville presents the possibility of a nostalgic encounter with history for African American visitors, something foreclosed at almost all other United States historic sites, including those affiliated with literary figures. Perhaps not surprisingly, then, the event has thrived: the National Trust for Historic Preservation praised the Hurston festival as "One of 25 Cultural Tourism Success Stories"; it received the "Regional Destination Award in the Humanities" from the Cultural Olympiad, was named "One of the Top 100 Events in North America" by the American Bus Association, and was listed as one of *Newsday*'s "Top Picks."[46] The photos on the website of this week-long event with singing, performances, reading, and dancing feature a far different demographic than do those on the Joseph Lloyd Manor website, reflecting the latter's location in Lloyd Neck, Long Island, where the Lloyd houses are fairly isolated in upper-class, predominantly white enclaves.[47] One would think the proximity to New York City might mitigate this isolation and racial exclusivity, until one considers that there are few other local activities and sites to attract African American visitors, who are statistically more likely to undertake group tours than white Americans.[48]

Anecdotal evidence would suggest that unless the isolation is part of the draw, such sites suffer. A correlative might be the House of the Seven Gables in Salem, Massachusetts. As its docents note, most people who visit the house have never read Nathaniel Hawthorne's famous book of the same name. They visit because it is in Salem, where they are drawn by the ghoulish witchcraft tourism. The Hawthorne site is an obligation, or one more thing to do. Houses lived in by Poe, Whitman, and others in isolated or impoverished neighborhoods struggle far more than those the same individuals inhabited in better-trafficked locations. The Paul Laurence Dunbar House shares this geographic fate; it was closed for a period in 2009 as a result of budget cuts—despite being named one of "10 great places to become well-versed in poets" by *USA Today*.[49] Susan Warner's home, discussed by Rebecca Rego Barry later in this volume, is even more compromised, located on an island. In some ways, what the example of Hurston, when contrasted with other authors, highlights is (1) the importance of location in tourism more broadly; and (2) the fact that literary tourism works best when it is organic, emerging from a groundswell of cultural goodwill. If the site is less convenient or desirable, the author must be very beloved to draw visitors, or the location must be central to the tourist's experience of the works, as Klara-Stephanie Szlezák notes in her consideration of Walden Pond in this volume. Houses associated with lesser-known authors like Susan Warner lack the fan base that would result in significant visitor numbers, which are quite often responsible for increases in revenue, grant opportunities, and corporate sponsorships. If a corporation had to choose between sponsoring a site associated with Hammon or one associated with Du Bois, the choice seems clear; likewise, people would much rather give money to a house that preserves the spirit of Laura Ingalls Wilder's spunky pioneering heroine than Warner's evangelical one—if they even know who Warner's heroine is. This is why the Mark Twain House and Museum dwarfs the nearby Harriet Beecher Stowe Center in Hartford, Connecticut: Twain is simply more fun, both in his literary output and in his public persona. Other examples abound: Hemingway attracts more tourists than Alcott; Poe draws more attention than Margaret Fuller. The consistent gender divide reflects historical realities and the limitations imposed on what women might do and the strictures placed on their behavior. In this way, foregrounding Hurston is a welcome intervention on more than one level. The Hurston festival is a recent creation, but the goodwill was there and growing; it simply lacked an outlet.

It seems redundant to point out that Hammon is no Hurston. There is not much to laugh at or with, or clap or sing along to, in his works. We have no dynamic, irreverent figure or sophisticated, earthy wit to carry us. In short: Hammon isn't *fun*. The problem, then, is how does one present Hammon to potential audiences? Joseph Lloyd Manor treats Hammon as an additive component. While the Lloyds remain primary, significant special events have been staged that celebrate Hammon, including a historical dialogue between Hammon and Phillis Wheatley, and a celebration of the three-hundredth anniversary of Hammon's birth.[50] At the same time, though Hammon is a central figure on the premises, and features prominently in a video, in scripted materials students are not asked to engage actively with him, his life, or his writings. Instead, other fictional samples are substituted in educational materials, both the "Slavery Program" and the "18th Century Childhood" unit. Henry Lloyd Manor House, which has fewer resources for the staging of special events, does foreground Hammon as a key component. Notably, Hammon is central to the site's marketing and promotions: of the seven tabs on its home page, only two are non-administrative, and these are labeled "Lloyd Family" and "Jupiter Hammon."[51] At Henry Lloyd Manor House, his presentation would seem to balance that of the Lloyd family, with interior and exterior representations. Lacking an identifiable gravesite—popular with literary tourists in particular, or those wishing to experience a more immediate sense of connection to an author or historical figure—Hammon is instead memorialized here by a plaque, presented in 1977 by what is now the Association for the Study of African American Life and History. Yet recognizing or even celebrating Hammon's presence does not appear to have fundamentally shifted the ways in which the Lloyds are conceived.

Therein lies both the problem in representing Hammon and a potential solution. As it stands, while Hammon is undeniably a valued component at both Lloyd houses, and in no way neglected in programming, current representations of his life still seem insufficiently contextualized. While significant work has been undertaken on black life on Long Island by Lynda R. Day and Grania Bolton Marcus,[52] and SPLIA actively and enthusiastically partnered with the Center for Public Archaeology at Hofstra University in excavating and exploring black life at Joseph Lloyd Manor and staging related events, educational materials and online and on-site exhibits have not yet used this information to enrich our understanding of Hammon as rooted within a black community.[53] Instead, he is presented primarily as a nominal member of the Lloyd family; the docent I met with repeated the unattributed claim that he may have slept in an upstairs room in Joseph Lloyd Manor.[54] This formulation of Hammon as a Lloyd production is not original to the Lloyd houses or SPLIA; indeed, it is a representation inherited from the preexisting Lloyd scholarship. This presentation as "honorary family member" parallels the tendency in previously published accounts to interpret Hammon's education, religious orientation, and activities as resulting from white interventions in his life, not as examples of black agency or ability.[55]

Concomitantly, reinscribing the notion that Hammon was singled out by the Lloyds because of his exceptional abilities ignores the way in which the concept of "exceptional" was highly constructed and necessarily excluded those who openly resisted the Lloyds' authority, thus implicitly undermining the capacity of Hammon's fellow slaves. To turn this on its head, instead of considering why Hammon was the beneficiary of "exceptional" treatment, this approach takes for granted the Lloyds' leniency as slaveholders in allowing him to publish. The impression one gets from established Lloyd scholarship is that Jupiter Hammon was more capable than his black peers, politically oriented toward black uplift certainly, but socially oriented toward his owners.[56] Uncomfortably, such scholarship implicitly invokes the mythic specter of the "happy slave." The related representation of the Lloyds is as slave owners who are strangely disconnected from the day-to-day operations and injustices of slavery which sustained their enterprises, instead functioning as seemingly enlightened benefactors when the opportunity arose.[57]

In all fairness, this dissonance we see in the representation of the Lloyds and Hammon is common in the presentations of many smaller house museums lacking the resources necessary to hire consultants, overhaul programming, and develop their exhibitions as they would like.[58] As Joanne Melish noted in 2006, "At the beginning of a new century, many historic sites still do not offer fully integrated histories."[59] Instead, "smaller museums . . . offer pictures of a white middle class endlessly absorbed in its cultural production. Even when these museums attempt to be inclusive they [tend to] reflect mainstream cultural prejudices and reinforce popular stereotypes."[60] Larger, more obvious sites are not exempt: African Americans continue to struggle for inclusion in Civil War sites, while Colonial Williamsburg has been characterized as "a celebration of European colonial history with enslaved Africans as an unavoidable incident, viewed from the perspective of those celebrating the European heritage."[61] Thus the current Hammon presentation is not uncommon in the representation of black peoples at historical sites originally conceived of as the literal and symbolic territory of whites. The inevitable tension arises from the foundational impetus to represent the home owners nostalgically while also celebrating the colonial past and revolutionary spirit—a tendency common to most house museums, if not the entire origin of historic preservation—and the impossibility of doing so in relation to slavery.

A productive public reconsideration of Hammon and his work might be facilitated by considering him not as exceptional, or as a treasured black member of a community of whites, but within the context of a slave-holding community and a vibrant black interrelated intergenerational community—where Hammon's own writings make clear he located himself. Concomitantly, the presence and history of black people could be more thoroughly understood as fundamentally constitutive of the narrative of the Lloyds. Such epistemological shifts have the potential to revitalize audience engagement across race with both Hammon and his writings. It is hard to read Hammon as insufficiently opposed to slavery when you place him in the context of a thriving business in which people who looked just like him—and indeed some of whom were probably related to him—were bought and sold with some regularity. For instance, Hammon's first published poem, a plea for salvation, was composed in 1760—the same year Henry Lloyd bought an eight-year-old girl, Hannah. Ten months later the enslaved Cyrus unsuccessfully attempted to escape from John Lloyd. While Hammon is best remembered for his "Address to Miss Phillis Wheatley," she is not the first Phillis he knew: Joseph Lloyd owned a woman named Phillis, born circa 1680, who alongside Maria and Aurelia (with her fifteen-month-old child) was appraised for sale in 1729 and 1730. A fellow Lloyd slave, Hester, apparently used every resource—including white community opinion—to ensure that she and her children would not be sold away from friends to South Carolina. "Let Cesar be sold for the most he will fetch if he continues sullen," Henry Lloyd Jr. wrote in 1770. Hammon's own father, Obium, ran away on at least two occasions preceding Hammon's birth.[62] Thus when Hammon cautions that he has "never said nor done anything, neither directly nor indirectly, to promote or to prevent freedom," a stance some might interpret as complacency, he equivocates in a way his black peers would recognize as tied to self-preservation—no doubt including the protection of his extended family, also owned by the Lloyds.[63] After all, by the very act of writing and publishing, Hammon covertly contested the justifications for racial bondage; overtly plotting or fomenting rebellion, he well knew, could result in his death, even in New York.[64]

While the Lloyd papers provide context for some of the specific practices of slavery within which Hammon was embedded, they are less direct in locating Hammon within a black community. This context, however, has the potential to be dramatically expanded by recent research. Charla Bolton and Reginald Metcalf have undertaken extensive genealogical and historical excavations which document Hammon's family ties and extended community, and have the additional benefit of expanding our knowledge of other members of his family and broader black community. Key among their findings is the possibility that Hammon spent the last years of his life not cared for by the Lloyds but rather, in all probability, in the home of his grandnephew, suggesting competing networks and orientations. From 2007 to 2009, Jenna Wallace Coplin and Christopher N. Matthews of the Center for Public Archaeology at Hofstra undertook excavations on the property of Joseph Lloyd Manor of a dwelling believed to have been once occupied by other black men, women, and children.[65] This is in many ways crucial, as from the perspective of African American tourism, historic houses work better when the dwellings were occupied by African Americans, not by whites with uncertainty as to just where their posited racial, social, and economic subordinates were quartered. Moreover, visitors to such sites, regardless of race, are "more willing to hear the story of slavery in the slave quarters than . . . in the main house."[66] Additionally intriguing at Joseph Lloyd Manor is the recovery of artifacts, numbering in the thousands, and awaiting full analysis.[67] As it stands at this writing, the representation of the Lloyds is grounded in material objects, while the lives of those they enslaved and their descendants are ephemeral and disembodied, unintentionally reinscribing their liminal status. Interpretations, re-creations, and presentations of such objects have the potential to rectify the imbalance in material representations of the lives of the inhabitants, thus bringing black life—including Hammon's—into sharper focus. Other literary tourist sites may benefit from a wealth of artifacts—a pen, a desk, a coat—but there is currently nothing personal or material at the Lloyd houses to enrich a visitor's sense of connection to Hammon beyond facsimiles of the texts themselves. Future archaeological endeavors may change this. While the excavations have been limited to the Joseph Lloyd Manor site, those associated with both sites have been active in encouraging and facilitating this work.

Expanding our understanding of Hammon beyond Long Island to New York City, where he also participated in black community activities, is likewise possible. For instance, it seems more than probable that Hammon knew individuals subsequently buried in the recently excavated African Burial Ground, which operated from the late seventeenth century to 1794 in lower Manhattan.[68] In this way, Hammon has the potential to be interpreted as representative of a broader community participating in extended networks of communication among the free and enslaved, native-born and African-born. Thinking about Hammon as part of an extended African diasporic community further disrupts the representation of him as exceptional or isolated, likewise making him a far more compelling figure for prospective visitors and reconfiguring how the sites might be interpreted.[69] To a certain extent, Joseph Lloyd Manor has already introduced such considerations by placing Hammon in dialogue with Wheatley, a position that echoes his own imaginative conceptualization.

Inevitably, enriching our understanding of Hammon and his black community would necessarily shift how the Lloyd family is presented in relation to slavery. While I am not arguing for renaming the sites after their best-known inhabitant, I would suggest that these sites might be productively reconsidered not as Lloyd houses first and foremost but as interstitial colonial spaces where black and white people lived together, experiencing the full, complex, messy world of slavery, steeped in both European and African traditions, and confronting the lived consequences of eighteenth-century religion, philosophy, and politics. Having said that, I believe it would be interesting to stop and consider how different these sites might be if they were treated not as Lloyd family sites or colonial spaces invoking nostalgia for simpler times, with black history added in, but first and foremost as African American sites, with all of the complications that would entail.[70] After all, they are undeniably and fundamentally black history sites, representing the rich complexity of black survival in the Americas, including African retentions, syncretic practices, and black creativity and ingenuity. Furthermore, it is Hammon who today is experiencing renewed attention, not the Lloyds. To a certain degree, such a paradigmatic shift has already been facilitated by the generation of additional events and outreach made possible by the involvement with Hofstra University and its scholars, who have partnered with the Joseph Lloyd Manor House on a number of activities, opening up new possibilities. The next step would seem to be to permanently root considerations of Hammon and the Lloyds in the same black context. What might it mean, for instance, to introduce Hammon and his work first as the product of a black community, rather than a white one, with the influence of Rose and Obium assuming primacy over that of the Lloyds?

At the very least, reconceptualizing the sites so that African American history is taken for granted as much as Lloyd history—meaning in both its specificity and its necessary interweaving with the Lloyds—has the potential to expand the appeal of the site. By this I do not mean imagining the two houses as the territory of African Americans alone. Indeed, as Rex M. Ellis observes: "Certainly, the African-American community should be involved in developing programming relating to that community, but one should not assume that that project would benefit or interest only African Americans. . . . Such assumptions and approaches actually ghettoize minorities and their history in a naïve and dangerous way."[71] Instead, I am arguing that there might be a broader population interested in celebrating emancipation, or exploring the influences of the Caribbean in eighteenth-century New York, or considering African retentions and related crafts, all of which build on the houses' place in the wider world. While those associated with Joseph Lloyd Manor in particular—which has greater resources available to it than LHHS and Henry Lloyd Manor House—have worked diligently to expand its reach to new audiences, this seems to be a matter of proposing innovations in temporary programming and outreach rather than reflecting on the way in which the site is fundamentally conceptualized.[72] This is not to say that the interest and goodwill are not there—I would actually argue the contrary, as the partnership with Hofstra and the related activities suggest—but the difficulties of realizing such a shift are compounded by the financial and resource challenges common to small house museums across the country.

Ultimately, my hope is that more concretely and thoroughly embedding Hammon in a black community or communities might further our understanding of his life and work, and draw additional attention to him, placing him within a broader narrative of black presence and life. Admittedly, this would be a narrative crafted by researchers, as opposed to first-person testimony from Hammon, but for better or worse, this kind of fabrication is part and parcel of what historical sites do.[73] Such an endeavor might help counter the fact that Hammon is not and never will be a traditional draw for literary tourism. If, as Nicola J. Watson argues, a precondition for literary tourism is a text "that invents and solicits tourism . . . a historically specific kind of text which converts readers into tourists," Hammon's writing falls woefully short.[74] Pilgrims will probably never seek out the Lloyd houses, hoping to enrich or indulge a deeply felt connection with Hammon, as they might with Thoreau's pastoral retreat, the heroines of Alcott's *Little Women,* the gothic chills of Poe, or the manly romance of Hemingway. Recognizing and exploring the contradictions, tensions, and ambivalences Hammon himself negotiated in relation to his world of enslavement—as evidenced by his own writing, and advanced by the Hofstra endeavors—might provide a constructive way to acknowledge and perhaps defuse any ambivalences Hammon now produces. Placing him within the context of black life more broadly makes his achievements, if anything, more admirable, and draws attention to his pronounced skill in navigating the racial politics of his world.

Considering Hammon in such a context might also temper our desire for uncomplicated narratives of exceptional people. It was one thing for Douglass—a young man with few attachments, as he represents it—to escape to the free North. But where exactly could Hammon, already in the North, and with close family ties, flee to? (Keep in mind that slavery was legal in what is now Canada until 1834.) The post-emancipation life of Wheatley demonstrates the difficulties of survival for African Americans.[75] But beyond troubling our ideas about how we define heroic figures from history, Hammon's life facilitates a meaningful discussion of the difficulties of doing history itself for historic sites. Notably, Hammon provides an ideal opportunity to discuss how sites construct their narratives through an assemblage of facts, in the process constructing as well a particular truth that is conveyed to visitors. Demonstrating the shifting interpretive possibilities over time also introduces a consideration of our own constructed moment, and the ways in which we choose to construct our own vision of the past based on the sites, objects, and narratives with which we choose to engage.

At the same time, it would be shabby of me not to admit that such a suggestion probably does not reflect the primary concerns or missions of either house, or of the organizations and numerous volunteers who generously give their time, resources, and creative and physical energy to staffing, promoting, and maintaining the sites. Yet, as Szlezák observes in her chapter considering Thoreau tourism and Walden Pond, multiple narratives and strands of touristic inquiry can coexist, "catering to the demands of different audiences." In the figure of Hammon there is an opportunity to capitalize on the interests of new audiences, including those drawn to the houses by literary tourism, while also improving their offerings for existing audiences and securing potential ongoing relationships with each. In cementing their existing base and cultivating a new one, both SPLIA and LHHS have the opportunity to ensure their sites' health and longevity. While it might ultimately be impossible to invent a successful literary tourism site, driven as most are by preexisting emotional connections to an author or his work (or both), it may be possible to capitalize more successfully on a literary figure of historic import by making him more accessible to the world at large. Expanding Hammon's biography and world in a manner that teases out its complexity would certainly go some way toward expanding his appeal to twenty-first-century readers and tourists.

## NOTES

I am indebted to the SSHRC Aid to Small University grant program, as well as Mount Allison University's CultureWorks, for funding for this project. Special thanks as well to the Canadian Association of American Studies for sponsoring the panel at the Northeast MLA where this research was first presented.

1. I cannot take credit for this observation: it was a passing remark made at "Editing Early African American Literature," Forty-Eighth Conference on Editorial Problems, Munk School of Global Affairs, University of Toronto, November 9–10, 2012.
2. I am indebted to Joan McGee and Ceil Stepanian for generously and graciously facilitating my visit to both houses on June 28, 2011.

3. Donna Ann Harris, *New Solutions for House Museums: Ensuring the Long-Term Preservation of America's Historic Houses* (Lanham, Md.: AltaMira, 2007), 8–15.
4. The LHHS was formed in 1974 and from the beginning celebrated Hammon. Thomas Lask, "18th-Century Black Poet Once Lived in Suffolk: Religious Fervor Familiar to Scholars," *New York Times,* April 8, 1973. In 1977 they received the plaque commemorating Hammon. Jonathan Coren, "A Black Poet's View on Christmas 1760: America's First Black Poet" *New York Times,* December 25, 1977. Hammon was equally recognized as important to the Joseph Lloyd property early on. See Rufus B. Langhans, letter to the editor, "Our Crumbling Shrines," *New York Times,* April 16, 1974, who also mentions the need to keep up another Long Island house museum, the Walt Whitman home in Huntington, now the site of the Walt Whitman Birthplace State Historic Site and Interpretive Center.
5. See Jean B. Osann, *Henry Lloyd's Salt Box Manor House* (New York: Lloyd Harbor Historical Society, 1982), 24; Charla Bolton and Reginald Metcalf, "The Migration of Jupiter Hammon and His Family: From Slavery to Freedom and Its Consequences," *Long Island History Journal* 23, no. 2 (2013), http://lihj.cc.stonybrook.edu. Bolton and Metcalf trace Hammon's family to Africa via Barbados.
6. Dorothy C. Barck, ed., *Papers of the Lloyd Family of the Manor of Queens Village, Lloyd's Neck, Long Island, New York, 1654–1826,* 2 vols. (New York: J. J. Little and Co., 1927), 1:187. A 1722 survey of the property includes the schoolhouse. See Osann, *Henry Lloyd's Salt Box Manor House,* 17. I have as yet encountered no primary source documentation for his attendance or that of other black children.
7. George Loveridge Bowen, *James Lloyd II, M.D. (1728–1810), and His Family on Long Neck* (N.p., 1988), 200; Barck, *Papers of the Lloyd Family,* 2:243; Jupiter Hammon, "An Address to the Negroes of the State of New-York," in *America's First Negro Poet: Jupiter Hammon of Long Island,* ed. Stanley Ransom (Port Washington, N.Y.: Kennikat Press, 1970), 107.
8. Bowen, *James Lloyd II, M.D.,* 12–13; Ransom, *America's First Negro Poet,* 14. The claim that Hammon's spelling required correction appeared in "To be Published and Sold by the printers of this paper: An Address to the Negroes," *Pennsylvania Mercury and Universal Advertiser,* March 8, 1787, 4. This claim is contradicted by the recently discovered poem in Hammon's own handwriting, "An Essay on Slavery," though there is a possibility that it was already corrected, or that his spelling was erratic, as was common during the era. Cedrick May and Julie McCown also remark on the quality of Hammon's penmanship, arguing it demonstrates a practiced hand. Cedrick May and Julie McCown, " 'An Essay on Slavery': An Unpublished Poem by Jupiter Hammon," *Early American Literature* 48, no. 2 (2013): 459.
9. Ransom, *America's First Negro Poet,* 107; Bowen, *James Lloyd II, M.D.,* 198, 200.
10. Bowen, *James Lloyd II, M.D.,* 199; Osann, *Henry Lloyd's Salt Box Manor House,* 24; Bolton and Metcalf, "The Migration of Jupiter Hammon and His Family."
11. Some have made much of Hammon's being mentioned in Lloyd family letters, whether it be the Lloyd family's consultation of a doctor on his behalf or their gift to him of an old saddle. See Barck, *Papers of the Lloyd Family,* 1:309, 2:694. But mentions of other people the Lloyds held as slaves suggest for the most part these are common matters of meticulous record keeping, and indeed the Lloyds seem to have been concerned that their slaves not be "spoiled." Barck, *Papers of the Lloyd Family,* 1:261. According to May and McCown, additional papers generated by a related family do mention Jupiter in a more personal way as "faithful Jupiter" (" 'An Essay on Slavery,' " 459).
12. Briton Hammon, *A Narrative of the Uncommon Sufferings, and Surprizing Deliverance of Briton Hammon, a Negro Man* (Boston: Green and Russell, 1760). In making this claim I am excluding criminal narratives and execution narratives, which were transcribed or even formulated by an amanuensis and whose reliability and authorship may both be questionable. For more on these forms, see Jeannine Marie DeLombard, *In the Shadow of the Gallows: Race, Crime, and American Civic Identity* (Philadelphia: University of Pennsylvania Press, 2012). The website for the Wells-Thorn House in Deerfield, Massachusetts, where

Lucy Terry Prince was enslaved, makes no mention of its famous resident. "Wells-Thorn House," Historic Deerfield, www.historic-deerfield.org. Despite painstaking research by Gretchen Holbrook Gerzina reconstructing the life of Prince and her family, no additional compositions by Prince have been located. See Gretchen Holbrook Gerzina, *Mr. and Mrs. Prince: How an Extraordinary Eighteenth-Century Family Moved Out of Slavery and into Legend* (New York: HarperCollins, 2008).

13. These form the basis of the Barck *Papers of the Lloyd Family* volumes, though more records are available. The three books are Bowen, *James Lloyd II, M.D.;* Osann, *Henry Lloyd's Salt Box Manor House;* and Kenneth Scott and Susan E. Klaffky, *A History of the Joseph Lloyd Manor House* (Setauket, N.Y.: Society for the Preservation of Long Island Antiquities, 1976).
14. Bowen, *James Lloyd II, M.D.*, 9–10.
15. For more on the day-to-day operations of the Lloyd enterprises, see Barck, *Papers of the Lloyd Family;* and Bowen, *James Lloyd II, M.D.* By 1687 or 1688, James Lloyd held at least five individuals in bondage: Rose, Tomeo, Gyon, Tony, and Obium. See Barck, *Papers of the Lloyd Family,* 1:105, 109. In March of 1716, Henry Lloyd listed the births of nine slaves, including Hammon, which suggests he held legal title to a significant number of people by that date. Bowen, *James Lloyd II, M.D.*, 197.
16. Bowen, *James Lloyd II, M.D.*, 14.
17. Harris, *New Solutions for House Museums,* 42–43.
18. Osann, *Henry Lloyd's Salt Box Manor House,* 24; Bowen, *James Lloyd II, M.D.*, 199.
19. Entries for John Lloyd, Oyster Bay, Queens, New York, and John Lloyd Senior, Oyster Bay, Queens, New York, 1790 United States federal census; Grania Bolton Marcus, *Discovering the African-American Experience in Suffolk County, 1620–1860* (1988; repr., Setauket, N.Y.: Society for the Preservation of Long Island Antiquities, 1995), 14–15.
20. Scott and Klaffky, *History of the Joseph Lloyd Manor House;* SPLIA website. Wood inherited the house from her father, the industrialist William J. Matheson, founder of the National Aniline and Chemical Company.
21. Amy Levin, "Why Local Museums Matter," in *Defining Memory: Local Museums and the Construction of History in America's Changing Communities,* ed. Amy Levin (Lanham, Md.: AltaMira, 2007), 10.
22. Hammon, "Address," 108.
23. Ibid., 112–13.
24. See DeLombard, *In the Shadow of the Gallows.*
25. Blyden Jackson, *A History of Afro-American Literature,* vol. 1, *The Long Beginning, 1746–1895* (Baton Rouge: Louisiana State University Press, 1989), 37; Sondra A. O'Neale, *Jupiter Hammon and the Biblical Beginnings of African American Literature* (Metuchen, N.J.: Scarecrow Press, 1993), 120. Phillip M. Richards takes this interpretation one step further, suggesting that Hammon is in fact arguing for black nationhood. See Phillip M. Richards, "Nationalist Themes in the Preaching of Jupiter Hammon." *Early American Literature* 12 (1990): 124. This contrasts starkly with earlier interpretations, such as Jackson, *History of Afro-American Literature,* 36–37, 122.
26. Cedrick May, "An Enslaved Poet on Slavery," *Yale Alumni Magazine,* May–June 2013, www.yalealumnimagazine.com.
27. Jupiter Hammon, "A Winter Piece," in Ransom, *America's First Negro Poet,* 73–75. At the time of writing, it is unclear who exactly circulated these rumors: White apologists for slavery? Black critics of Hammon? It is also unclear if these rumors pertained to Hammon's freedom alone or emancipation more broadly.
28. Given her focus, it makes sense that Trubek also does not include the Booker T. Washington birthplace memorial, or efforts to promote the birthplace of W. E. B. Du Bois. Anne Trubek, *A Skeptic's Guide to Writers' Houses* (Philadelphia: University of Pennsylvania Press, 2011). For the questionable nature of the Booker T. Washington site, see Patricia West, *Domesticating History: The Political Origins of America's House Museums* (Washington,

D.C.: Smithsonian Institution Press, 1999), 143–47. For the birthplace of W. E. B. Du Bois, see David Glassberg and Robert Paynter, "Du Bois in Great Barrington," in *Born in the U.S.A.: Birth, Commemoration, and American Public Memory,* ed. Seth C. Bruggeman (Amherst: University of Massachusetts Press, 2012), 240–57. More recently, efforts have been undertaken to save the home of the journalist and early civil rights activist T. Thomas Fortune. See Ariana Igneri, "Securing the future of the T. Thomas Fortune House," *Atlanticville,* August 1, 2013, http://atl.gmnews.com.

29. For more on the Margaret Mitchell House and local community support, see Harris, *New Solutions for House Museums,* 129–34. While the interpretive center at the Alex Haley House has featured exhibits related to slavery, it is notable that the site's newsletter, *The Front Porch,* evades the topic from its founding in June 2010 to June 2013. See www.alex-haley.com/alex_haley_museum.htm and www.alexhaleymuseum.org/newsletters.
30. A. V. Seaton, "Sources of Slavery—Destinations of Slavery: The Silences and Disclosures of Slavery Heritage in the UK and US," in *Slavery, Contested Heritage, and Thanatourism,* ed. Graham M. S. Dann and A. V. Seaton (Binghamton, N.Y.: Haworth Hospitality Press, 2001), 108; Patricia Hudson and Sandra L. Ballard, *The Smithsonian Guide to Historic America: The Carolinas and the Appalachian States* (New York: Stewart, Tabori, and Chang, 1989), 36. Even in the mid-1990s one could do plantation tours without ever hearing the words "slave" or "slavery." In 2001 David L. Butler published the results of a survey of brochures for 102 southern plantations and found that only 30 mentioned slavery. David L. Butler, "Whitewashing Plantations: The Commodification of a Slave-Free Antebellum South," in *Slavery, Contested Heritage, and Thanatourism,* 163–75, esp. 164–68.
31. James Oliver Horton, "Slavery in American History: An Uncomfortable National Dialogue," in *Slavery and Public History: The Tough Stuff of American Memory,* ed. James Oliver Horton and Lois E. Horton (Chapel Hill: University of North Carolina Press, 2006), 48; David Lowenthal, *The Past Is a Foreign Country* (Cambridge: Cambridge University Press, 1993), 341.
32. Lois E. Horton, "Avoiding History: Thomas Jefferson, Sally Hemings, and the Uncomfortable Public Conversation on Race," in Horton and Horton, *Slavery and Public History,* 138.
33. Horton, "Slavery in American History," 44.
34. While there are historic sites associated with slavery in the United States, they lack the imaginative capital of the slave forts, which repeatedly appear in genealogy programs featuring African American subjects as sites of origin, rupture, and pilgrimage. The proposed United States National Slavery Museum has yet to be realized.
35. Horton, "Slavery in American History," 51. See Lisa Woolfork, *Embodying American Slavery in Contemporary Culture* (Urbana: University of Illinois Press, 2009), for an extended treatment of Colonial Williamsburg and the dynamics of slavery. More recently, Azie Mira Dungey, a former slave reenactor at Mount Vernon, has staged a comedic Web series titled "Ask a Slave," www.askaslave.com, based on the questions she was frequently asked while in character. Dungey's sketches reveal both the depth of ignorance about slavery and the inevitable frustration of African American employees of such sites.
36. "Slave Auction at Colonial Williamsburg—Part 1," www.youtube.com; "Before a Slave Auction at Colonial Williamsburg—Part 2," July 9, 2009, www.youtube.com.
37. The volume *Interpreting Slavery at Museums and Historic Sites,* ed. Kristin L. Gallas and James DeWolf Perry (Lanham, Md.: Rowman and Littlefield, 2014), is intended to move thinking about how to present slavery forward.
38. The information on this unit was current as of August 9, 2014. See "On Site Education: Joseph Lloyd Manor," http://splia.org.
39. Society for the Preservation of Long Island Antiquities, "Voices from Lloyd Manor. Joseph Lloyd Manor House, School Group Discovery Programs at Lloyd Harbor, Long Island. An Eighteenth Century Childhood at Lloyd Manor," n.d. (educational material); Society for the Preservation of Long Island Antiquities, "Uncovering a Forgotten People: Enslaved Africans of Lloyd Manor and 18th Century Long Island," n.d. (educational material).

40. For some examples of protest, see Vanessa De La Torre, "Parent Files Complaint against Hartford Schools over Slavery Re-Enactment on Field Trip," *Hartford Courant,* September 20, 2013; Dorian Block, "New York Teacher Binds Black Students during History Lesson on Slavery," *New York Daily News,* December 5, 2008; Peter Hancock, "District Orders Changes to 8th Grade Slavery Lesson," *Lawrence (Kans.) Journal-World,* February 19, 2013; Iamseven, "School Ends Slave-Master Role Playing Teaching Exercise after Complaint," *Digital Journal,* January 18, 2007, http://digitaljournal.com; Thoai Lu, "Student Humiliated by Mock Slave Auction at Ohio School," *Colorlines,* March 11, 2011, http://colorlines.com; Kevin Sieff, "Va. Teacher Holds Mock Slave Auction," *Washington Post,* April 11, 2011; Alexis Garrett Stodghill, "School Near Atlanta Comes Under Fire for Slavery Recess Game," *the grio* (NBC), January 26, 2012, http://thegrio.com. For potentially more productive uses of role play, see Bob Peterson, "Rethinking the Constitutional Convention: A Role Play," in *Rethinking Our Classrooms,* vol. 2, *Teaching for Equity and Justice,* ed. Bill Bigelow (Milwaukee: Rethinking Schools, 2001), 63–69; and Kate Thomsen, *Building Resilient Students: Integrating Resiliency into What You Already Know and Do* (Thousand Oaks, Calif.: Corwin, 2002), 78.
41. Alan J. Singer, *New York and Slavery: Time to Teach the Truth* (Albany: State University of New York Press, 2008), 19.
42. It might be for this reason that some historic sites report problems hiring African American historic reenactors. See Woolfork, *Embodying American Slavery,* 163–68; J. Freedom du Lac, "Slavery Is a Tough Role, Hard Sell at Colonial Williamsburg," *Washington Post,* March 8, 2013.
43. Horton, "Slavery in American History," 51–52.
44. Roy Rosenzweig and David Thelan, *The Presence of the Past: Popular Uses of History in American Life* (New York: Columbia University Press, 1998), 156. Baltimore's National Great Blacks in Wax Museum might be an exception. Lisa Woolfork comments that its exhibits—which include a life-size reproduction of a slave ship characterized by the worst violence of the trade—are treated as more trustworthy by African Americans than those of Colonial Williamsburg, which boasts a team of historians. Woolfork, *Embodying American Slavery,* 110.
45. Cheryl Finley, "The Door of (No) Return," *Common-Place* 1, no. 4 (2001), www.common-place.org; Angela da Silva, "African American Heritage Tourism," *Preservation Issues* (Missouri Department of Public Resources) 7, no. 3 (September–October 2011): 10–12; "2012 Proclaimed 'Year of African-American Heritage Tourism,'" *Black Meetings and Tourism,* n.d., www.blackmeetingsandtourism.com (quotation).
46. "19th Annual Zora Neale Hurston Fest Set for Eatonville, FL," *Emerging Minds,* January 16, 2008, http://emergingminds.org.
47. According to the 2010 U.S. census, Lloyd Harbor is over 95 percent white, with the African American population hovering around 1 percent. This makes it one of the most segregated areas in the United States. The median income is almost $400,000, with fewer than 1.5 percent of residents living below the poverty line. "Lloyd Harbor Village," United States Census Bureau, 2010, http://factfinder2.census.gov.
48. Trubek, *A Skeptic's Guide to Writers' Houses,* 16–18. Approximately three times as many African American trips involve group tours as trips by travelers overall (10 percent versus 3 percent). Travel Industry Association of America, *The Minority Traveler* (Washington, D.C.: Travel Industry Association of America, 2003).
49. Trubek, *A Skeptic's Guide to Writers' Houses,* 115; Jim DeBrosse, "Ohio Historical Society Will Maintain Dunbar House; Residents Pitch in to Keep Doors Open," *Dayton Daily News,* April 8, 2009, www.daytondailynews.com.
50. Jenna Coplin, "Hammon and Wheatley Speak," October 7, 2009, Joseph Lloyd Manor House.
51. Lloyd Harbor Historical Society, "Jupiter Hammon: America's First Colonial Afro-American Published Poet," www.lloydharborhistoricalsociety.org.

52. See Lynda R. Day, *Making a Way to Freedom: A History of African Americans on Long Island* (Interlaken, N.Y.: Empire State Books, 1997); and Marcus, *Discovering the African-American Experience in Suffolk County.*
53. The Center's activities deliberately placed Hammon in conversation with others of African ancestry, and in support of this, numerous events were staged with SPLIA's wholehearted endorsement. These included talks on African American history and genealogy, an event with the E.R.A.S.E. Racism organization, and a 501(c)(3) grant regarding research and race in the region. Unfortunately the Center is now defunct, and it remains to be seen if this previous programming will have any influence on new materials when SPLIA has the resources to produce them. My thanks to Jenna Coplin for her generosity in sharing information about the Center's activities with SPLIA. Email to the author, October 2, 2013.
54. Undeniably there is evidence that northern enslaved peoples, usually household workers, lived in the homes of their masters, though this may have been less common in settings where larger numbers of people, including extended family units, were enslaved. See Gerzina, *Mr. and Mrs. Prince,* 69; James Oliver Horton and Lois E. Horton, *In Hope of Liberty: Culture, Community and Protest among Northern Free Blacks, 1700–1860* (New York: Oxford University Press, 1997), 16.
55. See Bowen, *James Lloyd II, M.D.,* 199–200, and Osann, *Henry Lloyd's Salt Box Manor House,* 24, who both suggest that Mrs. Lloyd (née Mary Atwater Clark) was Hammon's primary influence—though Bowen also credits Nehemiah Bull, who was a schoolteacher for the Lloyds in the 1720s. As Mrs. Lloyd was a published author herself, this seems plausible. Nevertheless, other religious black figures existed in the vicinity who did not have access to Mrs. Lloyd, including Blind Betty, a contemporary of Hammon's, who memorized the Bible. Day, *Making a Way to Freedom,* 29.
56. That visitors receive this impression is evident in the questions they are most likely to pose: "Why was he treated so nicely?"; "Why was he treated differently from the other slaves?"; "Maybe he was Henry's son?" Ceil Stepanian in discussion with the author, June 28, 2011. Bolton and Metcalf, "The Migration of Jupiter Hammon and His Family," is an important corrective.
57. While the materials for the specialized "Slavery Program" targeted toward youth more directly address the institution and ask children to consider what life might have been like for a enslaved child, black agency and resistance are absent. The exception would be the inclusion of activities based on the freedom quilt hypothesis, now widely accepted by academics and quilt and folklore historians as a twentieth-century invention. See Leigh Fellner, "Betsy Ross Redux: The Underground Railroad 'Quilt Code,'" Cottage Quilts, www.ugrrquilt.hartcottagequilts.com/.
58. Their historical owners' involvement is, however, more pronounced, including investing in slave-trading voyages and selling slaves as retail stock; see Barck, *Papers of the Lloyd Family.*
59. Joanne Melish, "Recovering (from) Slavery: Four Struggles to Tell the Truth," in Horton and Horton, *Slavery and Public History,* 103.
60. Levin, "Why Local Museums Matter," 12.
61. Erriel Roberson, *The Maafa and Beyond: Remembrance, Ancestral Connections, and Nation Building for the African Global Community* (Columbia, Md.: Kujichagulia Press, 1995), 19. I am indebted to Lisa Woolfork for pointing me toward Roberson.
62. Barck, *Papers of the Lloyd Family,* 2:584–85. Hannah is not the youngest child on record as being purchased or sold by the Lloyds without a parent; that would be Phebe, six years old in 1773; see 2:743, 571. For appraisal, see 1:307, 311. The negotiation appears at 2:746. For consequences of being sullen, see 2:723. Obium's attempted escapes are mentioned at 1:111, 144.
63. Hammon, "An Address," 73. Hammon's brother Richard is also recorded as the property

of the Lloyds. Richard's family has been traced by Bolton and Metcalf ("The Migration of Jupiter Hammon and His Family").

64. Horton and Horton, *In Hope of Liberty*, 28.
65. Jenna Coplin and Christopher Matthews, "The Archaeology of Captivity and Freedom at Joseph Lloyd Manor," African Diaspora Archaeology Network, December 2007, www.diaspora.illinois.edu/.
66. Rex M. Ellis, "Interpreting the Whole House," in *Interpreting Historic House Museums*, ed. Jessica Donnelly (Walnut Creek, Calif.: AltaMira, 2002), 68.
67. Jenna Coplin, "Preliminary Report Excavations at Joseph Lloyd Manor," submitted to Society for the Preservation of Long Island Antiquities, Robert MacKay, Ph.D., Director, September 17, 2009.
68. See Ned Kaufman, *Place, Race, and Story: Essays on the Past and Future of Historic Preservation* (New York: Routledge, 2009), esp. from 299 on.
69. On my visit to the Henry Lloyd House, I was told of possible examples of African retentions deployed during the 1711 building of the house and uncovered during maintenance work.
70. This is not to ignore the rich history of First Nations peoples on Long Island, nor to ignore possible interactions with or influences on the residents of both houses. Indeed, I recognize that this is an additional piece of the puzzle which I unfortunately do not have the space to address productively here.
71. Ellis, "Interpreting the Whole House," 76.
72. Center for Public Archaeology, *Connections: History, Preservation and Community, A Long Island Forum* (N.p.: Hofstra University, 2011), 2–12.
73. Ellis, "Interpreting the Whole House," 67.
74. Nicola J. Watson, *The Literary Tourist* (New York: Palgrave Macmillan, 2006), 12.
75. Vincent Carretta, *Phillis Wheatley: Biography of a Genius in Bondage* (Athens: University of Georgia Press, 2011).

# 2

# *"Step forth and again take up its magic pen"*

## The Author's House as Informal Memorial

ERIN HAZARD

*A collection concerned with the development of American literary tourism must include in its investigations Washington Irving. A preeminent literary tourist himself, and a soul keenly concerned with the preservation of George Washington's memory, Irving purchased the house that would become Sunnyside in 1835 with a goal of creating the ultimate American author's home. Despite this impulse, he, like Henry David Thoreau and Nathaniel Hawthorne, did not necessarily expect that this house and its contents would become a museum. Erin Hazard discusses the state of limbo that early literary tourist sites faced as they transitioned from nineteenth-century private homes and studies into public literary sites in the twentieth century. Along the way she uncovers what a series of individual curatorial and preservation acts reveal about Irving, his family, and popular interest in private literary spaces. While the preceding chapter establishes one of the major problems in literary tourism—the paucity of literary sites and museums devoted to African American authors and their literary creations—Hazard takes us to American literary tourism's formal origins in the nineteenth century.*

In the summer of 1835, Washington Irving purchased a small vernacular cottage on the banks of the Hudson River, with the intent of creating the first American literary tourist attraction. Irving was aware of the power of literary tourism: his project came at the end of many years spent traveling in Britain and Europe, where he had visited sites such as Shakespeare's birthplace in Stratford-upon-Avon and Sir Walter Scott's house, Abbotsford, using them as material for the essays he published under the literary persona Geoffrey

Crayon. Pondering the frustrations and enticements of literary attractions, Irving reveals in these essays a keen understanding of how nineteenth-century British literary attractions worked. Irving observed that visitors anticipate objects and locations securely linked to an author and his works—the lack thereof receives much commentary in "Stratford-on-Avon"—and that the ultimate thrill is a visit to a literary house and landscape in the company of the resident author, as he detailed in "Abbotsford." After Irving settled at Sunnyside on the Hudson, he deployed his knowledge of readers' desires when he published a letter to the editor of the *Knickerbocker Magazine* under the guise of his literary persona Geoffrey Crayon "documenting" his purchase of the Roost,[1] and as he undertook renovations that explicitly linked it to his existing writings about Dutch New York ("The Legend of Sleepy Hollow" or *History of New York*).[2] And he provided the greatest draw of all: himself as resident celebrity author.

Having imbibed the mores of literary tourism, in part from Irving's writings, American readers embraced the opportunity to travel on American soil as Geoffrey Crayon had done in Britain. Like Geoffrey Crayon, they sought out sites that linked authors' writings with objects, architecture, places, and of course the authors themselves. But as Irving's "Stratford-on-Avon" points out, this coordination of author, place, architecture, and objects falls apart easily after the death of an author. Taking Irving's Sunnyside, Henry David Thoreau's effects from Walden, and Nathaniel Hawthorne's Concord home The Wayside as my examples, in this essay I examine what happened to these sites and objects when their resident authors passed away. No longer inhabited or possessed by their luminaries but not yet properly historical in their literary associations, the first American authors' house attractions stood in limbo in the second half of the nineteenth century, a limbo that shows us something not previously revealed about how a house turns into a museum. Because these houses were exhibition sites while they were inhabited and then continued to be so during the decades when they turned from literary to literary *and* historical sites, there is an archive of information that allows us to see how they materially transformed from inhabited literary attractions into proper literary and historical house museums. Examining the historical link between the period when these houses were inhabited and the time when they became public museums not only demonstrates how a category of American houses became museumified but also offers a better understanding of historic house museums generally. Three later nineteenth-century posthumous authors' environments—Sunnyside, the display of Henry David Thoreau's effects at the Concord Antiquarian Society, and Nathaniel Hawthorne's Wayside—show a centrifugal tendency in their offering of exhibitions as substitutes for deceased authors as objects, then rooms, and finally itineraries in which visitors moved through the house and its surrounding landscape.

Admittedly, scholars from a range of disciplines have expressed interest in the question of how a house transforms into a museum. Existing studies are, for the most part, stories about how in nineteenth-century America it became possible for the public to *imagine* an American historical past and then to include already historical houses in the larger category of American public museums. Historical narratives of the American preservation movement run from the purchase of Mount Vernon to the purchase of Monticello and then often to the foundation of the Society for the Preservation of New England Antiquities.[3] Jan Cohn, in her study of the symbolic import of the American house *The Palace or the Poorhouse,* considers the role that the later nineteenth-century historical house essay genre plays in the advent of the conception of the house as a shrine.[4] Useful as these histories are, they seldom offer a glimpse of a house materially transforming into the historic house museum we are familiar with to this day. The case studies they examine are instances in which organizations or individuals had the idea of preserving a historical house first and then applied their ideas to already existing historical houses such as Mount Vernon or Monticello.

Given the historical position of nineteenth-century American authors' houses and the fact that many were attractions from the beginning, they offer a window onto exactly this transformation from house to museum in a way that historical houses of the same period do not. Writing generally about collections, Krzysztof Pomian argues that the collection is always a set of objects deprived of their usefulness, mediating between their audience and something invisible.[5] Applying Pomian's idea of the "invisible" to houses, and thinking of it more broadly as an intangible *something* that renders the material world fit for visual contemplation, reveals a significant difference between America's literary and historic houses during the second half of the nineteenth century. A historic house first had to acquire the "invisible" of historic significance over time, and then an individual, association, or community preserved it for that reason. Though books have their own histories as material objects, nineteenth-century literary tourists were drawn to authors' houses by the "invisible" of literary imaginings or the "invisible" of an author's celebrity during the author's lifetime and immediately after his or her death. While historians have examined the efforts to preserve sites associated with the Revolutionary War as well as the "colonial kitchen" displays at world's fairs and sanitary exhibitions, the informal preservation of authors' houses has received little attention. Their proto-curators devised strategies to re-create the appearance of houses' former resident authors using objects and architecture that foreshadowed, and indeed helped to form, many of the conventions now common in historic house museums.

### *Sunnyside: Irving's Relics*

During his tenure at Sunnyside, Irving allowed the house to mediate with a variety of, to use Pomian's term, "invisibles." Under Irving's direction, Sunnyside became a fantastic historicist environment, akin to Sir Walter Scott's Abbotsford.[6] In addition to serving as an invented literary landscape, Sunnyside was popularly presented as an emblem or physiognomy of Irving. As one author wrote, "It [Sunnyside] has grown up out of our author's own heart, and both in unity and in detail it is a striking reflex of his character, and even, fanciful as the parallel may seem to be, of his physique and manner."[7] While this thinking allowed Sunnyside to serve as a concrete counterpart to or even substitute for Irving, many visitors' accounts present the ultimate goal of a visit to Sunnyside as a visit with Irving. For these visitors, the house was nothing more than the container of Irving's genius. The abundance of visitors' accounts published after Irving's death suggest that the author greeted many traveling readers with hospitality, meeting with them in his study and inviting them to share in the family mealtime with his two resident nieces, Sarah and Catharine Irving.[8]

As the author aged and his health declined, visitors sought souvenirs attesting to his presence and also his writing practice; a number of visitors' accounts identify Irving's pen as exactly such a souvenir. Samuel Austin Allibone, the future editor of *A Critical Dictionary of English Literature and British and American Authors,* was brought to Sunnyside by Irving's publisher, G. P. Putnam. Allibone desired a glimpse of Irving's study:

> Some pens were on the desk. I took one in my hand: "How valuable one of these pens would be," I remarked "I am almost tempted to ask for one."
>
> He smiled and replied, "You are very welcome to any one of them;" and he took one up, and presented it to me.
>
> "Probably," said I, "this is the one you have used in writing the Life of Washington?" He replied that it was.[9]

The Tarrytown doctor who attended Irving on his deathbed would later recall another such pen: "He was physically unable at times to pursue his work, and began to fear that he should not be spared to finish it, and I recall the day when he in almost exultation said, 'I have finished my work, and, to fullfil [*sic*] a promise, I am going to take this *pen* to Mrs. Edwin Bartlett.' Mrs. Bartlett placed the *gold pen* in a handsome oval frame of black walnut, beautifully carved, representing the coat of arms of the United States and England."[10] Another visitor to Irving at this time reports on his peep into the author's study, describing Irving's pen in a manner that suggests its staging in a sort of proto–museum display with Irving's niece filling the role of curator: "The [study] walls are laden with books and pictures, which evidently are re-arranged every day by some delicate hand; for none of the books were tumbled into a corner, and no papers were lying loose upon the table. The pen, too, was laid precisely parallel to the edge of the inkstand—a nicety which only a womanly housekeeper would persevere to maintain!"[11] It is notable that this early collecting and curating of Irving's effects—whether in the instance of the pen carried away as a souvenir or the pen perceived by a visitor as in a tableau or the pen displayed in a frame on the wall—involve the objects with which Irving ostensibly wrote his epic *Life of Washington.*

In addition to writing a biography of Washington, Irving was involved in movements to turn two houses associated with Washington, the Hasbrouck House and Mount Vernon, into museum sites. In 1850 Irving and others successfully petitioned the State of New York to purchase Washington's headquarters in Hasbrouck, New York.[12] While researching his biography of Washington, Irving thanked Robert C. Winthrop: "I am also much obliged to you for the clippings which you send me from newspapers, giving familiar anecdotes of Washington. It is surprising how few anecdotes there are of him in his familiar life—but he was essentially a public character and so regulated in conduct by square and rule as [to] furnish very little of the amusing and picturesque anecdote that we find in the lives of more irregular men."[13] Irving the biographer appears to have recognized the potential of objects to suggest details of Washington's "familiar" life lacking in the archives. Immediately after Irving's own death, Charles Lanman published an account of a research trip Irving had made to the house of George Washington Parke Custis, Washington's step-grandson, who had resided at Mount Vernon with him: "Mr. Irving's main object in visiting Arlington [Custis's residence, Arlington House] was to gather items of personal information about Washington. . . . The pictures, the books, and the furniture—relics of Mount Vernon—were all exhibited."[14] After the publication of his biography in 1859, Irving deemed the Mount Vernon Ladies' Association's efforts to purchase Mount Vernon and transform it into a museum meritorious of a $500 donation.[15] The association was able to complete the purchase that year and open Mount Vernon as a museum one year later in 1860.

Following Irving's death in 1859, Sarah and Catharine Irving assumed a heightened importance in the mythology and history of his house. In his will, Irving took special care to ensure that Sunnyside remained in the Irving family, bequeathing it to his brother Ebenezer and then to Ebenezer's daughters (Sarah and Catharine), as long as they did not marry.[16] Popular features on Sunnyside during the nieces' tenure present the women as Irving's caretakers and curators. One visitor, recalling time spent at Sunnyside, writes that Sarah and Catharine Irving "were ever ministering to the slightest wish of their honoured uncle."[17] It is not surprising that the nieces' "ministering" to their uncle transformed into the curating of Sunnyside after his death, for a curator might be either a minister to souls or the caretaker of a property. But what were the possibilities facing these unlikely inheritors of a property deemed culturally significant on the basis of its very recent literary associations? While Irving used Sunnyside as a means of self-promotion during his lifetime and also participated in the nascent historic preservation movement, the Irving nieces' task of exhibiting Irving's former but not yet historical house on the basis of its literary associations was, as of 1859, uncharted. It is not surprising, then, that their preservation activities at Sunnyside were nearly undocumented. The visual and anecdotal evidence remaining from their tenure, however, shows the Irving sisters used a carefully arranged nexus of objects in Irving's study to substitute for the author's presence and create a family-tended shrine to the author.

The earliest attempts at memorializing Irving and Sunnyside suggest a will to restore Irving to the house, particularly to his study. Mere days after Irving's death on November 28, 1859, the art dealer Michael Knoedler commissioned the artist W. H. Powell to provide "a memorial which the lapse of time would only render more difficult to evoke from the resources of art."[18] According to Knoedler, the Irving family assisted Powell, allowing him to sketch inside the Sunnyside study and supplying him with a bust, portraits of Irving in his youth, and "a daguerreotype, which had been taken of Mr. Irving after he had entered his sixty-fifth year."[19] Today a watercolor by Powell of Irving in the Sunnyside study, similar to the full-scale "memorial" work later reproduced as an engraving, survives in the collections of Historic Hudson Valley.[20] The Sunnyside study has little visual significance in this image. It is reduced to a window seat, a curtain, and some scattered books. Of primary interest is the portrait of Irving, head in hand, with his elbow on the sill of the window. The painter's emphasis on Irving suggests that, in the period immediately following his death, an interest in imaginatively re-creating his residence trumped the arrangement or preservation of objects associated with him.

Later posthumous images likewise include Irving but start to emphasize the objects in the Sunnyside study as a means of memorializing him. In 1863 Christian Schussele painted *Washington Irving and His Literary Friends at*

*Sunnyside* after an engraving by Irving illustrator Felix O. C. Darley. Schussele's image, indebted to Thomas Faed's 1849 image of Scott and his literary friends at Abbotsford, restores Irving, with fourteen other American writers, to the Sunnyside study. Though the emphasis is admittedly on the figures, within the confines of the shadowed (and greatly enlarged) study, certain identifiable elements are discernible: the geometric carpeting, the curtains in front of the lounge with bookcases behind, and a painting on the left wall. Benjamin Lossing visited Irving at Sunnyside weeks before Irving's death and in 1860–61 published a series of views of Sunnyside in the *London Art Journal;* the same images were later included in Lossing's 1866 volume *The Hudson from the Wilderness to the Sea.*[21] Lossing depicts Irving in the room (again enlarged), as did Powell and Schussele, but here he seems one of the many fixtures of the study that demand Lossing's attention, like the curtained alcove with bookshelves and lounge, the partners desk given to Irving by his publisher G. P. Putnam, and the mantelpiece with candelabra and framed pictures.

In 1887 a photogravure of the Irving study included in the Putnam publication *The Land of Sleepy Hollow* shows the study's transformation into a reliquary for Irving's remaining effects (fig. 2.1).[22] Though the medium of the photograph rendered the imaginative return of Irving achieved in Powell's, Schussele's, and Lossing's images impossible, the photograph is no less a work of the imagination. The careful arrangement of a nexus of objects, obviously preserved by the Irving sisters, stands in for the author in his absence. The study alcove, Ball Hughes's bust of the author, and Irving's Voltaire chair and desk inhabit the now unused space, while the informal arrangement of papers and writing implements atop the desk conveys recent activity and the sense that the author is on his way to complete work yet undone. Some three decades after Irving's death, the "invisible" of Irving's former use of these objects elevated them into relics capable of mediating his former presence.

> She told us that they feared to remain there because of their remoteness from any neighbors. At that time there were no houses to be seen from the lane. The railroad, just below the house, was infested with tramps, who often alarmed them. Even as she spoke, a horrid hairy-faced figure appeared at the open French window leading to the porch. Stepping lightly toward the window, in a frightened, timid voice she said: "Go away, go away, this is a private house." And he went away with surprising agility. I was greatly relieved. "That is why sister and I cannot stay in this lovely place," she explained, as she resumed her seat.[23]

If Black's recollection is accurate, the Irving sisters struggled with intruders. At least toward the end of their residence, the Misses Irving used Sunnyside

FIGURE 2.1. Dr. J. L. Williams, "The quiet, secluded, poetic haunt in which a great author wrote his greatest works." From *The Land of Sleepy Hollow, and the home of Washington Irving; a series of photogravure representations, with descriptive letter-press by J. L. Williams* (New York: G. P. Putnam, 1887), 66.

as a summer house, leaving servants to care for the property while they spent their winters in Manhattan.[24] By the 1890s, the house was reportedly in need of repairs, which the Irving nieces were financially incapable of completing.[25] Respecting their uncle's expressed wish to keep Sunnyside in the Irving family, the nieces sold it to their nephew Alexander Duer Irving in March 1896.[26] Sarah Irving retained possession of the books and furniture in the study until her death, evidently feeling an obligation to their maintenance.[27] Before their nephew undertook any renovations, the Irving sisters saw that "the rooms were photographed, that everything might be arranged in exactly the same position as before."[28]

The Irving sisters' removal from Sunnyside signaled the close of that spirit of informality and compromise that had made possible their simultaneous inhabitation and exhibition of Sunnyside. Alexander Duer Irving sought to ensure the privacy of the property even as the community expressed a heightened sense of entitlement to the site. By the end of the nineteenth century, the precedent existed for such a house to be operated as a public museum. In 1893 the poet John Greenleaf Whittier's childhood house in Haverhill, Massachusetts, was purchased by the mayor and turned over to the Haverhill Whittier Club to be operated as a museum.[29] With the Irving sisters' departure from Sunnyside, community members organized to secure a similar future for that house. There was, evidently, some sort of a popular attempt to acquire Sunnyside at the time of its sale and transform it into a public museum. The scope and agents of this effort, however, remain elusive. In 1897 the *New England Magazine* lamented the failure of "the movement which was talked of last year to purchase Sunnyside . . . and preserve it as a literary landmark."[30] Sunnyside was not opened as a public museum until the mid-twentieth century.

No doubt motivated by the public claim to the property, A. D. Irving asserted his private ownership. Reacting to the frequent visitors, he closed off the two routes to the house—Sunnyside Lane, an old wagon road extending east from the Hudson River to Broadway, and the Hudson River path, a north-south footpath—with wire fences and "No Trespassing" signs.[31] Irving hired an architect, William H. Mersereau, to transform Sunnyside into a large country house and year-round residence for his family. An addition was built on the back, or north, side of Washington Irving's Sunnyside, thus maintaining the front and river-facing façades and the integrity of the original rooms. The renovation and fortressing of Sunnyside suggest that by the beginning of the twentieth century, A. D. Irving felt pressed to choose between using Sunnyside as a private residence or a house museum. Though the Irving sisters' experiment at combining these functions seemingly proved untenable, their curation of the Sunnyside study had opened up possibilities for the objects and spaces of not quite yet historical literary houses. On the basis of their associations with Irving, the sisters had elevated his former belongings to attractions in and of their own right, and, moreover, they showed that with proper arrangement, such objects could be used as substitutes for Sunnyside's deceased and celebrated tenant.

## *Walden: An Author's Room as a Museum Object*

By the late nineteenth century, not only might the author's study be conceived of as an informal museum room, but also its assemblage of furnishings and objects could constitute a museum object in and of themselves. Henry David Thoreau's effects from Walden, collected by the Concord community and exhibited in their local Antiquarian Society museum, constitute such an example. Housed in the historic Reuben Brown House beginning in the late 1880s, the Concord Antiquarian Society displayed a re-created colonial kitchen, and by 1905 its collections were organized by period groupings.[32] Scholars have identified colonial kitchen displays as significant precursors to museum period rooms; these kitchens were first displayed at sanitary fairs in the 1860s, then at the exhibitions of the 1880s and 1890s, and finally in the early twentieth century at sites like the Concord Antiquarian Society Museum and the Essex Institute in Salem, Massachusetts.[33] It is notable that at the Concord museum, alongside the historical colonial kitchen, Thoreau's ordinary objects were also displayed in a room-like setting but on the basis of their literary, rather than historical, "invisible." This "invisible" motivated the society to exhibit the quotidian and not yet properly historical in a museum setting.

Concord resident Cummings E. Davis, who ran a candy and newspaper stand at the Concord train station, also exhibited local antiques and curiosities in his rented rooms above the Concord courthouse. Davis has received some attention as an early collector of historical objects.[34] His collecting activities illustrate how an author's effects acquired an auratic potential before they had acquired any sort of historical value. *The Concord Guide Book,* first published in 1880, recommends a visit to Davis's rooms at the courthouse, likening his display of the collections to literary depictions of antiquarianism: "It would have delighted the heart of Dickens or Scott to be able to examine the remarkable collection of rare and curious articles which Mr. C. E. Davis had for years been gathering, and which can be seen in his rooms at the Court House. It is in reality, nothing less than a 'Curiosity Shop,' and embraces a greater variety of family relics than the great novelist ever dreamed of."[35] The text enumerates Davis's collection: "old family china, from one hundred to two hundred and fifty years old—furniture once belonging to Peter Bulkeley, and brought by him from England in 1635—many articles once belonging to Thoreau, among others, the cane bedstead on which he slept in his hut in Walden Woods, and on which he died; his desk and chair used at Walden, and the pen with which he wrote his last words—a very beautiful old clock."[36]

Davis appears to have had contact with Thoreau; the 1911 edition of the Concord Antiquarian Society catalog lists a "British Cartridge Box of 1775 . . . Presented by Henry D. Thoreau to C. E. Davis" among its collections.[37] As for the objects from Thoreau's Walden cottage, the same catalog states that the objects "were in H. D. Thoreau's room at his mother's house" and, following his mother's death, were sold by Thoreau's sister Sophia to both Davis and George Tolman, a Concord printer who copied the inscriptions in Concord's Sleepy Hollow Cemetery.[38] Davis's collection was remarkable not only for its abundance of early American artifacts, but also for its seamless incorporation of Thoreau's effects—only eighteen years after his death and thirty-five years after he moved to Walden—into such a collection, thus affording the literary object a value commensurate with that of a historic object.

In 1886 Davis handed his collections over to the new Concord Antiquarian Society in exchange for employment as the overseer of and guide to the society's collections.[39] The society eventually purchased the Reuben Brown House, a Concord Revolutionary War landmark, where it installed the collections. The *Concord Guide Book* description shows that the Thoreau objects were a part of Davis's collection when he turned it over to the Concord Antiquarian Society. When exactly they were installed in the society's museum is unclear. By the mid-1890s, however, the ardent Thoreau devotee Alfred Winslow Hosmer photographed the Antiquarian Society's installation of the Thoreau room. The photograph shows Thoreau's bedstead from Walden placed in the corner of the room, blocking what appears to be a closet door. In front of the bed and to the left stands Thoreau's Pembroke table and small rocking chair.[40] The author's writing desk and the Reverend Asa Dunbar's Chippendale chair, which had been in his room at his mother's house, are placed at the foot of the bed. The rather cramped arrangement of furniture, with the chairs and tables blocking the bedstead, suggests that perhaps these items were placed together exclusively for the purpose of being photographed. Smaller objects set on the tables and bed are unclear and thus difficult to identify. A book and a box (the Thoreau family Bible and Thoreau's Indian box?) are placed on the Pembroke table, while Thoreau's inkstand and perhaps his childhood ruler or one of his drafting implements sit atop the desk.[41]

While the Irving sisters displayed Irving's effects in the familial home as an informal memorial to Irving, the Concord Antiquarian Society acquired objects associated with Thoreau and then displayed them in a new site accessible to the public. Thus, by the end of the nineteenth century, recent literary associations not only elevated workaday objects into "museum objects" but also inspired their arrangement as a variety of museum room. Alongside the well-studied colonial kitchen at the Concord Antiquarian Society existed an equally intriguing display. A bed, a table, a chair, and a desk constitute one museum object: "Thoreau's room at Walden." Hardly idiosyncratic, the Sunnyside study was a precursor to a room re-created in a museum setting on the basis of its literary associations.

### *The Wayside: The Literary Itinerary as Memorial*

The Thoreau room at the Concord Antiquarian Society was not the only preserved author's environment in Concord. Just down the street, in Nathaniel Hawthorne's former residence, The Wayside, Hawthorne's study serves as yet another example of this phenomenon. In 1852 Hawthorne had purchased a house named The Hillside from Bronson Alcott and rechristened it The Wayside. Shortly after his purchase of the house, Hawthorne moved to Britain with his family to work as a consul and did not return to Concord until 1860. Upon his return, inspired by the architecture he had seen in Europe, Hawthorne built his tower study onto the colonial-era house. Rising from and above the center of the house, the tower was and is a space suspended in sky and sunlight. After Hawthorne's death in 1864, various inhabitants (the Hawthorne family, a Mrs. Abba Gray, and The Wayside School for Girls) cared for the house. Evidently, the house, like Sunnyside, continued to draw visitors in Hawthorne's absence. An 1879 *Concord Freeman* advertisement placed by Hawthorne's daughter Rose Hawthorne Lathrop (no connection to the Lothrops, subsequent owners of the house) announced that the path between The Wayside and Orchard House was private property.[42] During this period, Bronson Alcott acted as an informal tour guide to Wayside visitors. As at Sunnyside, the study space served as Hawthorne's informal memorial; Mrs. Abba Gray's son even painted seascapes on the ceiling and stenciled Hawthorne's birth and death dates as a tribute to the author.[43]

These associations drew Daniel and Harriet Lothrop to the property. They served as both proto-curators and residents of The Wayside. After Daniel's death, in 1892, Harriet was active in the preservation of several other Concord houses. The Lothrops' daughter Margaret, who inherited The Wayside in 1924 and soon thereafter officially opened it to the public, recalled that her parents "felt it a duty to preserve the physical structure as well as the fine traditions of the past, and they decided to repair, but not to change unless absolutely necessary."[44] Harriet Lothrop had an interest in the history and preservation of colonial Concord: in 1888 she wrote a guidebook, *Old Concord: Her Highways and Byways;* in 1895 she founded the Children of the American Revolution; and she was also the founding member of the Old Concord Chapter of the Daughters of the American Revolution.[45] Yet the particular historical era to which Daniel and Harriet Lothrop attempted to preserve The Wayside was not the colonial period but rather the period of Hawthorne's residence, from which they were separated by only decades. For Lothrop, in the case of The Wayside, its literary "invisible" trumped its historical significance.

Like the Irving sisters, the Lothrop family evidently experienced difficulties living in a house that was, partially through their own efforts, also an attraction. Theodore Wolfe, in his guide *Literary Shrines,* writes of Margaret Sidney's (or Harriet Lothrop's) "experience with a legion of unaccredited, intrusive, and often insolent persons who come at all hours of the day, and sometimes in the night, demanding to be shown over the place."[46] Hawthorne's son Julian likewise commented on such intrusions: "Nor is it easy to overstate the indignation and resentment of these same travellers, when an attempt is made to insinuate the idea that the house may even now be a private dwelling, not at all hours of the day and night open to the inquisitive presence of strangers."[47] Lothrop's daughter Margaret remembered that her mother's white curtains were kept drawn in the sitting room to stop curious sightseers from looking through the windows.[48]

Yet if strangers peered in the windows of The Wayside, it was certainly in part due to Harriet Lothrop's cultivation of the house as an attraction. As at Sunnyside, and to some degree the Concord Antiquarian Society, Hawthorne's study was presented as a memorial to the author. This presentation predated the Lothrops' residence, as the paintings completed during the Grays' residence indicate. Lothrop, however, possessing a keen interest in historic preservation, attempted not simply to memorialize the room but to present it as Hawthorne may have used it. A late nineteenth-century photograph of the room shows a portrait of Hawthorne, a counterpart to the bust of Irving displayed in the Sunnyside study, hung above the stenciled birth and death dates and encircled with pine boughs (fig 2.2). Hawthorne liked to stand when he wrote and had a special "standing desk" designed for this purpose, which Lothrop displayed in the southeast alcove of the tower with a standard writing table placed around the corner. A placard Lothrop placed in the room used text as a supplement to the staging of objects. It mentions the tower in Monte Outo, Italy, which had served as the architectural inspiration for the room, as well as the standing desk and the "the waving pines" and

FIGURE 2.2. Herbert W. Gleason, "Hawthorne's tower study, The Wayside," ca. 1900. From Thomas Wentworth Higginson, *The Hawthorne Centenary Celebration at the Wayside* (Boston: Houghton, Mifflin and Co., 1905), 112.

"the quiet country" where Hawthorne "paced to and fro," visible from the windows of the tower. While the Irving sisters used objects at Sunnyside to honor Irving and re-create his presence, Margaret Lothrop appears to have used these placards as a complement to the visual and spatial, allowing her textual voice to interpret the architecture, objects, and surrounding landscape for visitors.

Remarkably, Hawthorne's study was not the only room in which Lothrop hung such a placard. By the end of the century, she had placed signs around the entirety of the house indicating the Hawthorne family's use of the rooms. For Lothrop, these textual additions offered a solution to the quandary expressed by the Irving sisters at the end of their stay at Sunnyside: How can a house be at once a lived-in home and a memorial to a celebrated and deceased resident? The placards preserved and indicated the literary value of The Wayside's various spaces without intruding upon Lothrop's use of the architectural space. Similarly, Lothrop attempted to acquire and furnish the house with objects connected to both Hawthorne and Concord.[49] While these objects served a use value for the Lothrops, they also incorporated the literary and historic associations of the house into their daily activities. In addition to their maintenance of the Hawthornes' history in the house, perhaps the most intriguing aspect of Lothrop's placards is how their placement alone indicates that, by the end of the century, the significance of the author's house exceeded the memorial study. Present in the major rooms of the house, the placards instructed visitors to The Wayside to travel throughout the house as an environment, rather than simply to imagine Hawthorne's presence in his working environment. In short, they suggest that a visit to The Wayside at the turn of the century was not merely a visit to The Wayside study. Rather, it was an itinerary.

This itinerary transcended the interior of The Wayside, including the surrounding landscape as one of its stations. A path followed the hilltop behind The Wayside and, if the Hawthorne children's memories are to be trusted, in his last years Hawthorne spent his days walking along the ridge.[50] After Hawthorne's death, the hilltop path became a significant part of the author's posthumous mythology. *The Concord Guide Book* presented the relationship between tower and study as complementary: "A curving path, bordered by pines and locusts, leads to the top of the hill along which Mr. Hawthorne walked daily, and where he was wont to compose (he liked space for that) what he afterwards wrote in 'the tower,' as the room elevated above the front of the house was humorously called in memory of the tower of Monte Outo."[51] A newspaper account of a reception at The Wayside during the Lothrop years explains that the boughs adorning the tower study created a visual and olfactory link to Hawthorne's ridge: "The old staircase and walls below were wound with the same fragrant growth of the forest, where Hawthorne wandered daily as he wrought out his marvelous romances, slowly pacing back and forth on the 'Ridge.'"[52]

On July 4, 1904, Margaret Lothrop celebrated the 1904 Hawthorne Centenary at The Wayside. A gathering of Hawthorne's family and readers sat facing Hawthorne's hilltop path as the author's granddaughter Beatrix Hawthorne revealed a tablet on a boulder reading:

THIS TABLET PLACED
AT THE CENTENNIAL EXERCISES
JULY 4, 1904
COMMEMORATES NATHANIEL HAWTHORNE
HE TROD DAILY THIS PATH TO THE HILL
TO FORMULATE
AS HE PACED TO AND FRO
UPON ITS SUMMIT
HIS MARVELOUS ROMANCES[53]

The Hawthorne Centenary tablet extended Lothrop's circuit of placards to Hawthorne's outdoor study, and accordingly, after the unveiling, Lothrop invited her guests on a tour of The Wayside.[54] One hundred years after Hawthorne's birth The Wayside remained a private family home, but Margaret Lothrop curated it as an attraction that foreshadowed later twentieth-century American historic house museums. At The Wayside, visitors moved throughout the house, viewed objects associated with Hawthorne, interpreted those objects with the help of Lothrop's text panels, and continued their tour in the landscape that had inspired the author's works.

Why then does it matter that in the second half of the nineteenth century, alongside historical association, literary association motivated the exhibition of objects, rooms, and houses? Should we just drop the distinction between the two and say that in nineteenth-century America the associative value of objects and architecture inspired their exhibition? I hope this essay has demonstrated the value of attending to these houses. Because they were not founded as historical houses, their literary associations allowed them to develop into museum-like spaces while inhabited. Reviewing this transitional period in the history of American authors' houses shows the attraction of these houses extending outward from isolated objects to single rooms to the entirety of the house and even to its surrounding landscape. Part of the appeal of these authors' houses is the sheer after-the-fact luck of the historian. Because of an alignment of historical circumstances, these houses and objects do actually *show* this process in a way that a house that stood dormant until the public recognized it as historical simply does not.

Taking the time to trace this historical trajectory offers an additional benefit. Because these literary houses grew into literary *and* historical houses under the eyes of families, communities, sightseers, and chroniclers, caretakers preserved an unlikely body of ordinary and unfashionable objects and architecture. Moreover, caretakers, tourists, and communities hailed these objects and buildings as auratic. Take Irving's Sunnyside as an example. Surely, upon Irving's renovation of the house, its fanciful pseudo-historical detailing would have been recognized as novel. But in the early twentieth century, Irving's brand of historicism was dismissed as unfashionable and was not of much interest to architectural historians until the middle of the twentieth century, when, not coincidentally, John D. Rockefeller Jr. financed the formal museumification of Sunnyside. When architectural historians identified an aesthetic value in the house, Sunnyside was available as a well-preserved sample because of its literary associations. And this is not an isolated example: Margaret Lothrop preserved The Wayside as a mid-nineteenth-century house and, on the other side of the Atlantic, the Dove Cottage Trustees exhibited Wordsworth's former dwelling as a late eighteenth- to early nineteenth-century cottage before architectural historians or preservationists would have identified any intrinsic aesthetic value in houses from these periods.

In one sense, the literary "invisible" of these houses saved them for later generations of tourists, curators, and scholars who would project value onto them not present in the immediate period after their resident author's death. During the period when the exhibition of these sites was being negotiated on the basis of their literary associations, family members and proto-curators molded significant precedents for the exhibition of ordinary objects and architecture. To be sure, in the imagination of the exhibitors there was nothing ordinary about these environments; the genius of their celebrated former tenants had, of course, hallowed them. Materially, however, what we see in these houses are often ordinary workplaces and objects like pens, chairs, beds, and tables. These exhibitions, then, offer a precedent beyond the well-studied colonial kitchen displays for later twentieth-century historic house museums like Colonial Williamsburg, Henry Ford's Greenfield Village, or Sturbridge Village, which strove to re-create the everyday life of past periods.

## NOTES

1. Washington Irving, "The Crayon Papers," *Knickerbocker* 13 (March 1839): 209. The cottage became a fantasy of seventeenth-century Dutch architecture, replete with collected Dutch weathervanes, a tile roof, stepped gables, and mounted iron letters celebrating "1656," the imaginary date of the founding of his house.
2. Adam Sweeting writes, "If one views Sunnyside as a work of fiction, an architectural reconstruction of a nonexistent past, than [*sic*] 'Wolfert's Roost' can only be described as the fiction of a fiction." Adam W. Sweeting, *Reading Houses and Building Books: Andrew Jackson Downing and the Architecture of Popular Antebellum Literature, 1835–1855* (Hanover: University Press of New England, 1996), 139.
3. See Charles B. Hosmer, *Presence of the Past: A History of the Preservation Movement in the United States before Williamsburg* (New York: G. P. Putnam's Sons, 1965); and Edward P. Alexander, *Museums in Motion: An Introduction to the History and Functions of Museums*

(Nashville: American Association for State and Local History, 1979). Patricia West discusses Mount Vernon and Monticello as the historic house museum's "flagships" and Louisa May Alcott's Orchard House and the Booker T. Washington National Monument "for what they can tell us about the crucial issues of gender and social diversity." Patricia West, *Domesticating History: The Political Origins of America's House Museums* (Washington, D.C.: Smithsonian Press, 1999), xi.

4. Jan Cohn, *The Palace or the Poorhouse: The American House as a Cultural Symbol* (East Lansing: Michigan State University Press, 1979), 198–200. Sarah Burns builds on Cohn's thesis in her consideration of the use of American writers' homes in the last third of the nineteenth century, concentrating on their symbolic and nostalgic potential as "homesteads" rather than their status as pilgrimage sites. Sarah Burns, *Pastoral Inventions: Rural Life in Nineteenth-Century American Art and Culture* (Philadelphia: Temple University Press, 1989), 264–65.
5. Krzysztof Pomian, *Collectors and Curiosities: Paris and Venice, 1500–1800* (Cambridge: Polity Press, 1990), 9, 23.
6. Between 1811 and 1825, Scott transformed a farmhouse in the Scottish Borders into Abbotsford, a medievalist fantasy estate linked to his writings.
7. T. Addison Richards, "Sunnyside the Home of Washington Irving," *Harper's New Monthly Magazine* 14 (December 1856): 1–21, 12.
8. See, for example, "Irving at Sunnyside in 1858," *Hours at Home* 1 (October 1865): 507–21; and "A Morning at Sunnyside with Washington Irving," *Southern Magazine* 12 (January–June 1873): 710–16.
9. Samuel Austin Allibone, "A Visit to Washington Irving," June 12, 1855. Transcript of original in the Huntington Library, San Marino, California, in the collection of Historic Hudson Valley (Tarrytown, N.Y.).
10. Horace Caruthers, M.D., "Reminiscences of Washington Irving," *Tarrytown Argus,* April 5, 1890, 1.
11. Theodore Tilton, "A Visit to Washington Irving," *Littell's Living Age* 63 (October– December 1859): 824.
12. West, *Domesticating History,* 4. Charles B. Hosmer refers to the purchase of Hasbrouck House by the State of New York as the first victory, albeit unorganized, of the American preservation movement. Hosmer, *Presence of the Past,* 35.
13. Irving to Robert C. Winthrop, May 23, 1853, in Ralph M. Aderman, Herbert L. Kleinfield, and Jenifer S. Banks, eds., *The Complete Works of Washington Irving: Letters, Vol. IV, 1846–1859* (Boston: Twayne, 1978–1982), 401.
14. Charles Lanman, "A Day with Washington Irving," *Once a Week* 2 (December 31, 1859): 6.
15. "Washington Irving," *Mount Vernon Record* 2 (extra issue between November and December 1859): 97. Irving made his contribution a month after he refused a request that his photographic portrait be sold, with the profits being turned over to the Mount Vernon Ladies' Association. Irving to Thomas W. C. Moore, January 12, 1859, in *Letters,* 4:675.
16. Irving's will reads as follows: "I give and devise my lands and dwelling house in Westchester County, which I have called Sunnyside, to my brother Ebenezer . . . on his death I give the same in fee to his daughters or daughter surviving him and unmarried, trusting they will endeavour, as I have endeavoured, to make this homestead a rallying point, where the various branches of the family connexion may always be sure of a cordial welcome.

    "I trust, also, they will never sell nor devise this particular property, out of the family; though circumstances may render it expedient or necessary for them to rent it out or lease it for a term; but it is my wish that the last survivor of those to whom I bequeath my estate will, in turn, bequeath it entire to some meritorious member of the family, bearing the family name, so that Sunnyside may continue to be, as long as possible, an Irving homestead." Copy of the last will and testament of Washington Irving (not in his autograph), MA 919, Department of Literary and Historical Manuscripts, Pierpont Morgan Library, New York.

17. James Grant Wilson, *Bryant and His Friends* (New York: Fords, Howard, and Hulbert, 1886), 162.
18. *Full-length Portrait of Washington Irving in His Library at Sunnyside by W. H. Powell,* (New York: Goupil and Co., 1860), 3–4.
19. Ibid., 3–4.
20. Historic Hudson Valley has dated this image to 1855 on the basis of an inscription on its back, and commented on its peculiarity as "one of the few visual records of the cottage's interior during the author's lifetime." Historic Hudson Valley, *Visions of Washington Irving* (Tarrytown, N.Y.: Historic Hudson Valley, 1991), 119. As noted in the text, the Irving family supplied Powell with a daguerreotype of Irving for assistance in his completing the memorial image. Powell's rendering of Irving is clearly copied from a daguerreotype taken by John Plumbe in 1848 and later photographed for a *carte de visite* by Mathew Brady. Irving detested the likeness taken of him by Plumbe; the press noted that "Mr. Irving was ever afterwards strongly prejudiced against daguerreotyping." "Portrait of Irving," unidentified news clipping accompanying "Irving, Washington—Carte de visite photograph from negative by Mathew Brady, 1862," Washington Irving Collection, pictorial materials, box 21, New York Public Library. Why Powell, if he actually completed the image at Sunnyside in 1855, would rely on an 1848 daguerreotype of Irving, which the author despised, is inexplicable. The evidence suggests that the Powell image is connected to the "memorial" requested by Knoedler (as either a study or a reproduction), and furthermore, that it is not an exception to the emblematic exterior representations of Sunnyside circulated during Irving's lifetime, but rather exemplary of a shift in the representation of Sunnyside, from exterior to interior, following Irving's death.
21. Benson John Lossing, *The Hudson from the Wilderness to the Sea* (Troy, N.Y.: H. B. Nims and Co., 1866), 343.
22. See *The Land of Sleepy Hollow, and the home of Washington Irving; a series of photogravure representations, with descriptive letter-press by J. L. Williams* (New York: G. P. Putnam's Sons, 1887). There is another photograph of the study that dates from the same time, "Library, or Workshop of Washington Irving," in the collections of Historic Hudson Valley.
23. Black, *I Remember,* 17–18.
24. "Irving's Home in New Hands," *Tarrytown Argus,* May 30, 1896; and "The Misses Irving Have Returned," *Tarrytown Argus,* May 18, 1895.
25. Undated and unidentified news clipping, ca. 1896–97, in Washington Irving Collection, Irving Family Papers, Miscellany, 1882–1898, W3108, Historic Hudson Valley collection (hereafter HHV collection), Rockefeller Archive Center, Tarrytown, N.Y. (hereafter RAC).
26. A reproduction of a check made out to "Catharine Sarah Irving" for $10,000, dated March 9, 1896, remains in the possession of Historic Hudson Valley, Washington Irving Collection, Irving Family Papers, W3108, HHV collection.
27. Transcription of Sarah Irving's will, June 8, 1900, Sunnyside 32, HHV.
28. Beatrice Sturgis, "Irving's Home To-day," *Peterson Magazine* 6 (November 1896): 1116. I have been unable to locate the photographs taken before A. D. Irving's renovations.
29. Whittier not only lived in the house but also used it as the setting for his poem "Snow-Bound" (1866). William Corbett, *Literary New England: A History and Guide* (Boston: Faber and Faber, 1993), 126. On the Whittier homestead, see Cohn, *The Palace or the Poorhouse;* and Burns, *Pastoral Inventions,* 264–65.
30. Richard Burton, "Washington Irving's Services to American History," *New England Magazine* 16 (August 1897): 645. Another mention of this movement survives in the correspondence of John D. Rockefeller Jr. The president of the Staten Island Historical Society, Vernon B. Hampton, wrote to Rockefeller of a letter dated February 24, 1897, from a James Bryce to a J. B. Best, Esq., "referring to an early effort to acquire and preserve Washington Irving's 'Sunnyside.'" Vernon B. Hampton to John D. Rockefeller Jr., February 18,

1952, folder 1100, box 123, Cultural Interest Series, Record Group 2, Office of the Messrs. Rockefeller, RAC.

31. Untitled clipping, n.d., n.p., and "Sunnyside Closed to the Public," n.d., n.p., Washington Irving Collection, Irving Family Papers, Miscellany, 1882–1898, W3108, HHV collection.
32. Allen French, "The New House and the Old Collection of the Concord Antiquarian Society," *Old-Time New England: The Bulletin of the Society for the Preservation of New England Antiquities* 21 (April 1931): 148.
33. See Melinda Young Frye, "The Beginnings of the Period Room in American Museums: Charles P. Wilcomb's Colonial Kitchens, 1896, 1906, 1910," and Rodris Roth, "The New England, or 'Olde Tyme,' Kitchen Exhibit at Nineteenth-Century Fairs," in *The Colonial Revival in America,* ed. Alan Axelrod (New York: W. W. Norton, 1985), 217–40 and 159–83; and Dianne H. Pilgrim, "Inherited from the Past: The American Period Room," *American Art Journal* 10, no. 1 (May 1978): 5–23.
34. Davis has elicited a modest amount of scholarly attention, specifically as an early collector of Americana. Charles B. Hosmer fits Davis into his history of New England's early preservation efforts, presenting Davis as an early antiquarian with a collection local in scope. Hosmer, *Presence of the Past* 109. Elizabeth Stillinger suggests that Davis's collecting was motivated purely by the associational power of objects to the exclusion of their aesthetic potential. Elizabeth Stillinger, *The Antiquers* (New York: Knopf, 1980), 23. Will Fellows aligns Davis with New England's "likely gay men as pioneering keepers of culture." Will Fellows, *A Passion to Preserve* (Madison: University of Wisconsin Press, 2004), 37, 38.
35. George Bradford Bartlett, *The Concord Guide Book,* rev. 2nd ed. (Boston: Lothrop, 1880), 109.
36. Ibid., 110.
37. George Tolman, *Catalogue of a Portion of the Collection of the Concord Antiquarian Society* (Concord: Concord Antiquarian Society, 1911), 31.
38. Ibid., 45.
39. French, "The New House and the Old Collection of the Concord Antiquarian Society," 148; and Tolman, *Catalogue,* vi.
40. The Pembroke table remained in Tolman's possession until 1908. Tolman, *Catalogue,* 45. Tolman may have lent the table to the Antiquarian Society, as he did his ambrotype of Thoreau. If this is the case, however, the *Catalogue* does not note it. If not, this information might cast doubt on the dating of the photograph.
41. Tolman's 1911 *Catalogue* states that objects like the ruler and drafting tools were placed inside the desk (45).
42. Anna Toogood, *The Wayside: Minute Man National Historic Park, Massachusetts* (Washington, D.C.: Office of History and Historic Architecture, 1970), 74. Toogood cites a copy of the *Concord Freeman,* May 1, 1879, in the possession of Minute Man National Historic Park.
43. Toogood, *The Wayside,* 69–70.
44. Margaret M. Lothrop, *The Wayside: Home of Authors* (New York: American Book Company, 1940), 5. They did, however, add a piazza onto the house, installed a new furnace, and repainted when necessary (160).
45. On Harriet Lothrop's preservation activities, see ibid., 183–84; and Toogood, *The Wayside,* 80–81; and West, *Domesticating,* 39, 57–60, 52.
46. Theodore Wolfe, *Literary Shrines* (Philadelphia: J. B. Lippincott and Co., 1895), 60.
47. Julian Hawthorne, *Nathaniel Hawthorne and His Wife,* vol. 1 (Boston: Houghton Mifflin Co., 1884), 450.
48. Doris Fanelli, *Historic Furnishings Plan, The Wayside, Minute Man National Historic Park* (Harpers Ferry, W. Va.: United States Department of Interior / National Park Service, Harpers Ferry Center, 1983), 142.
49. Ibid., 306–7, 76.

50. *The Memoirs of Julian Hawthorne,* ed. Edith Garrigues Hawthorne (New York: Macmillan, 1938), 32; and Rose Hawthorne Lathrop, *Memoirs of Hawthorne* (Boston: Houghton, Mifflin, and Co., 1897), 448. Though such recollections connect Hawthorne with the path specifically at the end of his life, Anna Toogood states that he had already formed the path before leaving for Europe in 1853. Toogood, *The Wayside,* 43.
51. Bartlett, *Concord Guide Book,* 59.
52. "Reception by Mrs. Lothrop," *New Haven Courier,* July 31, 1903.
53. Thomas Wentworth Higginson, *The Hawthorne Centenary Celebration at the Wayside: Concord, Massachusetts, July 4–7, 1904* (Boston: Houghton, Mifflin, and Company, 1905), 12.
54. Ibid., 25.

# 3

# *Keeping (the Spirit of) Thoreau Alive in Concord*

## Reflections on Diversity and Innovation in American Literary Tourism

KLARA-STEPHANIE SZLEZÁK

*If remembering the way that literary homes linger in a kind of "limbo" on their way to museum and historic site status keeps us aware of the roles women and families play as gatekeepers of the literary past, what of those authors who didn't have homes of their own? Even as the objects from Henry David Thoreau's room at his parents' home have been carefully and creatively preserved at the Concord Museum in Concord, Massachusetts, Klara-Stephanie Szlezák shows us how different types of Thoreau literary tourism have developed in the twentieth and twenty-first centuries at the Concord Museum, Walden Pond State Reservation, and most recently the Thoreau Farm, the site of his birth. Building on the research of pioneering literary tourism scholar Lawrence Buell, Szlezák uncovers an expansive "Thoreau territory" that speaks to the experience and complicated search for authenticity at literary tourism sites.*

"I hate museums, there is nothing so weighs upon the spirits. They are catacombs of nature. They are preserved death. . . . The life that is in a single green weed is of more worth than all this death."[1] Henry David Thoreau wrote these lines in his journal on September 24, 1843, before the publication of his major works and before his stay by Walden Pond. At that time, writers' houses as museums, while fairly popular in Europe, had not yet appeared in the American landscape. Little did Thoreau anticipate then that he would one day be the subject of museal and touristic endeavors.[2] As Thoreau is known to celebrate nature and firsthand experience, it comes as no surprise that museums were institutions he viewed rather skeptically. The aversion to museums that he so bluntly expresses stems from their association with "preserved death"; in his eyes, they artificially try to keep alive phenomena for the sake of documentation and inspection by later generations. House museums dedicated to the life and work of a famous writer would certainly fall into that category. As a large part of the appeal of these houses arises from the fact that the revered writer is dead, they may be perceived as equally "weigh[ing] upon the spirits," to use Thoreau's own words.[3]

Interestingly, the "preserved death" aspect of museums has been avoided in Thoreau tourism, and the documentation and interpretation of his life have taken shape in ways that reflect the many shades of his biography. Early Thoreau tourism, in particular, has been studied previously, most notably by Lawrence Buell in his 1989 essay "The Thoreauvian Pilgrimage: The Structure of an American Cult." Buell analyzes the phenomenon of pilgrimage to Walden Pond and meticulously traces the transformation of Walden "from Thoreau's sacred place into the reading community's sacred place," which he embeds in several contexts: the characteristics of Christian pilgrimage as formulated by Edith and Victor Turner, the cultural significance of the pastoral retreat, Concord tourism at large, as well as the processes of canonization. Laying out and commenting on the celebratory rituals performed at Walden, Buell contrasts them with more abstract forms of Thoreau pilgrimage in which Walden is no longer a destination, such as homesteading experiments and individual withdrawal from society. Although the resulting "mainstream of Walden imitation" to some extent effected a "decentralization of the Walden pilgrimage," Buell argues that the mythicization of Thoreau continues and that Thoreau as "an American cultural hero" is pivotal for perpetuating Concord's national and international fame.[4]

Incorporating the findings of Buell's influential essay, I approach Thoreau tourism from a different angle. Instead of focusing on the Walden pilgrimage exclusively, I broaden the view to reveal a wide variety of shapes that Thoreau tourism takes in Concord. After briefly embedding Thoreau in the context of the Concord of his time, I outline the development of Thoreau-related literary tourism in Concord from a diachronic perspective. A subsequent analysis of the ways in which Thoreau is "visitable" today will show that there are distinct strands of Thoreau tourism, including both traditional and more innovative approaches, disintegrated over time and now catering to the demands of different audiences.

## *Thoreau and Concord: Then and Now*

The standard depiction of mid-nineteenth-century Concord, Massachusetts, is of a haven for American intellectuals and writers. Authors who represented New England's literary culture—if not the entirety of American literary culture—resided in this small town roughly twenty miles west of Boston: Ralph Waldo Emerson, Bronson Alcott and his daughter Louisa, Nathaniel Hawthorne, Margaret Fuller,[5] W. Ellery Channing, Frank B. Sanborn, and Henry David Thoreau all dwelt in Concord and knew one another. Other authors came to visit. While many of them were "like moths attracted by the . . . Emersonian beacon,"[6] Thoreau had been a Concord resident before Emerson's arrival; born and raised in Boston, Emerson purchased and moved into his Concord home in 1835. Unlike most of the writers in honor of whom visitors made and make their way to Concord, Thoreau was a Concord native. Born at Minott House, a farmhouse on Virginia Road, in 1817, he spent all his life in his hometown except for a few early childhood years, his time spent at Harvard College (1833–1837), and his many travels in the area.[7] He died in Concord in May 1862. More of a "Concordian" than his contemporaries, he would represent a particular case in Concord literary tourism.[8]

The seminal event in Thoreau's life that linked him to the Concord area in the public mind was undoubtedly the construction of, and his stay at, his small house on the shores of Walden Pond.[9] "I lived alone, in the woods, a mile from any neighborhood, in a house which I had built myself, on the shore of Walden Pond, in Concord, Massachusetts": thus reads the first sentence of *Walden; or, Life in the Woods.*[10] Walden Pond as a geographical location has become firmly associated with the book's author and his "experiment," all three of which—place, man, and venture—have since been inflated to mythical dimensions.[11] Although the time spent in his house at Walden Pond, from July 1845 through September 1847, constitutes only a small fragment of Thoreau's life, an almost metonymic relationship between location on the one hand, and author and work on the other, has evolved over time. Walden and Thoreau have become all but synonymous, and the immense reverence bestowed upon Thoreau is being projected onto a landscape that is "undeniably . . . rather ordinary." Thoreau's standing as an epitome of counterculture and resistance to norms is grounded in "the metaleptic association with a place," that is, Walden Pond, rather than in his character alone. While the scarcity of actual portraits of Thoreau himself is in part responsible for the fact that visualizations of the place came to substitute for the person, Thoreau's writings were central to informing popular images, particularly his "references . . . to forms of *being-at-homeness*" in nature, which, while not restricted to his experiences at Walden, came to be conflated and condensed in this one place.[12]

It is undisputed not only that Thoreau had an acute sense of place but also that the influence of place on man was a major theme of his literature.[13] That Thoreau came to be inextricably linked to Walden results both from his writings and from their reception. Thoreau consciously described a particular Walden in his work, "his" Walden, and thus contributed to founding the myth surrounding his Walden Pond dwelling. Don Scheese claims that "it was [Thoreau's] lifelong effort to create a sacred place, to compose 'a poem . . . called Concord.' " Being aware of the power of observation and perception as well as of the written word, Thoreau "created for himself a place of pilgrimage where he could continually reenact his vocation of inhabiter." That Thoreau ever considered creating a "place of pilgrimage" for others seems unlikely.[14] Still, it remains a fact for literary tourism that he did. While the origins of the conflation of Thoreau and Walden are found in his own writings, the reception and interpretation of Thoreau's works, specifically the overriding popularity and critical acclaim of *Walden,* contributed considerably to making Walden Pond a tourist destination. Buell argues that the success of Walden as a destination for literary pilgrims is "symptomatic not merely of the rise of Thoreau's personal reputation but, more broadly, of an American apotheosis of pastoral retreat that was inherent in the earliest institutionalization of Transcendental Concord as a cultural shrine."[15] In a way, Thoreau's *Walden* struck a chord with the public, not necessarily only in a literary sense, but in a broader cultural sense, which found expression in the public's response to the setting of *Walden.*

Other forces at work in the consolidation of the lasting and preeminent association between Thoreau and Walden are found outside the immediate context of Thoreau's writings. Portrayals of Thoreau as well as descriptions of Walden Pond published in guidebooks to the Concord area made sure to mention the two in one breath, while overlooking or downplaying other places in and around Concord that relate to Thoreau.[16] In addition, this prevailing association, which has become part of "common knowledge" and shared perception, was historically fueled by (at least) two forces characteristic of literary tourism: nostalgia and commodification. Though "nostalgia" is an intricate and much-debated concept, especially in the context of heritage tourism, I use it very generally, in the sense of an emotion that prompts acts of memorialization for the very purpose of creating and maintaining memory of past times, conditions, and people.[17] Walter Harding and Michael Meyer trace "the beginnings of a nostalgic view of Thoreau," which helped Thoreau tourism emerge, to the 1930s. This particular nostalgia for Thoreau overlapped with a more general sense of nostalgia throughout New England in its "desire to escape . . . into the simplicity of the past"—a simplicity that Thoreau's experiment put into action and that his oft-quoted, and mostly de-contextualized, motto "Simplify, simplify!" seemed to encapsulate. And "commodification" describes all those market forces that helped institutionalize tourism at a time when New England was economically on the decline.[18] Thoreau's Walden Pond house played a central role in the initiation of Thoreau tourism, as it offered a tangible destination for tourism as well as a marketable icon. Thoreau's growing "platial iconicity" (as Klaus Benesch puts it) was thus supported not only by *Walden*'s rise to the status of an American classic, but also by developments that popularized this iconicity for tourism.

## *Thoreau's "Cabin" Lost and Found? The Development of Thoreau Tourism*

It was during Thoreau's lifetime, in the mid-nineteenth century, that literary tourism emerged in the United States. Years before sites associated with Thoreau were given much thought, Concord was already a center of attention. Various publications from the second half of the nineteenth century onwards—forerunners of modern-day tourist guidebooks—represented Concord not only as a writers' mecca but also as a destination for literary pilgrims.[19] These early books mostly advise the Concord tourist to visit the homes of Emerson, Hawthorne, or the Alcotts. There are two basic reasons why Thoreau was neglected or appeared rather marginally in these publications. First, his writings were not very widely received and appreciated until the twentieth century.[20] Second, these early publications were specifically interested in presenting the writers in a context that reflected notions of domesticity. In the preface of *Homes of American Authors* (1852), the editors expressed "pride in showing [their] countrymen how *comfortably housed* many of their favorite authors are."[21] The mid-nineteenth-century notion of "comfortably housed" hardly would have corresponded to any of Thoreau's dwellings: before moving into his ten-by-fifteen-foot one-room house in the woods, he lived in Emerson's house in "the room at the head of the stairs, a little room"; after abandoning his Walden Pond house, Thoreau "had his den in the attic" of his father's house on Main Street.[22] Never striving for home ownership along the lines of nineteenth-century middle-class domesticity, Thoreau did not come to epitomize the values attached to such a lifestyle.[23] The myths, naturally based in part on misrepresentations, which emerged around Thoreau around the turn of the century, thus specifically created a counter-image to middle-class domesticity, creating a niche for Thoreau tourism. While most literary sites in Concord present tourists with domestic scenes in writers' houses, Thoreau tourism seeks to capture the writer outside domestic period rooms.

The homes of writers are widely believed to hold special interest for literary tourists,[24] and yet Thoreau-related sites turned into popular destinations for literary tourists despite the lack of a "writer's home" in the traditional sense. Primarily, literary tourists were attracted to the "only true house of his."[25] The initial interest in tracing Thoreau in Concord was directed toward the shores of Walden Pond. That this, the "only true house of his," was of course to some degree the result of purposeful construction went largely unnoticed. Walden Pond as introduced in *Walden* is "a carefully constructed literary site, less Thoreau's home than his home page, a virtual space he designed to represent himself and to promote his business."[26] Unlike many other writers' houses, in which the authors' personalities find expression within the framework of the domestic realm, incorporating specific gender roles and family values, Thoreau's Walden home did not readily fit in with these domestic standards. Apart from Thoreau's own intentions to depict Walden in a certain way, later generations continued to construct pastoral images of Walden. Purposefully idyllic descriptions, such as the "sylvan dwelling" in which Thoreau had "felt at home,"[27] contributed to inciting visitors' (almost sensationalist) curiosity and fascination, infused with a sense of romanticism. Yet the popular image of Thoreau and his house, secluded from the world at large, was not historically accurate. W. Barksdale Maynard, in "Thoreau's House at Walden," explores the house in the context of contemporary rustic architecture and draws the conclusion that Thoreau neither constructed a cabin nor sought the life of a hermit: "Far from abandoning societal conventions, Thoreau in moving to the pond instead participated enthusiastically in the general cultural conversation regarding retirement and the villa. He relocated not to the wilderness but to a recently logged clearing in an intensively used landscape just minutes' walk from town."[28]

The degree to which misconceptions became ingrained, especially in the tourism discourse, can be seen in the 1937 *WPA Guide to Massachusetts.* In the entry on Concord as a center of American literary culture, Thoreau's myth is central: "By the shores of Walden Pond, Emerson's intimate friend, Henry David Thoreau, the naturalist, fled from society, built his hut and studied the trees and birds he was to write about in 'Walden, or Life in the Woods.' "[29] This description reproduces several stereotypical notions: it affirms the established triad between man, place, and book, neglecting other places associated with Thoreau—and thus implicitly reducing the twenty-five years of his adult life spent in Concord to a two-year period. It also neglects other works, in particular *A Week on the Concord and Merrimack Rivers,* which Thoreau wrote while living by Walden Pond. Furthermore, it validates the romantic appeal of the "Walden myth" by reiterating the image of the house as a "hut" and the image of Thoreau as a hermit, who "fled from society"—suggesting an absoluteness that was not given: "Every day or two I strolled to the village to hear some of the gossip which is incessantly going on there . . . and which, taken in homœopathic doses, was really as refreshing in its way as the rustle of leaves and the peeping of frogs." Temporary retreat and hermitage are not quite the same thing.[30]

The fascination with Thoreau's temporary quarters, however exclusive and reductive, was not hindered by the fact that the structure was no longer standing.[31] On the contrary, the *absence* of material evidence that Thoreau had ever been *present* at Walden Pond may have fueled its appeal, lending the story and the place a touch of mysteriousness and generating a natural desire to retrieve what has been lost. The house was moved from its original spot soon after Thoreau's departure. Emerson bought and subsequently sold the house to his gardener Hugh Whelan, who was about to set up a farm on Emerson's land. After Whelan abandoned his plans, another farmer, James Clark, purchased the house and moved it to the other end of town, where it was used as a granary. In June 1868, having fallen into utter disrepair, it was demolished, its roof reused on a pigsty and some of its boards integrated in a barn on the Brooks Clark farm, on the north side of Concord.[32] Once the house was gone, all perceptible traces of its original location were blurred by erosion of the sandy ground around Walden Pond. The furniture fared slightly better. Thoreau took it to his father's Concord house, and it was later deposited in the Concord Museum, along with more than 250 other objects related to Thoreau and his family, directly and indirectly through his younger sister Sophia, who was "largely responsible for the preservation of his material legacy."[33] Thus, what survived on the shore of Walden Pond at the time was not artifactual but narrative and imaginary in nature.

One of the earliest responses to the lack of physical remnants at the site of Thoreau's house can be traced to the year 1872.[34] On the occasion of the tenth anniversary of Thoreau's death, Bronson Alcott, prompted by a letter from a Thoreau devotee from Iowa, laid down the first pile of stones that would develop into a steadily growing cairn. Having helped in the early stages of the house's construction in 1845, Alcott pointed out what he believed to be the site and instigated what was to become a decade-long tradition and one of the first memorials to Thoreau. While exposed later on to acts of disrespect, if not outright vandalism, the cairn and the tradition of laying down stones survives into the twenty-first century.[35]

The cairn at the site of Thoreau's house is an intriguing case of a site that has been created so people could visit it in honor of a person and perform a memorialization ritual. By laying down a stone, visitors have the chance to perform a symbolic act of veneration. In addition, the individual contribution to the cairn is often linked to the hope of having wishes fulfilled, turning the memorial into a "mound of wishes" at the same time.[36] While the cairn has no inherent connection to either Thoreau or his house, it has developed into a tourist site in its own right, on the basis of a presumed proximity to the original site of the house. This testifies to a number of factors central to the functioning of literary tourism. First, there is the need to relate the revered person to a particular place: literary tourism, like any kind of tourism, requires movement as well as a place to move toward. Second, there is a pronounced desire to encounter material evidence, to look at and to touch: in the absence of the revered person, some *physical* substitute has to substantiate the *spiritual* experience the visit offers. Third, the spatial context and the material object(s) have to be imbued with a sense of "authenticity": place and object can provide satisfaction only when they are thought to establish a connection to the revered person himself or herself.[37] Such forms of literary tourism have kinetic, visual, and haptic dimensions and are motivated by the prospect of experiencing "authentic" settings.

Even though the cairn is neither located at the exact spot nor specifically reminiscent of Thoreau's personality or dwelling, it has been formally recognized as a Thoreau site. Both its visualization, not least on picture postcards (fig. 3.1), and related commodification, and the signposting that inscribes it as an index into the landscape visibly legitimize it as a place worth going to. That the cairn appears as a legitimate Thoreau site despite the aforementioned absence of an immediate connection may be due, on the one hand, to a lack of alternatives at an early point in time. On the other hand, the ritualistic nature of the site, where every visitor can individually pay homage to Thoreau not just by *being* there but by *doing* something—laying down a stone—undeniably has a strong appeal.

Despite the formation and recognition of the cairn as a destination for Thoreau tourists, the ephemerality of Thoreau's house as a built structure that was so well documented remained unsatisfying. The supposed authentic encounter offered by the cairn proved not to be authentic enough, and given that there was no evidence confirming that the cairn indicated the original location, the desire to locate the site precisely and reliably persisted. In the 1870s, tourists started to dig for souvenirs, but more serious, yet sporadic, attempts at excavations also took place. The first half of the twentieth century saw the beginning of archaeological efforts to locate the foundations Thoreau had laid decades earlier.[38] In November 1945, Roland Wells Robbins, not a professionally trained archaeologist but "a self-styled Thoreauvian and 'Pick and Shovel Historian,'" excavated the foundation of Thoreau's chimney after three months of digging, just a short while after the centennial celebrations

FIGURE 3.1. Historic picture postcard, "Thoreau's Cairn, Concord, Mass." *Courtesy of American Antiquarian Society.*

of the beginning of Thoreau's "experiment."[39] Robbins writes: "At the turn of the twentieth century, with all material evidence lacking, hearsay had developed many legends about the house, its original site, its size, its construction and its fate. By July 4th, 1945, when the commemorative services were held at Walden Pond, marking the hundredth anniversary of Thoreau's moving into his home there, those legends still flourished." This passage, in which Robbins legitimizes his archaeological zeal and method by implicitly contrasting science with mere "hearsay" and "legends," is drawn from the account, published two years after his excavation, of how and why he engaged in the quest and how he succeeded. Not exactly a scholarly study, *Discovery at Walden* (1947) describes the excavation process and gives Robbins the opportunity to present himself as a true Thoreauvian—even if "the literary world" may not grant him this status. Arguing on the basis of the materially graspable findings he made—implicitly opposed to "merely" spiritual or intellectual findings—Robbins asserts that he has "probably come as close as any of [his] contemporaries to meeting and visiting with Henry David Thoreau in person"; the allure of a personal encounter is undiminished.[40]

In his introductory remarks to *Discovery at Walden,* Walter Harding, then secretary of the Thoreau Society and a dedicated Thoreau scholar, assesses

Robbins's discovery: it finally "authenticated the exact site of the cabin," which granted more precise knowledge "of just where Thoreau dwelt than on which boulder the Pilgrims landed in Plymouth Beach."[41] Harding's words are remarkable for two reasons: they emphasize once again the central role of "authenticity" in the endeavor, and, by drawing a comparison between the "cabin" site and Plymouth Rock, Harding elevates Thoreau (tourism) beyond the local and regional to the national level, and widens the context to include processes of national identity formation. Robbins's discovery thus not only constituted a major gain in the historical knowledge about Thoreau and his house but also altered and redirected literary tourism at Walden Pond. It necessarily diminished the attraction of the cairn and called for measures to consecrate the actual "cabin" site. The discovery led to systematic signage and demarcation of the spot where Thoreau's house once stood and where literary tourists from then on would be directed.

Yet, locating the original hearth "merely" enabled Thoreau enthusiasts to recapture the Walden house on a two-dimensional level, as coordinates on a map. A three-dimensional reconstruction held the promise of either transporting visitors back to the past or of making the past "alive in the present."[42] *Walden* contains detailed enough descriptions of the construction materials and process to make a reconstruction possible; Robbins was among the first to build and sell "Thoreau houses" in the 1940s. Visitors who come to Walden Pond, protected today by the Walden Pond State Reservation (operated by the Massachusetts Department of Conservation and Recreation [DCR]), will find both the "cabin" site and the "cabin" replica—just not in the same place. The replica of Thoreau's house, built in 1985–86 by carpenter Paul Reardon, was built according to the descriptions in *Walden,* entries in Thoreau's journal, and the drawing of the house by Sophia, printed in the first edition of *Walden* in 1854. Instead of being located at the original site, the reconstruction is adjacent to the State Reservation's parking lot, very close to the road.[43] While the current position is based on well-considered decisions by the DCR,[44] it is hardly the position one might expect, since it disrupts the unity between place and material object, and the house is not, unlike in *Walden,* at the shore of the pond. In front of the replica, tourists can see a bronze statue of Thoreau. The nearly life-size statue, whose form suggests both dynamism—Thoreau is widely known to have traveled long distances by foot—and deep reflection, functions as a visual, three-dimensional means by which to evoke Thoreau's spirit for the visitors and thus to turn the experience of the replica into a more vivid one.

Vividness of experience is further pursued in the replica's interior. The house is furnished with a bed, a chair, and a writing desk precisely modeled after Thoreau's furniture; furthermore, there is cooking equipment by the hearth, as well as a box of firewood. While these careful arrangements generate a sense of historical integrity and immediacy, implicitly suggesting that the logs will be used for a fire to cook a meal over, the "illusion" of the past (when the hearth would have been used and the bed slept in) is broken by a feature typical of tourist sites and exhibition spaces which firmly grounds the visitors in the present time: a guest register. Through the guest register, the room is unmistakably marked as an exhibitionary space; the house's interior is revealed to be a space for display and education (information about the furniture is provided on plaques right outside the house), rather than one of "staged authenticity" (to quote Dean MacCannell) or unmediated experience, which betrays its proximity to a museum space.

The replicas of the furniture in the interior bring to the fore two issues that are interconnected at the core: the question about the nature of museum display as well as the question of the relevance of original artifacts. The house replica neither displays original artifacts nor uses labeling. Inside, tourists can see exact replicas of the furnishings, fitted into the same amount of space as in the original, but the items on display are of recent production. The furnished replica is a permanent and publicly accessible installation meant to educate its audience. By contrast, at the Concord Museum, tourists can see the actual desk Thoreau wrote on while staying at Walden Pond, the bed he slept in, the chair he sat on, yet not *in situ* but arranged in an institutional setting (fig. 3.2).[45] Tourists desiring to see objects touched and used by Thoreau, and thus supposedly imbued with the writer's "aura," are well advised to see the Thoreau Collection at the Concord Museum, which holds about 250 artifacts formerly belonging to Thoreau and his family.[46]

From the angle of diversity in Thoreau tourism, the distinction between replica furniture and original furniture, between "constructive" and "objective authenticity," to borrow Ning Wang's distinction, is crucial since it expands the fields of interest and attraction. On relatively few square miles in the small town of Concord, very different tourist expectations are addressed. This is possibly owing not only to the availability of sites and materials but also to the conscious efforts of various agents to supply different (and of necessity somewhat competing) displays and narratives. Robbins's text, which, among other texts, legitimizes the (touristic value of the) "cabin" site, exemplifies how narratives are formulated to corroborate the establishment of a tourist site.

The same strategy can be observed with the Thoreau Collection of the Concord Museum. In a 2006 book on the collection, *An Observant Eye: The Thoreau Collection at the Concord Museum*, David F. Wood, curator of the Concord Museum, sketches an image of Thoreau that is firmly set in the context of material culture and advocates material objects and memorabilia

FIGURE 3.2. Thoreau's desk, bed, and chair (foreground) as well as three pieces of family furniture (desk, worktable, and chair; background), exhibited at the Concord Museum, Concord, Mass. *Photo by Klara-Stephanie Szlezák. Courtesy of the Concord Museum.*

for a better understanding of Thoreau's life and work. Not surprisingly, his view of the value of Thoreau artifacts betrays a notion of "authenticity" as reliant on original objects, as this passage shows:

> A simple green desk made in Concord, Massachusetts, in about 1838 by a cabinet-maker who charged perhaps one dollar for it, had a career in America's intellectual history *entirely out of proportion* to its humble origin, *because it was Henry Thoreau's* desk. Since it entered the Concord Museum collection, the desk has become a cornerstone of the museum and *a treasured American icon.* Henry Thoreau is best known as the author of *Walden,* universally acknowledged to be one of the great books of American literature, and of "Civil Disobedience," one of the most influential essays in the worldwide democratic tradition. Both were written at this desk.[47]

Clearly, through the association with Thoreau, the material object itself has assumed the status of a relic and is thus worth seeing with one's own eyes. The multiple objects exhibited in the museum's Thoreau Collection do not gain their significance from the association with Thoreau alone. Their value is augmented by a narrative that presents Thoreau as very fond of artifacts and appreciative of "old objects as direct, emotional connections" to past times.[48] The museum displays not only Thoreau's Walden Pond furniture but also a wide array of items and furnishings from his parents' house on Main Street and related to his work as a surveyor. By presenting the material dimension of Thoreau's life and works as no less important than the spiritual, this portrayal of Thoreau opens up a perspective that has been previously relegated to the background. Interestingly, the Concord Museum relies on conventional forms of museum display to communicate an image of Thoreau that deviates from the more conventional image of him as a man who detached himself easily from his material surroundings and for whose understanding the material is secondary to the spiritual.

With these two visions of Thoreau clearly at odds with each other, discussing which vision of Thoreau might be more accurate is, however, not most relevant here. It is instead important to recognize that the various destinations offer different experiences to Thoreau tourists according to what they *can* offer, and that these different sites and sights are accompanied by legitimizing narratives which all draw from Thoreau's life and works and set different emphases according to their position in the field of Thoreau tourism. The Concord Museum is a peculiar case within the field of literary tourism as it offers a kind of "meta"-tourism by presenting present-day tourists with the vestiges of other, earlier forms of tourism: on display in one of the glass cases are stones from the Thoreau cairn, inscribed by the visitors who had placed them on the pile (fig. 3.3). Strictly speaking, these are not Thoreau artifacts, since they have no immediate connection to Thoreau, be it a connection of former ownership, of production or creation, or of representation. The stones relate to Thoreau only through literary tourism: they are not evidence of Thoreau but evidence of tourism memorializing Thoreau. When viewing the cairn stones outside their original context, displayed in a glass case, present-day literary tourists direct their "tourist gaze" (to refer to John Urry's influential concept) to another form of the very activity in which they are themselves engaging at that moment.[49]

This object-based image of Thoreau proposed by the Concord Museum is all the more significant as it points toward more innovative forms of Thoreau tourism. By presenting a Thoreau who is firmly rooted in his Concord surroundings, who is situated in a distinctly material context, and whose life outside the Walden years is increasingly taken into account, the image proposed runs counter to many aspects of the Walden myth. The same tendency can be discovered in more recent forms of Thoreau tourism that not only leave the shores of Walden Pond but also depart from the enclosed space of

FIGURE 3.3. Wood fragment from Thoreau's house at Walden Pond, two cairn stones, tin star, and jail lock, displayed in a glass case at the Concord Museum, Concord, Mass. *Photo by Klara-Stephanie Szlezák. Courtesy of the Concord Museum.*

the museum building. The early twenty-first century is witnessing the "rapid development" of literary tourism, and Thoreau tourism is no exception.[50] Established forms of Thoreau tourism are complemented, and potentially rivaled, by more recent forms that are meant to build on and preserve Thoreau's spirit.

### *Beyond the "Cabin": Innovative Forms of Thoreau Tourism*

When Lawrence Buell observes that "a situated Thoreau makes for a more attractive as well as a truer version of him than a freestanding Thoreau," he underlines the centrality of Thoreau's connection to place—not only in Thoreau's life but also retrospectively, for those who want to learn about him.[51] Yet, this "situatedness" is not to be confused with fixedness or stagnation. Situatedness allows for mobility and evolution within a spatial dimension; detaching Thoreau from Walden Pond is not equivalent to divesting him of his situatedness. Present-day visitors to Concord can experience Thoreau as multiply situated, and they can do so in various and somewhat unconventional ways.

The Thoreau Society aims "to stimulate interest in and foster education about Thoreau's life, works, legacy and his place in his world and in ours" and sees outreach as one of its organizational pillars.[52] Those visitors who only pass through Concord and limit their visit to Walden may benefit from the Thoreau Society's activities as it runs the Thoreau Society Shop at Walden Pond. The featured products, besides books, include T-shirts, jewelry, and other ephemera. Drawing extensively on Thoreau's writings, these products testify to the claim that Thoreau is "one of the most quoted of American authors on posters, calendars, greeting cards, and even in the comic strips. Such phrases as 'different drummer' and 'lives of quiet desperation' became commonplaces."[53] While the Thoreau Society puts a major emphasis on research related to Thoreau, it also aims "to stimulate interest in and foster education" through a broad offering of activities. Educational programs, including lectures, classes, and performances are not limited to Concord residents; excursions take Thoreau admirers outside Concord, to places Thoreau himself visited, such as Mount Katahdin and Cape Cod.[54] The shared experience of the outdoors is regarded as an alternative approach to Thoreau and his ideas.

Thoreau Farm, the birthplace on Virginia Road, which was reopened in 2010, takes a new approach to Thoreau and is a further enrichment for Thoreau tourism in Concord. Run by a trust and envisioned as "a thought leader in 'green preservation,'" Thoreau Farm follows a clearly educational mission, which is expressed in its book and acorn logo: it declares itself to be "a place to examine [Thoreau's] timeless ideas about life, nature, and civic responsibility."[55] The trust furthers its goal "to make Thoreau Farm more than just a historic site—we want it to be a place of ideas" by sponsoring various media channels for the expression and exchange of ideas and thoughts: in addition to a Facebook page and a Twitter account, a blog and a forum ask visitors for responses and comments.[56] Electronic communication, however, is not meant to replace the on-site experience. Thoreau Farm is open to visitors five days a week and also offers a broad program of classes and workshops for writers of all ages. The farm departs significantly from other Concord sites associated with Thoreau by addressing an audience that is not only interested in tracing Thoreau's biography but also eager to engage actively in a dialogue with Thoreau and other Thoreau devotees. The connection to the deceased writer, which is a vital motivator for literary tourism, is established not through visiting and gazing but through putting into practice Thoreauvian ideas, in varying workshops and programs. Such forms of Thoreau tourism, no longer hinging on the Walden experience alone but aiming to portray a more diversified and complex Thoreau, go beyond the experience of platial (archaeological) or material (objective) "authenticity" and reflect the lasting influence of Thoreau's thinking, rather than stages of his biography.

Concord is indisputably "Thoreau territory," and sites associated with the writer abound. Among the many Concord writers who attract literary tourists to the small New England town, Thoreau is a special case. Notably, unlike in the case of the two Concord homes of Nathaniel Hawthorne, the Alcott family's Orchard House, and Ralph Waldo Emerson's house, there is no historic house museum in which visitors can take a guided tour to see the rooms Thoreau inhabited and to learn about his life and work. Nevertheless, tourism surrounding Thoreau is thriving. Literary tourists can trace Thoreau's biography to one place: Concord is the location of his birthplace on Virginia Road; he died in his parents' house on Main Street; within walking distance from there, visitors can see the modest headstone, simply inscribed "Henry" and perennially decorated with flowers, which marks his grave in Sleepy Hollow Cemetery. Concord is moreover the locale of his literary achievements, epitomized by the lasting fascination with Walden Pond and Thoreau's temporary residence there. The "tendency to over-pastoralize Walden" despite its popularity as a tourist destination, as well as to "protest, starting at least as early as the 1890s, against the exploitation of the pond area," is unbroken to this day.[57] Yet the subject of Thoreau tourism in Concord is not exhausted by taking into consideration tourist activities surrounding Walden Pond.

The sheer extent and variety of Thoreau tourism in and around Concord makes it hard to provide a coherent and encompassing survey and analysis and necessitates particular emphases. In this chapter I have sought both to uncover the cultural forces that initiated and shaped Thoreau tourism and to point toward more recent trends. These recent developments in Thoreau tourism, more so than the earlier forms that centered on *Walden* (and thus Walden), reflect Thoreau's inclusion in the American canon.[58] Earlier forms of Thoreau tourism revolved around Walden Pond, his house, and its furnishings, reflecting a concentration on *Walden* as the work most readily associated with Thoreau. A Thoreau tourism that reaches beyond "the Walden experience" can be read as a sign of a more holistic reception of Thoreau's writings. Heightened interest in innovative forms of Thoreau tourism betrays a larger familiarity with his formerly lesser-known works. Familiarity with Thoreau's principal ideas through his writings inspires interest in forms of tourism that favor nature over institution, and active participation over passive reception, and endorses a particular worldview and lifestyle.

Does literary tourism in Concord contribute to keeping Thoreau and his spirit alive? Admiration for and remembrance of Thoreau and his work has been active and unbroken since his death in 1862 (admittedly to varying degrees), so I would indeed argue that twenty-first-century Thoreau tourism in Concord is about *keeping* Thoreau alive. It is not a case of *revival,* as could have been the case, given Thoreau's rapid yet belated rise from relative obscurity to the forefront of American literature. It is remarkable that keeping (the spirit of) Thoreau alive hinged on the adaptability of Thoreau tourism to changed audiences and expectations. The most palpable modification Thoreau tourism in Concord has gone through is that of "cutting the cord" between Thoreau and Walden Pond. The centrality of Walden Pond to Thoreau tourism is beginning to give way to a more diversified picture of Thoreau, ultimately diversifying the experiences available to Thoreau tourists themselves.

## NOTES

1. Henry David Thoreau, *Journal,* vol. 1, *1837–1844,* ed. John C. Broderick et al. (Princeton: Princeton University Press, 1981), 465–66.
2. Using the term "museum"/"museal" is somewhat problematic, given the lack of a universally valid definition in the face of the wide variety of competing definitions with the potential to include many buildings and sites in the category. While I am aware of this, the scope and focus of this chapter do not allow me to address any related questions.
3. See Nicola J. Watson, introduction to *Literary Tourism and Nineteenth-Century Culture,* ed. Nicola J. Watson (London: Palgrave Macmillan, 2009); and Harald Hendrix, "Writers' Houses as Media of Expression and Remembrance: From Self-Fashioning to Cultural Memory," in *Writers' Houses and the Making of Memory,* ed. Harald Hendrix (New York: Routledge Taylor and Francis, 2008), 1–11. To my knowledge, Thoreau's view on house museums is not known. In fact, he may not have had an opinion on them, since the first sparks and the first big wave of preservation efforts, which gave rise to the establishment of historic house museums on a larger scale, only occurred in the 1850s and 1880s, respectively. See Patricia West, *Domesticating History: The Political Origins of America's House Museums* (Washington, D.C.: Smithsonian Institution Press, 1999). In his lifetime they were still rather scarce.
4. Lawrence Buell, "The Thoreauvian Pilgrimage: The Structure of an American Cult," *American Literature* 61, no. 2 (1989): 184, 188, 197.
5. While Margaret Fuller had no permanent residence in Concord, she spent weeks at a time there, staying at Emerson's house. Meg McGavran Murray, *Margaret Fuller: Wandering Pilgrim* (Athens: University of Georgia Press, 2008), 84, 90–91, 180–81, 233–35.
6. Van Wyck Brooks, *The Flowering of New England, 1815–1865* (1936; repr., New York: Modern Library, 1952), 288.
7. A few years after his birth, the family moved to Chelmsford, then to Boston, and returned to Concord in 1823. Raymond R. Borst, *The Thoreau Log: A Documentary Life of Henry David Thoreau, 1817–1862* (New York: Hall, 1992), 1–5.
8. Thoreau was subsequently singled out as the true "Concord son." W. Ellery Channing's 1873 biography relates that "Henry, from his childhood, had quite a peculiar interest in the place of his birth," and states that there was "no better place for his business." W. Ellery Channing, *Thoreau: The Port-Naturalist* (1873; repr., New York: Biblo and Tannen, 1966), 21. Frank B. Sanborn writes in his 1883 biography *Henry D. Thoreau:* "Of all the men of letters that have given Concord a name throughout the world, he is almost the only one who was born there. . . . Thoreau was native to the soil." Frank B. Sanborn, *Henry D. Thoreau* (Boston: Houghton Mifflin, 1883), 63. For an early twentieth-century account that portrays Thoreau as deeply rooted in Concord, see chapters 15 and 19 in Brooks, *The Flowering of New England.*

9. Following W. Barksdale Maynard's observation that Thoreau himself mostly called his construction a "house," I use neither "cabin" nor "hut" in this discussion. W. Barksdale Maynard, "Thoreau's House at Walden," *Art Bulletin* 81, no. 2 (1999): 305.
10. Henry David Thoreau, *Walden; or, Life in the Woods* (1854; repr., Princeton: Princeton University Press, 2004), 3.
11. W. Barksdale Maynard, *Walden Pond: A History* (Oxford: Oxford University Press, 2005), 4.
12. Klaus Benesch, "Where I Lived, and What I Lived For? Thoreau's Platial Iconicity," in *American Cultural Icons: The Production of Representative Lives,* ed. Günter Leypoldt and Bernd Engler (Würzburg: Königshausen & Neumann, 2010), 110–13. For a detailed survey of all the likenesses of Thoreau known to this day, see Thomas Blanding and Walter Harding, "A Thoreau Iconography," in *Studies in the American Renaissance,* ed. Joel Myerson (Boston: Twayne, 1980), 1–35. For more detail on Walden iconography, particularly in photography, see Leslie Perron Wilson, "Walden: Pilgrimages and Iconographies," in *The Oxford Handbook of Transcendentalism,* ed. Joel Myerson, Sandra Harbert Petrulionis, and Laura Dassow Walls (New York: Oxford University Press, 2010), 659–70.
13. See, e.g., Richard J. Schneider, ed., *Thoreau's Sense of Place: Essays in American Environmental Writing* (Iowa City: University of Iowa Press, 2000); and Taimi Anne Olsen, *Transcending Space: Architectural Space in Works by Henry David Thoreau, E. E. Cummings, and John Barth* (Lewisburg, Pa.: Bucknell University Press, 2000).
14. Don Scheese, "Thoreau's *Journal:* The Creation of a Sacred Place," in *Mapping American Culture,* ed. Wayne Franklin and Michael Steiner (Iowa City: University of Iowa Press, 1992), 141, 146. Scheese is certain that Thoreau did not "realize that his modest surroundings would become a sacred place in American culture, a Mecca luring over 400,000 pilgrims annually" (146)—a claim with which I agree.
15. Buell, "Thoreauvian Pilgrimage," 189.
16. The guidebook's chapter on Walden Pond and Thoreau is a case in point. See Miriam Levine, *A Guide to Writers' Homes in New England* (Cambridge: Applewood, 1984), 115–20. Levine's timeline of Thoreau's life prints the years Thoreau stayed at Walden in bold, and she mentions Thoreau's life outside of his Walden house in only one opening and one closing paragraph of the chapter. William Corbett calls Walden "first among American sacred literary places" in *Literary New England: A History and Guide* (Boston: Faber and Faber, 1993), 110.
17. See David Lowenthal, *The Past Is a Foreign Country* (Cambridge: Cambridge University Press, 1999), 4, 11, 13.
18. Walter Harding and Michael Meyer, *The New Thoreau Handbook* (New York: New York University Press, 1980), 209. See Dona Brown, *Inventing New England: Regional Tourism in the Nineteenth Century* (Washington, D.C.: Smithsonian Institution Press, 1995).
19. See, e.g., George Tolman, *Concord: A Few Things to Be Seen There* (Concord, Mass.: Patriot Press, 1902); and Perry Walton, *Concord: A Pilgrimage to the Historic and Literary Center of* America (Boston, 1922).
20. Harding and Meyer, *New Thoreau Handbook,* vii. *Walden* and Thoreau's posthumously published works did not have the same circulation and stature as most of the works of his Concord contemporaries for quite a while.
21. Preface, *Homes of American Authors; Comprising Anecdotal, Personal, and Descriptive Sketches* (New York: G. P. Putnam's Sons, 1852), iv, emphasis added.
22. Brooks, *The Flowering of New England,* 295, 434. The Thoreau family had moved to the Main Street house in 1850, when the pencil business made the purchase of a larger house possible, and Henry lived there for the rest of his life. Harding and Meyer, *New Thoreau Handbook,* 10. The Main Street house, called the Thoreau-Alcott House (the Alcotts moved there in 1877), still stands but is privately owned.
23. See David P. Handlin, *The American Home: Architecture and Society, 1815–1915* (Boston: Little, Brown and Co., 1979), chap. 1.

24. See, e.g., Mike Robinson and Hans Christian Andersen, "Reading Between the Lines: Literature and the Creation of Touristic Spaces," in *Literature and Tourism,* ed. Mike Robinson and Hans Christian Andersen (London: Continuum, 2002), 1–38.
25. Channing, *Thoreau,* 7.
26. Robert Sattelmeyer, "Depopulation, Deforestation, and the Actual Walden Pond," in Schneider, *Thoreau's Sense of Place,* 243.
27. Brooks, *The Flowering of New England,* 370.
28. Maynard, "Thoreau's House at Walden," 303. See also Sattelmeyer, "Depopulation," 243. In his intriguing analysis, Maynard further elaborates on the connections between Thoreau's Walden house, the mid-nineteenth-century villa movement, and the emerging suburban culture, and sees the house as participating "in a variety of architectural traditions: the summerhouse, the literary hermitage, and the wilderness retreat." Maynard, "Thoreau's House," 322. The Walden house further calls to mind the specific notion of an author's retreat, which provides the calm and the liberation from day-to-day obligations that are necessary to accomplish creative work. The Walden house was, among other things, meant to serve as an author's retreat and give Thoreau the freedom to write "his long-gestating book manuscript." Maynard, *Walden Pond,* 65.
29. *Massachusetts: A Guide to Its Places and People, written and compiled by the Federal Writers' Project of the Works Progress Administration for the State of Massachusetts,* American Guide Series (Boston: Houghton Mifflin, 1937), 213.
30. Thoreau, *Walden,* 167. Later on in the same chapter of *Walden,* "The Village," Thoreau writes: "I had gone down to the woods for other purposes. But, wherever a man goes, men will pursue and paw him with their dirty institutions, and, if they can, constrain him to belong to their desperate odd-fellow society" (171). This passage makes clear that being critical of, or rejecting, forms of societal organization is not equivalent to being antisocial. The latter, not the former, is likely to result in hermitage.
31. (At least) as early as 1866, people gathered at Walden, having a picnic to celebrate Thoreau's birthday. Letter from Sophia Thoreau to Daniel Ricketson, quoted in David F. Wood, *An Observant Eye: The Thoreau Collection at the Concord Museum* (Concord, Mass.: Concord Museum Publications, 2006), 128.
32. Walter Harding, *The Days of Henry Thoreau: A Biography* (Princeton: Princeton University Press, 1992), 222–24. William E. Griswold's "After Walden: A Biography of Thoreau's Hut" (unpublished research paper, 1954, series III.W.6, Walter Harding Collection, Thoreau Society Collections at the Thoreau Institute at Walden Woods, Concord, Mass.) not only traces the fate of Thoreau's famous house but also testifies to the degree to which the material object had assumed iconic status, resulting in the house's "biography."
33. Wood, *An Observant Eye,* 9. Sophia (1819–1876) not only preserved Thoreau's belongings but also helped create the Walden iconography by drawing the sketch of Thoreau's house by the pond which would appear on the title page of the first edition of *Walden.* Wilson, "Walden: Pilgrimages and Iconographies," 665. Maynard justly ascribes Sophia Thoreau a crucial, active role in the memorialization of her brother. For instance, she arranged for the removal of Thoreau's body from the town cemetery to Sleepy Hollow, where she knew his name would be seen next to Hawthorne's; she prepared his political papers for posthumous publication and authorized the publication of excerpts from his journal (Maynard, *Walden Pond,* 159, 185–86); and she closely observed and documented the growing popularity of Walden as a literary site.
34. If 1872 marks the onset of a tradition that set off Thoreau tourism, this year roughly coincides with the "new surge of interest in Thoreau in the 1880s," the decade when the first volumes of his *Journal* were published. Harding and Meyer, *New Thoreau Handbook,* 206.
35. Roland Wells Robbins, *Discovery at Walden* (1947; repr., Stoneham, Mass.: Folcroft, 1970), 4.
36. Ibid., 3.

37. The very concept of "authenticity" has developed into an issue indelibly ingrained in any discussion concerning (literary) tourism, originating with, or at least intensified by Dean MacCannell's claim that all tourists ultimately set out on a "quest for authenticity." Dean MacCannell, *The Tourist: A New Theory of the Leisure Class* (1976; repr.; Berkeley: University of California Press, 1999), 105. "Authenticity" has been the subject of scholarly debates and numerous publications that tend to draw into question the notion of objective authenticity and propose an understanding of the concept that foregrounds the individual's subjective expectations and experience. See, e.g., Erik Cohen, "Authenticity and Commoditization in Tourism," *Annals of Tourism Research* 15, no. 2 (1988): 371–86; Gordon Waitt, "Consuming Heritage: Perceived Historical Authenticity," *Annals of Tourism Research* 27, no. 4 (2000): 835–62; Ning Wang, "Re-thinking Authenticity in Tourism Experience," *Annals of Tourism Research* 26 (1999): 349–70. For reasons of scope and focus, I do not engage here in a theoretical discussion of the role and meaning of authenticity. I do, however, use the term in quotation marks to indicate my awareness of the ambiguity and disputability of the concept; if needed, I specify the kind of "authenticity" to which I refer.
38. The Reverend C. A. Cress in the 1870s and Wade Van Dore in 1922 both unearthed bricks in the immediate surroundings of the cairn. Maynard, *Walden Pond,* 175, 180, 232.
39. "Roland Wells Robbins Slide Images of Concord, Massachusetts, People, Places, and Events and of Other Locations (Primarily in Massachusetts), 1947–1981" (finding aid), Concord (Mass.) Library, www.concordlibrary.org.
40. Robbins, *Discovery at Walden,* x, 59, 60.
41. Walter Harding, introduction, ibid., xvi.
42. Lowenthal, *The Past Is a Foreign Country,* 248.
43. Another full-scale model of the house stands on the grounds of the Concord Museum in downtown Concord, donated by the Thoreau Society in 1995.
44. I am grateful to a park interpreter who, in an email exchange in September 2010, explained to me the DCR's motivations for this decision: apparently a major factor was accessibility. The original location is comparatively hard to reach and would thus have excluded a number of visitors from seeing the house. Furthermore, a position in the woods, out of the (constant) sight of park rangers, would have risked potential acts of vandalism. The third reason the interpreter named was particularly interesting: since the original site is considered "sacred," positioning the replica there would only have been a way to "profane it." While this is of course one individual's opinion, I do think it is to some extent a statement representative of the current operators. It necessarily brings up the issue of "authenticity" again: however accurately the house is rebuilt, it will never be the "original" and thus creates a noticeable disharmony with the "original" site, leading to a sense of profanity. Such a view is clearly founded on a rather conventional notion of "authenticity."
45. Both displays meet different tourist expectations according to the tourists' respective perception of "authenticity" (see note 36). In this context, Ning Wang's differentiation between various understandings of "authenticity" proves useful. The display of the replica furniture in the replica house would not content an audience for which the experience of authenticity consists of "an epistemological experience . . . of the authenticity of originals" (called "objective authenticity" [Wang, "Re-thinking Authenticity in Tourism Experience," 352]). Yet it caters to an audience for whom authenticity is given if the display allows for the projection of expectations and images of a symbolic nature (which Wang calls "constructive authenticity" [353–56]). "The Henry David Thoreau Collection," Concord Museum, www.concordmuseum.org.
46. I use the term "aura," drawing on Walter Benjamin's seminal essay "Das Kunstwerk im Zeitalter seiner technischen Reproduzierbarkeit" ("The Work of Art in the Age of Mechanical Reproduction," 1936), in which the notion of the "aura" is grounded in the notion of "uniqueness" (*Einzigkeit*). While formulated with reference to works of art, Benjamin's observations are applicable to artifacts whose fascination stems from the sense

that they are unique and/or uniquely connected to an "auratic" person. Walter Benjamin, "Das Kunstwerk im Zeitalter seiner technischen Reproduzierbarkeit," in *Illuminationen* (Frankfurt: Suhrkamp, 1969), 148–83.

47. Wood, *An Observant Eye,* 11, emphasis added. Wood uses the same rhetoric with reference to Thoreau's bed: "This bedstead is famous for having made up part of the furnishings of Walden Pond" (57), claiming "fame" for the material object itself.
48. Ibid., 20.
49. John Urry, *The Tourist Gaze* (London: Sage, 2009). Encountering an older and markedly different form of Thoreau tourism in the display of the stones might in turn make viewers of the Thoreau Collection at the Concord Museum aware of their own role as Thoreau tourists and encourage them to participate in these older rituals of "Thoreauvian pilgrimage" as well.
50. Watson, introduction, 3.
51. Lawrence Buell, foreword to Schneider, *Thoreau's Sense of Place,* x.
52. Home page, Thoreau Society, www.thoreausociety.org.
53. Harding and Meyer, *New Thoreau Handbook,* 210.
54. See www.thoreausociety.org.
55. Ibid. Interestingly, Lawrence Buell was involved in the preservation of Thoreau's birthplace and its subsequent use as a space for education and encounter and has served on the board of trustees. His active involvement counters widely held beliefs that studying literary tourism is incompatible with supporting and/or participating in it.
56. Ibid. Such forms of responses and "visits" reach into the domain of virtual tourism, as Thoreau Farm welcomes visitors to the actual site as well as to the website. On the theory of virtual tourism, see, for instance, chapter 7 in Bella Dicks's *Culture on Display: The Production of Contemporary Visitability* (Maidenhead, Berkshire: Open University Press, 2003).
57. Buell, "Thoreauvian Pilgrimage," 180.
58. When I use the term "canon," I am fully aware of its being a thorny issue. Most important, when I speak of "Thoreau's inclusion in the American canon," this may suggest two kinds of reduction which I do not wish to imply. First, one insight gained from the canon revisions starting in the 1980s is that the singular use of "canon" implies a universality that is not given. The singular does not suffice to reflect the diversity of literatures produced and read in the United States. Second, speaking of inclusion in a canon might be read as implying stagnation. "Inclusion" does not, however, preclude a future exclusion. Taste changes, and thus any canon is naturally dynamic. Thoreau's inclusion thus refers to the development of the past 150 years. Thoreau's inclusion in the "canon" signifies the frequency with which his works appear on school and university curricula as well as his growing popularity inside and outside academia.

# 4

# *The Wide, Wide World beyond a Tiny, Deserted Island*

## At Home with Susan and Anna Warner

REBECCA REGO BARRY

---

*If literary tourists have a difficult task in finding an existing home where they might encounter Thoreau and his work, tourists interested in Susan and Anna Warner are faced with an abundance of authenticity at Constitution Island (papers, furnishings, and a decrepit home)—and no ability to access it. The Warner sisters, best-selling and tremendously influential authors in their day, are largely forgotten by all but literary and religious historians today. Outlining her exploration of the now closed Warner House on Constitution Island, Rebecca Rego Barry dares to ask: What happens when interest in an author is no longer sufficient to keep the doors open to a historic house museum that tells an essential story of nineteenth-century American women's experiences?*

---

Visiting the Susan and Anna Warner House is almost like touring a famous prison; for one quiet moment when the door slams shut, you can be transported. These two literary sisters shared the most unlikely home: a deserted 280-acre island in the Hudson River, just off the coast of West Point, New York. Even more improbable, perhaps, is the fact that this is where one of nineteenth-century America's biggest best sellers was written. Under the pseudonym Elizabeth Wetherell, Susan Warner wrote *The Wide, Wide World* (1850) while living on Constitution Island. She wrote every morning before dawn, until her father rose, when she had to prepare breakfast. Her younger sister Anna lit the fire, boiled water for tea, and then took up her own pen. They toiled together, producing an astonishing eighty-nine books between them. After her death, the *New York Times* wrote of Susan, "In this secluded corner of the world, one of the most remarkable and at the same time retiring of American women accomplished her lifework."[1]

The house where literary history was made is modest, not at all like the Gilded Age mansions that dot the Hudson River Valley. The oldest part includes a thick stone wall dating from Revolutionary War days, when the site was very likely a barracks. The island is, after all, the location of a strategic victory over the British; it is where troops constructed a "Great Chain" to block British naval vessels headed upriver. A new wing of eight rooms was added in 1836, after the Warner sisters' widowed father, a New York City attorney named Henry Warner, purchased the island.

When I visited in the spring of 2009, I thought the décor might be called genteel Victorian—threadbare area rugs, dark wood furniture, a cabinet full of china, and piles of books in decorated nineteenth-century bindings—but it had, as I described it then, "a rare authenticity that restorations often lack," because these were not reproductions; they were the Warners' things (fig. 4.1).[2] Which is to say, there didn't appear to be any "staging" or overt "curation" of the site; there was a want of neatly typed labels, an audio tour, or a gift shop. That was just before the house closed, before the Warners' belongings were removed to storage. Returning to the house seven years later—psychologically, if not physically, since it remained shuttered—in this chapter I explore the house and the island as tangible "objects" and seek to demonstrate the effect they had on the Warner sisters and American literary history and to explain what they tell us about the experiences of American women in the nineteenth century.

After Henry Warner lost his fortune in the Panic of 1837, he moved his two daughters—then aged eighteen and thirteen—and their aunt Fanny (their mother had died when the girls were young) from Manhattan to the island. To have relocated two teenage girls accustomed to city life and relative wealth to an island where they were forced to chop wood and churn butter seems stunning to a modern reader, and it is one of the most interesting aspects of the sisters' story.[3] These women were isolated geographically, financially, and socially from the life they had known. Incredibly, the Warners lived there until their deaths, Susan in 1885 and Anna thirty years after that. The solitude must have been almost unbearable. They filled it with words, songs, and prayers, but their creations were products of a nineteenth-century set of circumstances that cannot be overlooked, among them the belief that daughters were safer at home than in pursuing outside work. Women—even a well-educated best-selling novelist like Susan Warner—felt powerless to shape their own destinies.

I first traveled to Constitution Island when I was writing a short article for *Preservation* magazine about the temporary closure of the Warner House.[4]

FIGURE 4.1. The room where the Warner sisters wrote is referred to as the Revolutionary Sitting Room because of the Gilbert Stuart portrait of George Washington over the fireplace. The room pictured here, post-1933, looks tidier and less cluttered than it was when the Warner sisters lived there. U.S. Military Academy, Warner House, Constitution Island, West Point, Orange County, N.Y. *Photograph, post-1933, Historic American Buildings Survey/Historic American Engineering Record/Historic Landscapes Survey.*

Since 1908 the island and the Warner House have been owned by the United States government and utilized by the United States Military Academy at West Point. The Warners' house is surrounded by a military reserve that is used by cadets for training exercises. Until 2009, tourist access was seasonal and limited, and historic preservation was a low priority. Long after the "temporary closure," the situation remains uncertain. The house sits empty and awaiting funding mandates to pay for what a West Point spokesperson called a "fairly extensive" and "fairly costly" renovation,[5] even though a preservation architect told me back in 2009 that the structure was essentially good, and that what it needed most was replacement of the rotting sills, installation of a ventilated roof, and a better drainage system.[6] All of the Warners' furnishings are in storage. The archives, housed on the West Point campus until their "arbitrary" eviction by the army in the fall of 2012, were removed to secondary spaces as of January 2013—a main archival research space at Locust Grove (once the property of Samuel F. B. Morse) near Poughkeepsie, New York, and an office / ancillary archival space in Cold Spring, New York.[7] The army had succeeded in fully occupying the island.

Why does it matter if the Warner sisters' house is closed, their furniture is in storage, and their archives are in Poughkeepsie? There are those who would tell us that writers' houses and their artifacts are insignificant, that biography itself is beside the point, and that it is the text we should revere. But the Warner House is both a physical structure and a symbol. It embodies the physical and mental confines to which women of the Warners' time and class were subjected. Prefiguring Charlotte Perkins Gilman's yellow-wallpapered room by forty years, the Warners' captivity was real. Essentially, their isolation was the story behind the story that can provide us with a deep understanding of Susan and Anna Warner—and that story plays out in a secluded house on an otherwise deserted island.

The Warners, of course, did not always reside on Constitution Island. Susan Bogert Warner was born in New York City in 1819. Her father hailed from upstate New York, and his legal practice necessitated frequent travel to Albany. Her mother, Anna Marsh Bartlett, had five children between her marriage in 1817 and her death in 1826, only two of whom survived into adulthood. The youngest, Anna Bartlett Warner, born in 1824, was to become Susan's constant companion. Although motherless, the girls were reared by their aunt Fanny, and their childhoods, especially Susan's, were filled with events and accouterments typical for young women of their age and status: French and Italian lessons, piano practice, reading, museums, silk dresses, and calling cards. Susan was acquainted with Julia Ward Howe, a well-to-do friend who would go on to write "The Battle Hymn of the Republic."[8] They were also friendly with the famous Phelps Stokes clan of "Old New York," multimillionaire bankers and philanthropists; one of its members, Olivia E. Phelps Stokes, corresponded with them and compiled a very affectionate book of their letters after Anna's death.[9]

In the 1830s, during a profitable time for Henry Warner's real estate speculations, the Warners lived first in a town house at 461 Broome Street in New York City and then in a mansion at 10 St. Mark's Place. They also kept a summer home in Canaan, New York, where Henry had grown up and where his family had been substantial farmers. The Warner sisters were on a path toward increasing wealth and social prominence, and with 90 percent of her female peers set to marry, surely Susan was destined for a good match.[10]

Scholars differ on whether Susan could or should have married when her father's fortunes began to decline in 1837. After Susan's death, Anna recalled in the biography she wrote how timid and nervous a person her sister was.[11] The archivists at the Constitution Island Association describe her as "high-strung" and ill-suited to marriage.[12] She was awkwardly tall and slender, and exceedingly bookish. But all that may be beside the point, because by 1838, when their St. Mark's mansion was sold, Susan's prospects for a lavish coming-out and a marriage to someone of her class were all but gone. Instead, Henry decided to "tuck her away at home," to use cultural historian Mary Kelley's phrase.[13] He had purchased Constitution Island in 1836, intending to build a grand summer residence. In July of that year, after her father began to talk about moving to the island, Susan realized that the life she had imagined was slipping away. In her diary on her seventeenth birthday she wrote: "I am anything but joyful, be it what day it might. I had formed delightful anticipations, but they must be only *hopes* now. I had such bright visions, but they have faded."[14] Is she talking about losing her home in New York City, or her way of life, or a good match? She seems aware of a sea change, and yet it is impossible to know, because she stopped writing in her diary. Anna later recalled, "For well nigh a year and a half she either wrote no journal, or afterwards destroyed it."[15] Susan was known to excise pages from her diaries with a razor, and that year and a half was likely the most traumatic time in her life. The family's circumstances were greatly reduced, and Susan's life was rapidly becoming very different from the one she had begun to enjoy.

Henry was forced to move his daughters to the island indefinitely. Instead of the mansion complete with ponies he had promised, they moved into an antiquated cottage. The economic panic of 1837 had hit many elite families hard, and the Warners were no exception. Retreating to Constitution Island offered Henry a chance to recover. It is not known whether or how much he consulted his adolescent daughters about the relocation; as the literary critic Nina Baym reminds us: "Society was based on money, and men had all the control—the power to make it, to disburse it, to keep it, and the terrifying power to lose it. . . . Daughters were economically ruled by their fathers."[16] Indeed, Henry sent Susan away to visit relatives when the family made its final move in the spring of 1838, perhaps to soften the blow.

Of this time in their lives and Susan's experience of it, Anna later wrote: "From waiter and coachman and cook to the skill of our own hands (chiefly) was a broad step. . . . [F]rom dainty silks and laces, we came down to calicoes, fashioned by our own fingers. . . . [F]or my sister in the bloom of her young womanhood it must have been hard. . . . She wanted to go about, to talk, to entertain."[17] By the following year, Susan and Anna were chopping firewood, gathering sticks for kindling, and churning butter. The girls knew they were "ruined." As Susan wrote, "The journal lags, and how should it not? for I am turned housekeeper!" She added later: "I am not able to do all I would. I do not study Italian. I play but very little on the piano, I do not read much, I do not even write every day."[18]

Ever mindful of their father's "heavy burden" (as well as the empty oil can), the Warner sisters lived parsimoniously, and when things became truly dire in the mid-1840s, they began to think about ways to generate income of their own. According to Nina Baym, "Between 1820 and 1870 there were virtually no satisfying and well paid occupations for women."[19] Partially this was due to the limited educational opportunities for women; but that was not necessarily the problem for Susan. For her there were several issues in play. First, white middle-class women occupied a domestic sphere and were conditioned to live privately, away from public scrutiny. As one scholar of the period asserted, "After all, [a woman's] proper sphere was the home."[20] Second, the isolation of Constitution Island, with nary a neighbor in sight, eliminated the genteel option of teaching or giving music lessons. And third, it turns out that although Susan was schooled, her education had been designed for a "social purpose," that is, middle-class marriage.[21] She was, as Baym suggests, much like her most famous character, Ellen Montgomery, who enters the real world and "discovers how deplorably she has been fitted by education or upbringing to deal with it."[22]

And yet the financial panic had created a need for women to participate in the economy as providers. It was Anna who first showed entrepreneurial initiative: she created a children's game based on natural history called Robinson Crusoe's Farmyard, painstakingly painting each card and sending them off in batches for sale. It was around that time that Aunt Fanny suggested to Susan that she try writing a novel. It must have seemed rather shocking to the sisters, considering how they had been brought up; there had been a time when Susan was forbidden to read the novels of Sir Walter Scott. But by 1849, they had little left to lose, except the roof over their heads. Besides, she was not the first woman to respond to the dire financial times by turning to writing. In the preceding decade, as literary scholar Mary Templin observes, "an outpouring of dozens of novels and stories—nearly all by white, middle-class, Northern women—responded to the national threat of financial failure."[23] Susan, always an avid reader, had female literary role models. Like Catharine Sedgwick, she could write from the privacy of her own home. The pressure was on.[24]

So began a writing routine now famous among Warner aficionados. Even with the thermometer reading twenty-eight degrees in their shared "study," Anna would be the first up, "generally by half past four."[25] She would have kindled the fire and made the tea by the time Susan joined her, and the two would then write for several hours in silence. The room was decorated in the Victorian style—paintings covering the walls, full bookcases, ornaments on every surface—and yet the chair cushions were thin, and the throw rug was frayed. And until a few years ago, this setting remained in place, chilling visitors even on the warmest summer day.

It was there that Susan produced *The Wide, Wide World,* a novel that became a literary phénomenon. Literary scholar Jane Tompkins has dubbed it "the Ur-text of the nineteenth-century United States. More than any other book of its time, it embodies, uncompromisingly, the values of the Victorian era."[26] Those values were self-sacrifice, submission, and evangelical faith—all of which were demanded of Susan, and she, in turn, enforced them in her fiction. The novel was an example of what has since been labeled "domestic fiction"; she was a member of the "damned mob of scribbling women" against which Nathaniel Hawthorne railed.[27] Nina Baym explains the genre this way: "In essence," these books tell "the story of a young girl who is deprived of the supports she had rightly or wrongly depended on to sustain her throughout her life." This young woman "is faced with the necessity of winning her own way in the world."[28] Baym describes not only the perfect genre plot for the domestic novel but also the biography of Warner herself. Warner's young heroine, Ellen Montgomery, is shuttled from one contemptuous relative to the next after her mother dies. In the end, Ellen earns her reward—wealth, marriage, and city living—by remaining faithful to her Christian values. Did Susan give Ellen the happy ending she would have wanted for herself? Did she, as Jane Tompkins suggests, dream "of luxury and access to the world"?[29]

Susan would never have those things in any great measure. Marriage was increasingly unlikely; when *The Wide, Wide World* was published, she was already thirty-one years old. At first she eschewed fame (and the access or re-entrance to society that it might bring) by publishing under a pseudonym, Elizabeth Wetherell; she later dropped the pen name. Money was always needed. (Susan opted for outright payments for her copyrights, unfortunately ensuring that there would be no further income from royalties.) And although they traveled regionally in their later years, the sisters lived sheltered lives, never straying too far from their island residence. Susan used a stereoscope to "research" worldly locations for her novels. Some literary critics now view *The Wide, Wide World* as evocative of Susan's homesickness, a novel of "dislocations and separations."[30] Their point is apt and manifests how significantly the move to the island changed her. As for so many women, her home was her world. The move to Constitution Island was not simple; it changed her address, but also her social standing, her marriage prospects, her relationships, her educational opportunities, and her ability to participate in a larger culture that the city had offered. The relocation and the financial strain that precipitated it gave rise to a new set of mental anxieties and physically demanding duties.

While Susan's novel was perhaps more oblique about these issues, the plot of Anna's first and most popular novel, *Dollars and Cents* (1852), is strongly autobiographical—and critical. It is the story of the Howards, a wealthy Philadelphia family that loses everything as a result of the father's financial speculations. Mr. Howard moves the family to the country, where his poor planning, bad management, and legal entanglements make matters worse. In the end, however, Anna rights the situation by giving the Howards what the Warner sisters may have wanted: a secure job for the father and an ideal marriage for the older daughter.

From these literary beginnings, the Warner sisters launched their careers. According to the Constitution Island Association, the grand total of their output is eighty-nine original books, with an additional thirty-five variant titles and three magazine articles.[31] In addition to novels, there were children's collections, religious stories, and hymns. When Anna Warner is remembered today, it is either as the woman who wrote the lyrics for the hymn "Jesus Loves Me," or as the author of *Gardening by Myself* (1872), a practical guide which advised that middle-class American women actually do their own gardening. Perhaps because of the triumph of *The Wide, Wide World,* Susan was always the more prominent and better-selling writer. Her follow-up, *Queechy,* though not as popular as her debut, was well received; Elizabeth Barrett Browning recommended it.[32] Her literary star seemed to be on the rise. But the contrast between Susan's reclusive home life and her reception and recognition in the wider world is sharp. As her fame increased and opportunities presented themselves, she was unable to wrest herself from her father or her home for too long. Susan Geary called Susan Warner "the obscurest of scribblers,"[33] a reference to Hawthorne's oft-quoted crack, and one wonders why she chose obscurity when success finally arrived on her doorstep.

Nothing manifests Susan Warner's anxiety over these famous/obscure, worldly/isolated juxtapositions more clearly than her private writings about the trips she took and the people she met in Boston and New York, before and after her literary debut. She had mixed feelings about traveling to Boston, but during her time there in 1846–47, she met with some of the leading cultural figures of the day. At a lecture, Catharine Beecher, supporter of female education, "made a most agreeable impression upon me," she reported.[34] At a party she mingled with novelist Catharine Maria Sedgwick, Harvard professor Louis Agassiz ("a perfectly charming man"), Ralph Waldo Emerson, and her old acquaintance Julia Ward Howe. "Mr. Emerson I didn't fancy," she wrote to her aunt.[35] She felt she had displayed composure and intelligence among this group; in other words, she fit in.

There was also a brief period in the fall of 1850 during which she lived at publisher George Palmer Putnam's Staten Island home while she proofread

*The Wide, Wide World.* Putnam, a founder of the major publishing company Wiley and Putnam, was situated at the center of New York's literary world. Among others, he published Washington Irving, James Fenimore Cooper, and Edgar Allan Poe. While staying at the Putnam home, Susan worked on her book, but she also had tea with "society" folks and went to the theater to see Jenny Lind. She enjoyed the theater immensely. Nine years later, back in New York City for a winter, she struck up a friendly relationship with the recently divorced actress, abolitionist, and author Fanny Kemble, a rather racy acquaintance for Susan.

For a modern reader, it is difficult to imagine why Susan did not harness these contacts more and break out of her sequestration. Some might argue that she loved Constitution Island—there are certainly entries in her diary that attest to happy times, particularly later in life, when she finds purpose in offering Bible classes to West Point cadets—but in her youth, it is clear she felt ambivalence. During that Boston trip, she confided, "Oh how I like to see and hear intelligent people!"[36] And just after *The Wide, Wide World* was published, as the sisters wondered where they would reside for the winter, Susan wrote, "The Island, alas! looks to me a dismal place for us to be locked up in for the winter; without a grown servant, without books, without a piano, without church, without a friend's face . . . without any brilliant prospects for the future."[37] Two pages later she added: "Home has ceased to be very lovely to me. How I do enjoy myself when I get away from it!"[38]

Susan's use of the words "locked up"—such a direct reference to a feeling of imprisonment—renders the reader speechless. She was now a poor, unmarried young woman, and the only thing to do with her was to "lock" her up or "tuck" her away, somewhere safe. Did she feel like a prisoner of her father's, of society's expectations, or of the island's inaccessibility? As Jane Tompkins put it, "Harder than the household drudgery was the isolation."[39] It was around this time—after writing *Wide, Wide World* but before its success—that she considered a position as a governess, as a way to earn money and, perhaps, freedom from isolation.

It is also interesting to note that while all this was happening, the women's rights movement was well under way. The Seneca Falls Convention occurred in 1848, 250 miles away from the Warners' desert isle. The Warners were not involved or perhaps even interested in the issue of women's rights, but they would not have been completely unaware of the movement. In fact, during the trip to New York when she met Fanny Kemble, Susan wrote about a gathering to discuss "the woman's sphere" in which "Mrs. F. and I [were] the chief talkers."[40]

So why didn't Susan "run away from home," so to speak? After the success of *The Wide, Wide World,* she had some money and some power to combat the subjugation she had experienced upon the family's relocation. Why didn't she row to the mainland, hop a train, head for the big city, and contact one of her literary acquaintances? It would have been challenging, but not unheard of, to make a new life. Other contemporaneous female writers had crafted successful careers to varying degrees, including Elizabeth Palmer Peabody, Sarah Josepha Hale, and Harriet Beecher Stowe. But as Jane Tompkins reminds us, "Women writers of the era, unlike their male counterparts, could not walk out the door and become Mississippi riverboat captains, go off on whaling voyages, or build themselves cabins in the woods."[41] Options for women were limited, and mistakes could be devastating.

Partly, Susan stayed because of her sense of familial duty. Once her pen proved profitable, she became the family's breadwinner—a family that included an elderly father and aunt, both of whom were incapable of financially supporting themselves, as well as her younger sister. The responsibility of that role would not have eluded Susan, a woman whose sense of self-sacrifice and moral obligation could be severe. Scholar Susan S. Williams believes that Susan Warner was feeding the machine, caught in a vicious circle: "The need to continue earning money encouraged her to depend on the support and assistance of her sister and increasingly her public, despite some discomfort with her role as a sentimental novelist."[42] In other words, writing sentimental novels was (or later became) a means to an end, instead of a passion.

Susan was uncomfortable and uncertain of herself as a successful writer. When she was staying at Putnam's house, one visitor asked her if she had met a Mr. James.[43] Susan wrote in a letter home to Anna: "I told her I had been living on a desert island. . . . I took my place in the literary world quietly, and said nothing."[44] The physical seclusion, which excluded her from the literary mainstream, was exacerbated by the fact that she very likely had reservations about her role—a woman's role—as a literary being. She eventually dropped the charade of a pen name, but the upper-middle-class values of her youth were too ingrained for her to market herself as an author. Twenty years after the publication of *The Wide, Wide World,* Susan listed her occupation as "Keeping House" in the 1870 U.S. census (echoing a time in 1830 when Catharine Sedgwick informed a bank that she had no profession).[45] Mary Kelley writes of this trend: "The literary domestics did not in their own minds become legitimate economic providers or businesspeople. Instead, they remained fundamentally private domestic women. . . . Basically unrecognized by or unacceptable to their society as economic providers, they had difficulty recognizing or accepting it themselves. In many ways they did it and denied it."[46]

In other words, writing may have been a necessary evil to keep tea and butter on the table, but it wasn't something that made a woman proud or happy. Which leads to the question: Would Susan Warner have published anything if not for the extreme circumstances of losing her financial, physical, and social home base? Williams tells us that George Haven Putnam, son of Warner's original publisher, took up the question, saying, "Susan always had literary ambitions, but it was the pressure for money that constituted the immediate incentive to the writing of *The Wide, Wide World*."[47] He believed she never would have written the novel if her prospects had not been "ruined" in the economic panic. To some extent her biographer Edward Foster agrees. He wrote that he was "almost certain" Susan would have married if her father had remained solvent, and that one change would have had an enormous effect on Susan's life.[48] She would have had no need for her own income, and besides, her husband and their surrounding society would likely have disdained literary ambitions.

The only trouble with these theories is that they overlook the fact that Susan Warner was an obsessive reader and, according to her contemporaries, a good writer.[49] Her writing tapped into the consciousness of her age. No less a personage than Henry James praised her work, and many critics have admired the sisters' local color writing. So when scholars propose that Susan Warner prefigured Charlotte Perkins Gilman and Sarah Orne Jewett in the female literary landscape, we must also ask: Would she have embraced a more literary stance had she had the leisure to do so?[50] We can only guess.[51]

If not marriage or writing, it is possible that the Warner sisters' talents might have been directed somewhere else altogether. The Constitution Island Association archives contain hundreds of fine drawings and sketches that hint at their artistic abilities. We also know that both Susan and Anna went on to become quite beloved religious instructors to the West Point cadets, who would row over for tea and Bible class starting in 1875 until Anna's death in 1915. That was a great source of pride and purpose for the sisters; it is easy to imagine one or both of them in a religious profession. Gardening, too, was an activity of great importance, particularly to Anna, whose *Gardening by Myself* is tellingly titled.

They spent their time, as they matured, engaged in extra-vocational pursuits, and considering that each sister lived all the remainder of her life on the island, they evidently adapted to their isolation. Sometime around 1870 Susan wrote in her journal, "I have been thinking, if this great loneliness and isolation is to make us do more work or do it better, with more entireness of heart or strength of desire,—why I am content."[52] Their father died in 1875, followed by Susan at age sixty-five in 1885, and Aunt Fanny, who had been confined to a wheelchair, later that same year. That left Anna alone on the island, except for what help she might hire here and there, for another thirty years.

Seven years before she died, however, Anna Warner did a very patriotic thing. She sold Constitution Island to the philanthropist Mrs. Russell Sage, who agreed to buy it and then turn it over to the United States as a gift, per Anna's wish.[53] The transaction seems to have been motivated entirely by Warner's connection to the cadets she and her sister befriended over the years. (So close was the relationship that the two sisters are even buried in the military cemetery there.) Anna was allowed to continue living on the island until her death, at which time West Point received a significant parcel of land to enlarge and buffer the military academy. President Theodore Roosevelt himself wrote a personal note to Anna in 1908, stating: "I write to thank you for the singular generosity which has prompted you and her [Mrs. Sage] to make this gift to the Nation. You have rendered a real and patriotic service, and on behalf of all our people I desire to express our obligation and our appreciation."[54] In 1916, the year following Anna's death, the Constitution Island Association (CIA) was founded by a handful of blue-blooded members with family names like Roosevelt and Livingston, and funding from J. P. Morgan.[55] A similar effort to preserve the Warner legacy came in the form of a bronze historical marker at the Jason Warner House, the Warners' summer home in Canaan, New York, in 1936.[56] But the Warners' star has faded in the past century, and a makeshift historical "friends" group was never likely to be much of a match for the United States Army.

The situation at Constitution Island was then, and is now, problematic. The United States government owns the land and the house, while the CIA retains the Warner family's archives and furnishings and has a mandate to protect and preserve them. Although a 2006 article characterized the relationship between the association and the military as synergistic, it is hardly so.[57] The CIA is a 501(c)(3) nonprofit that relies on fund-raising to provide preservation of and reference assistance for the Warners' archives and collections, as well as interpretive, educational, and recreational activities related to the Warner House and gardens. Funding for direct construction or renovation to the house, however, is subject to the army's budget process. Also, the CIA's volunteer board must seek approval from the USMA's garrison commander to run its programs; in essence, it is always at the mercy of the army.

Over the years, there have been good times and bad. There is a swift rate of replacement in West Point leadership, which means that any agreement regarding preservation or access can be reversed by a succeeding official with different sympathies. In the 1960s, West Point considered turning the island into a golf course.[58] In the 1990s, West Point covered the existing milk-painted interior with latex paint, which began to peel almost immediately, something called the "potato chip" effect. In 2002, West Point undertook a very expensive reconstruction of the island's old boathouse. The former executive director of the CIA questioned the preservation standards and called the results "really disturbing."[59] What becomes clear is that however much West Point officials may continue to talk about restoration of the Warner House, it is neither their strength nor truly a priority.[60] Of course, there is also the inevitable lack of federal funding, which in this case is complicated by the fact that a historic home's preservation budget must be carved from the larger federal budget of the United States Army and the Department of Defense.

In the spring of 2009, West Point declared the house "unstable." CIA members were caught off guard by the announcement since they had been lobbying for some basic repairs for years. The house needed a water remediation system and a new roof, but a preservation architect had declared the structure essentially sound. The interior was in good shape. I walked through and saw the Warners' cradle, their mother's wedding china, a medicine chest full of bottles, and hundreds of books. I stood in the room where Susan composed *The Wide, Wide World.* It was spare and shabby, retaining its original furnishings, but moving: two women sat right here, huddled in front of the fire, writing for their lives. It was, quite literally, a Victorian's vista, and I was able to experience it firsthand.

Constitution Island is still deserted—with the exception of the caretaker's cabin—with admittance only by boat or an officials-only access road, and the Warner House is remarkably unchanged but for some dim-witted paint choices and indifferent preservation protocols. When I last saw it, there was no evidence of a professional curator's touch, no design to show or teach anything at all—and therein, perhaps, lies part of the problem. Literary tourists in search of the Warners, having persevered in setting foot on the island at the right time of year, may not mind minimal signposting, but those who are unaware of the Warners' books or who lack a connection to Victorian literature and material culture need less regulation and more interpretation. While the CIA has cared for the collections, it is an all-volunteer effort of local history enthusiasts pitted against the United States Army, which controls access, funding, and the physical structure. In managing the site with little or no oversight from (civilian) preservation specialists, curators, or scholars for more than one hundred years, West Point has undercut the Warner House and the Warners.[61]

After that closure, West Point required the CIA to remove the house's contents. The original budget appropriation for structural repairs expired, and no new appropriation was ordered.[62] It had been suggested that the CIA break ties and relocate the Warners' possessions to another building—something in a nearby town, perhaps in cooperation with a local historical society—that would provide access for scholars and tourists and give the CIA control over its collections. In August 2012, New York senator Charles Schumer publicly recommended that the army transfer the island to the Department of the Interior in an effort to promote tourism. Later that year, the army expelled the CIA office and archival facility from the West Point campus.[63]

Even if the archives are safely stored somewhere else, the house itself is a powerful object lesson in women's history and women's writing. I don't celebrate Susan Warner because I loved reading *The Wide, Wide World.* Rather, I am intrigued by her life and the scraps of it that remain: her house, her books, her (self-expurgated) diaries, her letters, her furniture, and her view down to the river, all of which have much to tell us about American history and heritage. This is what Jane Weiss dubbed the "intertextuality" of Warner's life and novels.[64]

This feeling is not nostalgia, for this was not a "better, sweeter America."[65] It is, in some ways, just the opposite. Being in this old house makes a visceral connection to a world in which American women were largely governed by forces beyond their control; suddenly Susan's reference to being "locked up" isn't so enigmatic. Surely the experience of physically touring the island and the home imparts valuable intelligence about the Warners, American fiction, and the country's financial history. We all read Harriet Beecher Stowe and marvel at her ability to reach the American reading public with her abolitionist platform—and we revere her and visit her Hartford home, now a National Historic Landmark. But what about Susan Warner, author of America's first best seller, the "Ur-text of the nineteenth-century United States"? *The Wide, Wide World* might not be a popular read these days,[66] and most of the Warners' work is out of print, but scholars and creative writers continue to find material of interest in their stories.[67] With that in mind, what cultural responsibility does the army bear in protecting the Warners' literary legacies? And, if a well-kept author's home or literary tourist site encourages and promotes an author's reputation, then what share of the blame does West Point have for the Warners' diminished status?

West Point's desire to command and control the situation was so great that it successfully lobbied for the resignation of longtime CIA board members. In 2013, former New York governor George Pataki asked Frederick Osborn III to join the board and "rescue" it.[68] Osborn, himself an army veteran, started anew. He called on West Point's superintendent and was met with unexpected enthusiasm. The CIA officers were allowed to return to the island the following year, although the house itself was, and still is, off-limits. Then West Point announced that the West Point Association of Graduates (*not* the CIA) would begin to collect funds from private donors for the restoration of the Warner House. The presiding West Point commander Colonel Dane D. Rideout said, "We're all anxious to improve access to beautiful

Constitution Island, and to restore the Warner House, a place steeped in history and meaning."[69] His comment inspired cautious optimism for the house's future—tempered by the fact that everything (or nothing) will be done on West Point's terms, and access will necessarily be restricted so long as the army stewards the island.

Indeed, as the saga of the Warner House continues after nearly a decade of turf war, there is renewed hope that a happy ending is within reach. In the autumn of 2015, West Point issued a press release stating that an education center would be built on the island.[70] According to the release, "The project was awarded Sept. 30, and represents the initial phase of a holistic upgrade of facilities on Constitution Island which has been in planning for several years." The CIA was "stunned," according to its chairman, who noted that construction was slated to begin in April 2016. Why an education center would be constructed before restoration of the actual historic site was a mystery, but preliminary plans for the new education center indicated that the Warner sisters would split the curatorial space with Revolutionary War and Native American topics.[71]

Osborn attributes this victory to the new board's change of tactics in dealing with West Point. "We've made a point to be very grateful to the army," he told me. "It's a matter of understanding that they own [the island], that they have the responsibility for it, and if we run around saying we want to take it away from you and give it to the Department of the Interior, or are furious that you haven't fixed the house, and we can't do anything and we are angry at you and all that, that doesn't help. None of that helps. So we stopped saying that, stopped doing all that, and look what happened."[72]

Then, only two months after the education center revelation, there was another shocking development: the army asserted its plan to finance a $3.5 million restoration of the Warner House. Initial design and engineering estimates had placed the total cost around $6 million, and the revised lower figure reflects the army's scheme to restore only parts of the home—including the roof, footings, sills, foundation, and porches—while it solicits donations for the living spaces. The news has energized the CIA, which celebrated its centennial in 2016, but it also takes all of the decision making out of its hands. And while funds have been earmarked for this project, the CIA was warned that the army might need the money for something else, and should that be the case, another delay would ensue. "That has happened before," said Osborn.[73] The uncertainly was heightened by the fact that West Point would have a new garrison commander in July 2016, and if the new leader didn't share a sympathy for the Warner sisters, the house would continue deteriorating.

In 1903, Charlotte Perkins Gilman attacked domesticity and wrote about the oppressive role of the home, particularly for women.[74] Gilman was also, incidentally, against turning authors' homes into literary pilgrimage sites,[75] and yet her declaration stands as testimony for why the Warner House still matters. The Warner House looms over everything the Warner sisters wrote. The house, the island, and the isolation are integral to understanding not only the Warners' fictional characters but also their personal character. It adds texture to American literary history, but also to the history of American wealth and speculation, social mores, and women's history. The sisters' lives show us in bleak detail that the place for genteel white women, particularly unmarried women, was in the home, no matter how dire the circumstances or how great the need. They are part of a much bigger American story, of which a very substantial portion threatens to slip away under the army's watch.

Is it true that no (wo)man is an island? In the case of Susan and Anna Warner, the sad fact is that their crippling isolation cultivated their creativity. It can be argued that without the island, there would be no *Wide, Wide World* or any of the other books, hymns, and artworks they produced. Their home, the landscape, and all it entailed—social demotion, financial insecurity, mental anguish, physical hardship—set the stage for a blockbuster, and in their seclusion, they reached millions.

## NOTES

1. Edgar Mayhew Bacon, "Susan Warner: Her Home on Constitution Island, Near West Point, Her Sister Still Living There," *New York Times,* September 3, 1898.
2. Rebecca Rego Barry, "Alone on an Island: West Point Closes Writers' Home," *Preservation,* July 7, 2009, www.preservationnation.org.
3. Just writing this makes it sound like a nineteenth-century version of the reality television series *The Simple Life,* in which two wealthy young women struggle with manual labor.
4. Barry, "Alone on an Island."
5. Theresa Brinkerhoff (United States Military Academy) in discussion with the author, March 22, 2013.
6. Stephen Tilly in discussion with the author, June 15, 2009. Tilly had worked and consulted on other historic buildings at West Point.
7. The furnishings have been in storage since 2009. In late 2012 the army requested that the Constitution Island Association (CIA) remove its archives from campus. A series of emails to CIA researchers kept me informed of the dire situation. One email said that the closure was due to "an arbitrary decision of the United States Military Academy to stop providing office and storage space to the Constitution Island Association." The USMA, for its part, has not released any information on the eviction. On March 22, 2013, a West Point spokesperson told me she was unfamiliar with it.
8. For biographical research I found two works most useful: Anna Warner, *Susan Warner* (1909; repr., New York: Constitution Island Association, 2009); and Edward Halsey Foster, *Susan and Anna Warner* (Boston: Twayne, 1978).

9. Olivia E. Phelps Stokes, *Letters and Memoirs of Susan and Anna Bartlett Warner* (New York: G. P. Putnam's Sons, 1925). Additionally, Anna Warner wrote a biography, *Some Memories of James Stokes and Caroline Phelps Stokes, arranged for their children and grandchildren* (Cambridge, Mass.: Riverside Press, 1892).
10. Mary Kelley, *Private Woman, Public Stage* (New York: Oxford University Press, 1984), 34.
11. This depiction of Susan as shy and nervous seems to evolve throughout the biography.
12. During my March 2012 visit, I met with Bryan Dunlap and Faith Herbert.
13. Kelley, *Private Woman,* 34.
14. Warner, *Susan Warner,* 162.
15. Ibid., 169.
16. Nina Baym, *Woman's Fiction: A Guide to Novels by and about Women in America, 1820–1870,* 2nd ed. (Chicago: University of Illinois Press, 1993), 40.
17. Warner, *Susan Warner,* 176–77.
18. Ibid., 181, 192.
19. Baym, *Woman's Fiction,* 30.
20. Kelley, *Private Woman, Public Stage,* 111.
21. Ibid., 92.
22. Baym, *Woman's Fiction,* 20.
23. Mary Templin, "Panic Fiction: Women's Responses to Antebellum Economic Crisis," *Legacy: A Journal of American Women Writers* 21, no. 1 (2004): 3.
24. Perhaps this is one expression of what Frances B. Cogan called the "survival ethic" for women in this time period. Frances B. Cogan, *All-American Girl: The Ideal of Real Womanhood in Mid-Nineteenth-Century America* (Athens: University of Georgia Press, 1989), 4.
25. Warner, *Susan Warner,* 379, 381.
26. Jane Tompkins, afterword to Susan Warner, *The Wide, Wide World* (New York: Feminist Press, 1987), 585.
27. The much-discussed remark was originally made in a private note from Nathaniel Hawthorne to his publisher and friend William D. Ticknor on January 19, 1855; see *Nathaniel Hawthorne: The Letters, 1853–1856,* ed. Thomas Woodson et al., vol. 16 of *The Centenary Edition of the Works of Nathaniel Hawthorne* (Columbus: Ohio State University Press, 1987), 304.
28. Baym, *Woman's Fiction,* 1.
29. Tompkins, afterword, 601.
30. See, for example, Sara E. Quay, "Homesickness in Susan Warner's *The Wide, Wide World,*" *Tulsa Studies in Women's Literature* 18, no. 1 (Spring 1999): 39–58.
31. These numbers from an untitled document dated February 24, 2012, were given to the author by Faith Herbert at the CIA archives.
32. Foster, *Susan and Anna Warner,* 67–68.
33. Susan Geary, "The Domestic Novel as a Commercial Commodity," *Papers of the Bibliographical Society of America* 70 (1976): 381.
34. Warner, *Susan Warner,* 232.
35. Ibid., 252.
36. Ibid., 242.
37. Ibid., 323.
38. Ibid., 325.
39. Tompkins, afterword, 590.
40. Warner, *Susan Warner,* 388. The Mrs. F is either Mrs. Cyrus Field or Mrs. H. M. Field, sisters-in-law. Cyrus Field was a financier who helped create the Atlantic Telegraph Company and laid the first telegraph cable across the Atlantic Ocean in 1858. Henry Martyn Field was a pastor and an author. From 1854 to 1898, he was editor and proprietor of *The Evangelist,* a Presbyterian journal based in New York.
41. Tompkins, afterword, 593.

42. Susan Williams, "Widening the World: Susan Warner, Her Readers, and the Assumption of Authorship," *American Quarterly* 42, no. 4 (December 1990): 569.
43. Meaning Henry James Sr., I presume, a contemporary of Susan's, who traveled in literary circles.
44. Warner, *Susan Warner,* 293.
45. In the 1870 census, the sisters are "keeping house" and Aunt Fanny is "at home." They have two farm laborers in the household and two domestics at the time of the census taking. The presence of live-in servants may have lessened the loneliness of their island life, and yet no one servant seems to have stayed long enough to become part of the Warner narrative. See 1870 U.S. census, Putnam County, N.Y., population schedule, Phillipstown, 105–6, dwelling 661, family 870–871, Henry Warner and Susan Warner. Digital images, Family Search, January 5, 2016, https://familysearch.org/.
46. Kelley, *Private Woman,* 177.
47. Williams, "Widening the World," 565.
48. Foster, *Susan and Anna Warner,* 79.
49. In Anna Warner's *Susan Warner,* Susan is portrayed as a voracious reader in her teens, reading works by Sir Walter Scott, Shakespeare, Dante, and Cervantes.
50. See Catherine O'Connell, "'We *Must* Sorrow': Silence, Suffering, and Sentimentality in Susan Warner's *The Wide, Wide World,*" *Studies in American Fiction* 25, no. 1 (Spring 1997): 21–39; and Baym, *Woman's Fiction,* 161.
51. I find it fascinating that in Sarah Orne Jewett's *Country of the Pointed Firs* there is a Miss Joanna Todd who lives on an island off the Maine coast, who, despite her slightly different locale, seems quite familiar. Jewett writes, "There is something in the fact of a hermitage that cannot fail to touch the imagination; the recluses are a sad kindred, but they are never commonplace." Sarah Orne Jewett, *The Country of the Pointed Firs,* (Boston and New York: Houghton Mifflin, 1896), 127.
52. Warner, *Susan Warner,* 459.
53. "Mrs. Sage May Give Isle to West Point: She Is Considering the Purchase of Constitution," *New York Times,* August 6, 1908.
54. The letters between Mrs. Sage and President Roosevelt explaining the details of the deed and the one of thanks from Roosevelt to Anna Warner are transcribed and published online at www.constitutionisland.org. Anna also gave the family's treasured portrait of George Washington, by Gilbert Stuart, to the nation.
55. Foster, *Susan and Anna Warner,* 108.
56. The marker, on Paper Mill Hill Road, states: "Many of [the] scenes in 'Wide Wide World' and 'Queechy' were laid in and around this house where Susan and Anna Warner, noted American authors, spent several summers." According to the database maintained by the Association of Public Historians of New York State (www.aphnys.org), the marker is still in place.
57. Jessica Campilango, "The Constitution Island Association," *Hudson Valley Review* 23 (September 2006): 56–63.
58. Conversation with the CIA's former executive director Richard de Koster during an interview in 2009.
59. Ibid. Even the *New York Times* picked up the story, highlighting the amount spent by the army to restore the shed-sized structure and the controversy surrounding it. See Christopher West Davis, "An Island of American History," *New York Times,* July 21, 2002.
60. I have often stopped to ask myself if it should be a priority. West Point is first and foremost a military training school, not a museum. But then, why not turn the property over to a public or private organization that will care for it properly? Ethically, it must be one or the other. I am not alone in this opinion. See Michael Randall, "Constitution Island Pitched for Public Use," *Times Herald-Record* (Middletown, N.Y.), August 7, 2012.
61. In a letter of resignation from the CIA board dated April 2, 2014, Bryan Dunlap asserted

that West Point had "methodically reduced the Association's scope of operations, community reputation, and revenues nearly to zero."

62. Bryan Dunlap, in discussion with the author, March 2012.
63. I wrote a brief commentary on this, "Army Targets the Historic Home of Two Literary Sisters in the Hudson River Valley," published on the *New York Daily News* book blog on March 25, 2013, www.nydailynews.com/blogs.
64. Jane Weiss, "Many Things Take My Time: The Journals of Susan Warner" (Ph.D. diss., City University of New York, 1995).
65. Anne Trubek, *A Skeptic's Guide to Writers' Houses* (Philadelphia: University of Pennsylvania Press, 2011), 10.
66. According to the Feminist Press, only two hundred copies sold in 2011. This doesn't account, however, for digital downloads of the book—via digital readers or from free archival sources like the Internet Archive.
67. Three recent projects come to mind: an essay by Jennifer L. Brady, a lecturer in history and literature at Harvard University, titled "Loving *The Wide, Wide World:* A Novel, Its Fans, and Their Fictions" *Common-Place* 12, no. 1 (October 2011), www.common-place-archives.org; a study of editions of *The Wide, Wide World* being made by Jessica DeSpain, an assistant professor of early and nineteenth-century American literature at Southern Illinois University, who runs the remarkable hypermedia archive Susan Warner's *The Wide Wide World* Digital Edition, https://widewideworlddigitaledition.siue.edu/; and Robert J. Morgan's 2006 picture book *Jesus Loves Me, This I Know: The Story behind the World's Most Cherished Children's Hymn* (about Anna Warner).
68. Frederick Osborn III, discussion with author, February 5, 2016. Osborn was at the time of writing the CIA board chairman.
69. "Constitution Island Association, U.S. Army Garrison at West Point Sign New Document," *Highlands Current,* April 13, 2014, http://highlandscurrent.com.
70. "Education Center to Be Built on Constitution Island Near West Point," October 5, 2015, www.army.mil/article/156641.
71. Osborn, discussion with author.
72. Ibid. Osborn, incidentally, feels that the Department of the Interior handover idea "may have some merit but we're not even bringing it up these days." Furthermore, in his opinion, Senator Schumer handled the proposal badly and too publicly, and "the brass [at West Point] were understandably furious."
73. Osborn, discussion with author.
74. Charlotte Perkins Gilman, *The Home: Its Work and Influence* (New York: AltaMira, 2002).
75. Trubek, *A Skeptic's Guide,* 9.

# 5

# *"Afoot with my vision"*

## Whitmania and Tourism in the Digital Age

MARA SCANLON

*Literary tourists today—and arguably always—have found ways to "visit" with authors beyond traveling to their homes: seeking out graves, touring the landscapes of novels, journeying to the sites of long-destroyed writers' retreats, and even paging through a guidebook to authors' homes and haunts. Today, digital opportunities for such tourists abound. Mara Scanlon recounts her adventure with both digital and physical literary tourism in pursuit of a such a "visit" with Walt Whitman. In exploring the digital, she also uncovers the complicated dual role of literary scholar and de facto literary tourist: as she puts it in a summary of a class trip to find Whitman in the Library of Congress, in "those magical hours . . . we were (good) old-fashioned groupies, we were Whitman lovers." Delving into some of the least tangible elements of literary tourism, Scanlon reminds us that there are many routes through which we can find Whitman.*

In his famous American epic *Song of Myself*, Walt Whitman provides the reader with an image of an odd pre–Wright brothers aerial expedition over the United States: "My ties and ballasts leave me, my elbows rest in sea-gaps, / I skirt sierras, my palms cover continents, / I am afoot with my vision."[1] In these lines, Whitman is buoyed by his revelatory poetic powers, traveling freely above the nation he loves in a way that is both surreal (drawing to mind something like a massive bearded balloon escaped from the Macy's Thanksgiving Day Parade and bumping slowly and awkwardly across the landscape) and yet somehow, even now embodied—after all, he has elbows, palms, and eyes.

Bizarre as is the image of a Whitman blimp traveling the fruited plain, the poet's lines, from which I draw my title, articulate well the best promise of digital resources and technological connectivity for the literary tourist. Without the ties and ballast of travel arrangements, of financial constraints, of overly sincere volunteer tour guides or reenactors, we can be borne aloft on the powers of a good Wi-Fi signal; we can move through eras and places with rapidity and freedom; we can, like Whitman's "palms cover[ing] continents," stretch ourselves in time and space well beyond what was formerly thought possible. "No guard can shut me off," boasts Whitman, "no law prevent me."[2] That's the freedom of the Internet, or at least it should be. Emily Dickinson's small writing table, positioned in her bedroom in Amherst, Massachusetts, by the basket she used to lower baked goods to children; the faded name and gravel on Gertrude Stein's grave in Paris; fog on Walden Pond, just before sunrise in Concord, Massachusetts; Mark Twain's white shirt, spread wide for easy study; a sterling silver nail file that Edgar Allan Poe gave to his proofreader—these and many more literary or authorial sights/sites, of varying degrees of strangeness and intimacy, are easily available on the Internet, and today we take our ability to access such things for granted.[3] In truth, the "open road" of the Internet recalls Whitman's free-spirited, encompassing poetic voice much more powerfully than does the old-fashioned doctrinaire guidebook or TripTik we might have used in days of yore to travel to Whitman's birthplace on Long Island, his final home and grave in New Jersey, or anywhere else the great poet of liberty, justice, and unlimited data plans for all may have slept. And navigating the Web, as Christian Krug also notes, is an action already steeped in the discourses of movement: "Using the internet," he writes, "is metaphorically conceptualized as 'physical travel': We 'visit' a homepage by entering an 'address' and clicking a 'go'-button."[4]

In the digital age these mobilities, formerly restricted to tourists with means, are now easily available to anyone with Internet access and a working knowledge of Flickr, Google, literary blogs, and house museum websites—and yes, there *are* apps for literary tours of many major cities, and for various authors (e.g., the Thomas Hardy Trail) as well.[5] Although, like the Whitman blimp on high, we might, strictly speaking, be looking at something from a physical remove, the perspective is usually even closer or clearer than one could get in the flesh from behind velvet ropes, is available well beyond the typically limited hours of operation at most physical spaces, and can be accessed without hefty entrance fees. Ideally, as in Whitman's imagined voyage, the experience of such digital travel is marked by vitality ("Storming, enjoying, planning, loving, cautioning, / Backing and filling, appearing and disappearing, / I tread day and night such roads")[6] and somehow still feels "real," retains "vision" that is not just dreamy or prophetic but shows us things with our own eyes, things we might never have seen in past circumstances.

Whitman, in his attempt to represent the diverse peoples of a young nation, often relates human events very far from his own experience in his poetry, but he nevertheless insists on a primary connection with them, forged through his imagination and language: "All this I swallow, it tastes good, I like it well, it becomes mine, / I am the man, I suffer'd, I was there."[7] So too may we theoretically establish intimacy even as digital tourists. Indeed, when we discuss the benefits of blogs, social networking technologies, and the unharnessed power of the Internet, we often use words like "connection" and "immediacy." Even in earlier forms, technology has long conveyed (or at least promised) such imminence, whether in newsreels of battlefields or radio broadcasts by the president. Some readers will recall the old Bell Telephone tagline designed to encourage long-distance phone calls: "The next best thing to being there."

Nevertheless, the term "digital tourism" is commonly used much more concretely, in the context of digitally supported tourist enterprises and "destination marketing": agencies and sites that use online booking and business management, social networks that are used for sharing information and reviews of tourist attractions and lodging, social media and electronic communications for customer service, and coordinated business communities that cluster their information online. You can program specific tourist attractions, including literary ones, into geospatial platforms like GoogleEarth and the global positioning system in your car. A special summer school opportunity focused on digital tourism and offered by the University of St. Andrews Computer Human Interaction (SACHI) Research Group in the United Kingdom describes itself as being "in the context of applications, services and technologies for tourists (referred to as Digital Tourism)," and the program focused heavily on digital tools ("multimodal input and output interfaces, data fusion techniques and hybrid architectures, vision, speech and conversational interfaces, haptic interaction, mobile, tangible and virtual/augmented multimodal UIs, tools and system infrastructure issues for designing interfaces and their evaluation").[8] I'm not saying that this form of digital tourism doesn't sound like fun, but it does feel a long way from the promise of "I know I have the best of time and space, and was never measured and never will be measured."[9] In other cases, such as an online photo essay on "digital tourism," the phrase is used pejoratively; a photography student in Belgium exhorts tourists to "please just look the beauty of the world few moments [*sic*]" before worrying about recording it digitally. "I tell you," he writes, "today, when people travel they think more to take pictures, go back to their homeland and show their pictures to their friends and family to make them jealous." Worse, "they will never watch them again or even upload them on a computer. I don't understand this."[10]

When I talk about digital literary tourism, it seems important to specify that, rather than just making travel more efficient, pleasurable, affordable, or jealousy-inducing, the technology actually provides access to the artifact or place. As I suggested in comparing it to Whitman's amazing journey powered by poetic imagination and sustained by words (the poet says in delight and triumph, "I fly those flights of a fluid and swallowing soul"),[11] it not only supports tourism or records tourism; it *is* tourism of a sort.[12] And because in literary tourism, as many people have observed, the (usually deceased) body, lodging, and belongings of the writer merge in strange and inseparable ways with the corpus of writing in drawing the tourist's interest, digital resources that provide access to manuscripts, as well as views of graves and walking sticks and teapots and vests, can act as a kind of "attraction" even for those whose purpose in viewing/visiting them is far from, or more than, scholarly. Whitman's words are stirring on the printed page of a book mass-produced in New York in 1996; how much more so are they when viewed in his own writing on an image of thick, yellowed paper digitized by the voluminous and marvelous Walt Whitman Archive or by the Library of Congress? They can raise a sensation not unlike that of running one's hand over the banister that you know a poet touched many times himself as he made his way up and down narrow stairs—a sensation that is intellectual but also, or more so, somehow made flesh, felt physically as a thrill or shiver, even if the manuscript itself is digital rather than material.[13]

I myself have felt this electric reaction or frisson, this shiver of union and immanence, not only when I peered through the door at Whitman's bathtub ("And we *know* he was naked here," breathed a student who was with me), but also when I look, for instance, at Whitman's "Hospital Notebook" from the Civil War years, when he served as a volunteer aide (a "spiritual wound-dresser") in the hospitals of Washington, D.C. Is that a pathetic, even delusional, fiction of connectivity that reductively sees the textual page or image as an extension of an author's self? Should we eschew our experience as literary tourists seeking connection to writers we love in the same way we might avoid tacky tourist clothing and memorabilia?[14] In her 2011 book *A Skeptic's Guide to Writers' Houses,* Anne Trubek calls such a quest "literary voyeurism, worship, or, more crudely, lit porn," observing, "Readers desire an impossible intimacy, a desire at once central to the pleasure of reading but ultimately insatiable."[15] As an academic trained in critical analysis, I feel I ought to adopt a similar stance. This essay feels like resistance to, or even a subversion of, my education. Because I must confess that I am finally quite sympathetic to the desire for fantastic intimacy with an adored author and am not always disappointed in my attempts to fulfill it. (In full disclosure, I am a woman who was so excited to find herself at the Emily Dickinson

Homestead that she got out of the rental car without putting it in park.) And if the Internet can enable that thrill ride, well, bravo.[16]

Interestingly, although I am talking about some of the newest technologies in interrogating the opportunities and limits of digital (literary) tourism, the model I discuss could fall naturally into the long tradition of "armchair tourism," and indeed "virtual tourism" and "armchair tourism" are frequently linked under one definition since neither requires much physical movement beyond clicking or turning pages. The blogger Dot Creations, on her site "Confessions of an Armchair Tourist," humorously lists the "service providers" of armchair tourism as "Books, Travel Literature, Television, Movies & other Audio Visual media, and Internet."[17] Like the Internet now, books have been published for years with narratives of travel to exotic or famous places, and with photographs that allowed those at home to feel as if they, too, had access to the attraction, including authors' houses.[18] Nicola J. Watson, for example, tracing the rising fascination with the homes of British writers in the mid-nineteenth century, lists several such books of that period focused specifically on literary persons and places.[19] When this genre is being discussed in a scholarly way, it is called "travel writing," and deemed worthy of critical analysis. But to many of us, it is essentially tourism, the (guilty? voyeuristic?) pleasure of experiencing what is unfamiliar and desired, even if one doesn't cross the border of the front door. Also marking this tension, her study of literary tourism has as its "origin, stuff and subject," Watson says, "the amateur, the sentimental, the autobiographical and the bodily," which are "all normally excluded from academic discourse."[20]

Whereas "armchair tourism" might connote today a passivity uncomfortably close to "couch potato," as though one becomes a seasoned traveler just by watching Rick Steves every Sunday morning while consuming one's Cheerios, "digital tourism" could suggest a more active mental journey, guided heavily by the choices of the tourist through the nonlinear spatial labyrinth of hyperlinks and search engines. Discussing Web navigation in relation to the historic house Castle Leslie, for example, Elizabeth Grubgeld says, "The web text, and the means by which it is navigated, offer the illusion of intimacy with family members who are inextricably identified with particular rooms within a specific house and whom the visitor accesses by moving at will through various rooms."[21]

In fall 2009, in my capacity as an English professor, I had the opportunity to reflect on these matters while teaching Digital Whitman, an undergraduate course that was running as part of a multi-university project, funded by the National Endowment for the Humanities, called "Looking for Whitman: The Poetry of Place in the Life and Work of Walt Whitman."[22] Deep studies of Whitman, of course, are not unusual; he is frequently lauded, with Emily

Dickinson, as one of the most important American poets, whose free-range poetics and expansive, gregarious persona ("hankering, gross, mystical, nude")[23] charted new paths in literature that challenged traditional notions of poetic form, sexuality, class, race, liberty, America, nature, the soul, and much more. Nevertheless, the project was unusual and experimental in its pedagogy. Linking five simultaneous courses on Whitman, both graduate and undergraduate, via intricately networked blogs and social technologies, and making rich use of digital resources, the project also focused strategically on physical geographies that were important to Whitman (Brooklyn; Manhattan; Camden, New Jersey; and, in my case, Fredericksburg, Virginia, and Washington, D.C., the landscapes of the poet's Civil War experience). All classes, of course, had equal access to the stellar digital collections on Whitman, chiefly the pioneering and thorough Walt Whitman Archive, directed by scholars Ed Folsom and Kenneth M. Price, but also the various manuscript and artifact images available through the online site of the Library of Congress.[24]

The tourist opportunities in the physical locales, by contrast, varied quite a bit. In Brooklyn, for instance, one can at least visit the dock where the Brooklyn Ferry still crosses, many years after it was lauded by Whitman, and see quotations from his poetry etched in the concrete, but his homes in Brooklyn, as in Manhattan, have been largely swallowed by the growth of the city. West Hills, Long Island, which maintains Whitman's Birthplace, State Historic Site, and Interpretive Center on Old Walt Whitman Road, is accessible.[25] In Camden, one can tour the Whitman house museum, an unassuming narrow dwelling in which the poet died, on the former Mickle Street, now Martin Luther King Jr. Boulevard. The house is staffed by knowledgeable volunteers and holds many of Whitman's own belongings, or objects that match those found in the photographs of his home's interior in the nineteenth century.[26] Camden also has Whitman's burial site and thus, with both house and grave, was the richest of the geographic locations for the venture. The task of the "Looking for Whitman" project was therefore not only to embrace digital communication, publication, and research in scholarly work, and in forms that were both textual and multimedia, but also to explore these local sites physically, to become Whitman tourists, in thinking about the importance of place to Whitman and to our encounter with him 150 years later.[27]

My class (obsessed with the Good Gray Poet in a way that, to be honest, far exceeded the mannerly writer-reader dynamic) did take full advantage of this invitation to play geeky literary-historical tourists: we toured the Fredericksburg battlefield on which Whitman's brother was wounded, which is now protected by the National Park Service; the site of the Union camp where Whitman found not only his brother—after seeing George's name among the lists of injured in a New York newspaper and, as was common in the Civil War, coming in person to seek him—but also his calling to serve as a nurse; sites on the streets of Washington, D.C., where Whitman lived and worked in the 1860s and early 1870s;[28] and Ford's Theatre, where his beloved President Lincoln was killed on a night when Whitman's partner Peter Doyle was in the audience. In the Library of Congress, we were given a private (and transformative) viewing of dozens of Whitman artifacts (letters, personal effects, manuscripts, diaries).[29] The following semester, after the class had technically ended, we also traveled to Camden, to meet with other students and professors from the "Looking for Whitman" project for a conference and to tour Whitman's final home and burial site.

Notwithstanding these universally thrilling opportunities, it does take a lot of work to corral undergraduates into literary tourism on three different Saturdays of the academic year—even those undergraduates who came to love Whitman, including the one who fantasized about being a wounded soldier boy nursed by the hirsute poet. This was especially true of our day in the nation's capital, which was about thirteen or fourteen hours long, most of it in pouring rain and very chilly temperatures, and of the 5:30 a.m. departure time for our visit to Camden. If I tried to explain theoretical models of tourism to my class, that the "ceremonial ratification of authentic attractions as objects of ultimate value [is . . .] measurable to a certain degree by the time and distance the tourists travel to reach it," they weren't mollified by it.[30] And, given the strength of digital resources on Whitman and of the innovative technologies shaping our specific "Looking for Whitman" experiment, my students were increasingly comfortable and content with the access that digital technologies provided us, including not only pdf images of every edition of Whitman's oft-published *Leaves of Grass* on the Walt Whitman Archive, but also video testimonies from Serbian students in the project, reading in a nation fresh from war and dictatorship, about their encounter with the American poet who is a mouthpiece for radical equality and democracy. But getting ourselves physically to these places in Virginia, D.C., and New Jersey had its payoffs.

For instance, at Chatham Mansion, which sits on the bank of the Rappahannock River overlooking Fredericksburg, my students and I saw a landscape relatively unchanged since Whitman stood there in the Union camp in 1862, in the days following the slaughter of thousands of northern soldiers on Marye's Heights, where our university, and my home, now exist. Here he decided that his calling was to be a spiritual wound-dresser to the nation's injured, a role he held through and well beyond the Civil War, faithfully, daily making his rounds of the horribly maimed, the weak, the dying, the lonely. Excerpts from Whitman's book *Memoranda During the War,* which would be re-collected into *Specimen Days,* itself eventually woven into *Leaves of Grass,* describe his stay at Chatham:

> FALMOUTH, VA., *opposite Fredericksburgh, December 21, 1862.* —Began my visits among the camp hospitals in the army of the Potomac. Spend a good part of the day in a large brick mansion on the banks of the Rappahannock, used as a hospital since the battle—seems to have receiv'd only the worst cases. Out doors, at the foot of a tree, within ten yards of the front of the house, I notice a heap of amputated feet, legs, arms, hands, &c., a full load for a one-horse cart.[31]

The trees described by Whitman, knobby catalpas, are still standing at Chatham, within tossing distance of the window of the former amputation room, in which visitors, largely ignorant of the room's prior use, now watch an introductory movie to the National Park site.[32] Sometimes called the Witness Trees, the silent catalpas still communicated deeply to us as we used Whitman's own words to transport ourselves back in time, touching the gnarled trunks and listening as this letter was read aloud (*shiver*). Similarly, when we stood on a street in D.C. and our guide told us it was the spot where Whitman had suffered his first major stroke, my students looked at me in horror and seemed transfixed to imagine Whitman limping across the street, assisted, to his boardinghouse room, from which he would never again emerge a hearty, healthy man.

What separates these events in our experiences of Whitmanic tourism is that they brought us to things, places, and experiences that, at least at the time of this writing, are not available on the Internet. Online, not only couldn't we feel the bark of the catalpa trees, but also we might not even find a good photo. My interest in accessibility, immediacy, and presence was further complicated by our trip, at the end of our long wet day in D.C., to the Library of Congress. Here, after closing time, an exceptional librarian had organized a private exhibit of Whitman artifacts for us. We did not know in advance what or how much to expect—though I was heard to say beforehand that if we didn't see a Civil War hospital notebook I would sit down and wail. But thankfully I didn't have to, because the librarian had created a once-in-a-lifetime display for us, much of it specifically chosen to complement our study of the poet's Civil War years: dozens of Whitman's letters, manuscripts, publications, journals. We saw Whitman's pen, and his letters to (and the hair of) his longtime companion Peter Doyle; Whitman's own hair from shortly before his death, and his eyeglasses, one lens frosted protectively after his strokes (*shiver*). These items seemed especially thrilling because they were artifacts, not easily digitized. Or so I thought: when I Google-image searched "Whitman's eyeglasses," I got a beautiful picture from the Library of Congress website, much clearer than my own photograph from that rainy night.[33]

This raises many questions for me about what "seeing things" really means, questions that are entwined for me with Whitman's own exhortations: "You shall no longer take things at second or third hand, . . . nor feed on the spectres in books," he tells us. "You shall not look through my eyes either."[34] What is the difference between our eyes and the lens of the digitizing scanner or photographer? How do we "remember" something we see in person when the digital images of it that are available are all of higher quality but framed by someone else? When we tour online, are we taking things at second or third hand? Or, instead, are we fooling ourselves that we are really, truly seeing through an author's eyes and not just our own when we stand in the author's prior physical spaces?

Mónica Risnicoff de Gorgas writes: "Fiction is portrayed as reality in these 'theatres of memory' that are house museums. This kind of stage-management provides, on the one hand, the indelible traces of those who lived and used the original objects and whose ghosts can still be felt, and, on the other, the meanings ascribed by conservators, researchers and museographers."[35] This is to argue, of course, that physical spaces are just as mediated and controlled as the digitized representations, that neither provides the sort of direct and personal access that the tourist most desires.[36] Considering the "virtual tourism" available for ecotourists, Krug queries, "How far do digital environments differ conceptually from non-digital, but equally 'virtual' environments such as 'managed, constructed, or disturbed landscapes' . . . which is in effect what most nature preserves or national parks are?"[37] So can we make a case, when excellent visual representations and explanatory text are available online, that seeing things in person is worth the expense and time, if it is even possible for us to summon those very rare luxuries? To his readers, those who encounter him textually, Whitman promises the kind of intimacy that we seek in literary tourism; he says, in lines that demand to be read in a murmur, "This hour I tell things in confidence, / I might not tell everybody, but I will tell you."[38] With the use of tourist technologies, is that electrifying intimacy violated, stretched beyond any meaning, or simply made easy and more democratic, as surely Whitman might have wished?

I don't know that there are easy answers to these questions, and in some ways I find the questions more interesting anyway. Digital tourism may indeed be the "next best thing to being there," as armchair tourism books were in their day, and it gives access to manuscripts and editions, an important but unusual aspect for the specifically *literary* tourist, that is otherwise extremely constrained by the mechanisms in place to protect such fragile artifacts. I'll even say that sometimes it may be the better thing, giving more immediate and egalitarian access, allowing smitten readers to be afoot with their own visions.

And yet being the next best, or the better, is not being the *same* thing. Before we visited the Library of Congress, my class had read Whitman's accounts of his time in Fredericksburg, as I noted in discussing the catalpa trees. Using the electronic Walt Whitman Archive, for instance, we read this letter from Whitman to his mother, written on December 29, 1862 (exactly 106 years before my birth—*shiver*), about finding his brother George at the Union camp close to Fredericksburg: "Dear, dear Mother, . . . I succeeded in reaching the camp of the 51st New York, and found George alive and well—In order to make sure that you would get the good news, I sent back by messenger to Washington (I dare say you did not get it for some time), a telegraphic dispatch, as well as a letter."[39] The handwritten version of this priceless letter was one of the items that the librarian had pulled for us at the Library of Congress (fig. 5.1). What is not visible in the transcribed version of the letter we had seen in the online archive, or in the published version of Whitman's letters, is the revision Whitman made: the words "alive and well" are inserted into the sentence with a caret, no doubt anticipating the anxiety with which

FIGURE 5.1. Detail of letter from Walt Whitman to his mother, Louisa Van Velsor Whitman, December 29, 1862, from the Union camp near Fredericksburg, Va. Library of Congress. *Photo by Mara Scanlon. Courtesy Library of Congress.*

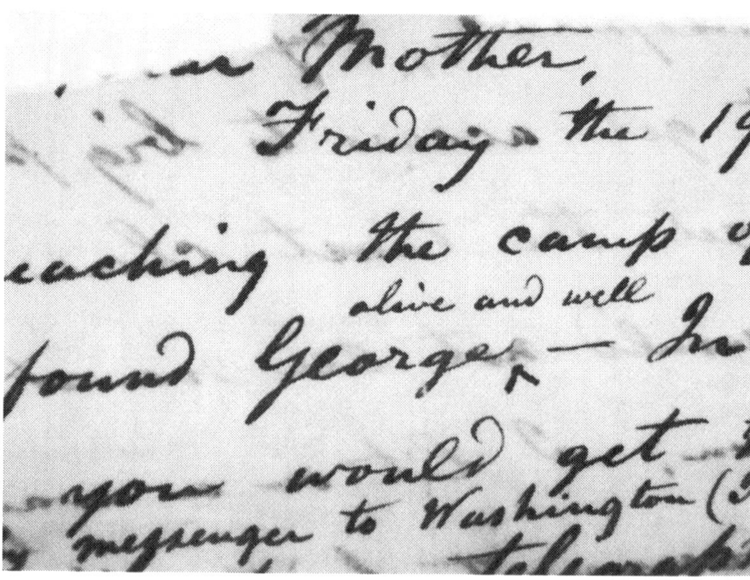
Mother,
Friday the 19
the camp
alive and well
found George —
would get
messenger to Washington (

his mother would scan the more ambiguous words "found George" if she had not received the "telegraphic dispatch" or was desperate for information about her wounded son. Certainly this letter could be digitized so that the revision was visible to all interested parties—but for me, and I believe for the students as well, there was something so heartrending, touching, and human about the insertion that seeing it in person made all the more powerful.

In other cases, the benefit of seeing things with my own eyes, not at second or third hand, was less clear. For instance, I compare photographs that I took myself at the Library of Congress of Whitman's hospital notebooks, in which he meticulously, lovingly records soldiers' names, conditions, and desires (something to read, a German Lutheran minister, some milk), with those from the Library of Congress American Memory site.[40] Undoubtedly, the publicly available archive image, for which one need not travel beyond the journey to the LOC website, is clearer, more easily read, and therefore arguably more powerful in that, after all, it is Whitman's *words* that touch and fascinate us. To be honest, in the Library of Congress's weird institutional room with lockers, blackened windows, and government-issue tables, nothing was very easy to read, even in close physical proximity, which we found as we stumbled reading aloud; the writing was still spidery, the ink bled through the paper, the plastic protection on many items reflected the awful fluorescent glare. We couldn't touch anything, couldn't feel the paper, the wood, the leather, the hair. I couldn't even smell the leather of Whitman's haversack or the odor of its decay.

But let me pause on this haversack (fig. 5.2). We had no idea that the librarian would show it that evening. In fact, we had specifically been told that this item, which Whitman brought with him daily as he made the rounds of the hospitals caring for soldiers, loaded with his notebooks and pens and the comforts he carried to the wounded, is so fragile, so light-sensitive now, that it is almost never displayed. But cue this scene: as my class moved through the tables at the library, the haversack was concealed in a large flat box. When the librarian removed the lid and we saw what was inside, most of us present burst into tears. Why? Were we just exhausted, soaked to the skin, in the twelfth hour of our tourist-acolyte odyssey? Maybe. But what I want to claim (in a way that requires a leap of faith of the kind that Anne Trubek comes to deride in her travels and writing) is that it was something hard to define: *presence*.[41] The truth is, the artifacts we saw with our own eyes, not at second or third hand, at the Library of Congress archive were in some ways no more accessible or immediate (indeed, arguably *less* accessible or even immediate if we mean time rather than proximity, or if we mean simple legibility) than the digitized images of those artifacts online. I saw that the inside of the

FIGURE 5.2. Walt Whitman's leather haversack, used during the Civil War in Washington, D.C., as Whitman served the wounded in hospitals. *Photo by Mara Scanlon. Courtesy Library of Congress.*

haversack is brown canvas. One of my students found an inky fingerprint and would *not* entertain suggestions that it belonged to anyone but Walt Whitman. But tears?

I have come to no further understanding of those magical hours than to say that we were (good) old-fashioned groupies, we were Whitman lovers, and we were wet, exhausted bodies. We desired the physical—the textured, the pasted, the water-stained. We may have cried because the broken skins of brittle pages and fragile covers, the light-sensitive and subsequently entombed haversack, and the tickets to a lecture on Lincoln long since delivered were as close to Whitman the man (light-sensitive, brittle, untouchable, entombed . . .) as we are ever going to get, as present as we can be. Unlike the wounded soldiers, we won't ever get the spoon-fed ice cream or the quiet healing presence of his two-hundred-pound, maroon-coated, deep-pocketed self. But it turned out that the digitized couldn't hold a gas lamp to the physically present, and even if it was paper and not exactly flesh, I wanted it.

There are so many reasons why Whitman is a rich poet through which to interrogate digital and corporeal tourism, and one of them is that he himself reflected on similar issues. Physical presence was essential to Whitman; he writes: "I merely stir, press, feel with my fingers, and am happy, / To touch my person to someone else's is about as much as I can stand."[42] Unable bodily to reach all physical corners of these United States, however, Whitman understood that his poetry was his emissary. The body and the imagination were not fully separable to him, and he claims at times that language gives full, essentially embodied, and even sexualized access, as when he writes in some of my favorite lines,

> Camerado, this is no book,
> Who touches this touches a man,
> (Is it night? are we here together alone?)
> It is I you hold and who holds you,
> I spring from the pages into your arms.[43]

But also, in his own day Whitman thoroughly embraced technologies—the photograph,[44] and especially typography, setting a good bit of *Leaves of Grass*'s type himself and even revising from printed drafts. What would he make of our fetishization of his handwritten manuscripts, of my anxiety that the digital image, more democratically accessible, may still not be more powerful?

Let me conclude not with interrogations but with a story—in fact, with a quest narrative of sorts. At the end of my class's field trip (pilgrimage) to Camden, we were awash with emotion after our visit to Whitman's Mickle Street house museum, where the students were in raptures over Whitman's huge boots ("If you touch those, I'll kill you," I hissed behind the guide's back, wanting desperately to slide my own feet into them) and his rocking chair, positioned, as in his lifetime, for looking out at the people and commerce of the street (but now looking at a large, institutional regional jail—*oh, Walt*).[45] We quivered with morbid excitement to stand in the very room where he died. Risnicoff de Gorgas, in her discussion of house museums, explains that "a particular type of mental and emotional reaction [is] produced by the presence and absence of the people who once lived in the house. But, above all, these houses are perceived as 'true reality' and therefore free of any kind of manipulation. As if in a time machine, visitors feel they are travelling to a 'frozen' past which also offers the possibility of a day of self-knowledge during which they can learn about themselves."[46] Okay.

*But:* we saw among the papers there a letter of sympathy from a European woman after the tragedy of September 11, 2001; seeking to reach an entire nation, she had chosen to mail her personal letter to the Whitman house address, an astounding testimony to the importance of place and to Whitman's central role as an American poet. That letter was about Whitman, and it was about the nation he loved to distraction, and it was about us, contemporary American tourists who live and study poetry fifty miles from the Pentagon, who were clasping hands with joy and grief as we climbed the stairs of a dead poet's house a hundred miles from Ground Zero at the former World Trade Center.

Ready for the final chapter, we went to the Harleigh Cemetery. Harleigh (which advertises itself as "Camden County's Most Exclusive 'Gated' Community") clearly highlights its main tourist attraction on its website with three photos of Whitman's grave, which is a large stone construction designed by the poet himself and set into the rocky earth. The website also boasts on its home page an electronically framed photo of the aged poet and his apropos lines "So welcome death; whene'er the time That the dread summons must be met, I'll yield without one pang of awe, Or sigh, or vain regret."[47] "Harleigh Cemetery," reads the website text, "with its peaceful and lush grounds allow [*sic*] Walt Whitman's words to be realized."[48] It is a strong example of the nineteenth-century garden cemetery, its rolling hills and greenery inviting a sense of tranquillity.

But on this particular visit, it was closed. The wrought-iron gates had been locked five minutes before our arrival, two hours before our trip coordinator had suspected, and we were feeling far from tranquil. As I looked back at them, the students on the bus fell into silence. Their faces were in disbelief bordering on despair, their fingers poised on the pages of the poem "So Long!" that they had intended to read at the gravesite, which ends:

> Dear friend whoever you are take this kiss,
> I give it especially to you, do not forget me,
> I feel like one who has done work for the day to retire awhile,
> I receive now again of my many translations, from my avataras ascending,
>     while others doubtless await me,
> An unknown sphere more real than I dream'd, more direct, darts awakening
>     rays about me, *So long!*
> Remember my words, I may again return,
> I love you, I depart from materials,
> I am as one disembodied, triumphant, dead.[49]

Now, we had seen the grave in a dozen very clear digital pictures online, photographed from different angles. We had seen an excellent digitized image of Whitman's own drawings for the grave and his clear specifications for its design. But (even though this is a clear case of "necro-tourism," which makes me feel sort of creepy)[50] we wanted to be *there,* to see it with our own eyes, to stroke the stones and press close to the bars while we looked inside the mausoleum. To shiver.

I risk my credentials as a responsible professor when I reveal that there is a narrow gap in the black metal fence of the Harleigh Cemetery. We didn't make it, but we found it. And we were happy. "Failing to fetch me at first keep encouraged," says Whitman. "Missing me one place search another, / I stop somewhere waiting for you."[51]

## NOTES

1. Walt Whitman, *Poetry and Prose* (New York: Library of America, 1996), 219. All quotations from this volume are from the 1891–92 edition of *Leaves of Grass.*
2. Ibid., 223.
3. The items and places specifically mentioned here are available to view through private photographs posted by other literary pilgrims on sites like Flickr, through communal aggregate sites like findagrave.com, or on the "official" websites of the Emily Dickinson Museum, the Mark Twain House and Museum, and the Museum of Edgar Allan Poe. Massive archives like those of the Library of Congress are also increasingly available for digital viewing. One of the many ways in which digital tourism challenges traditional models, of course, is that "official" access is complicated, undermined, and/or enabled by the ease with which prior physical visitors can make artifacts and places visually available online.
4. Christian Krug, "Virtual Tourism: The Consumption of Natural and Digital Environments," in *Nature in Literary and Cultural Studies: Transatlantic Conversations on Ecocriticism,* ed. Catrin Gersdorf and Sylvia Mayer (Amsterdam: Editions Rodopi, 2006), 251. Nevertheless, drawing on Anne Friedberg's theorization of the "mobilized virtual gaze," Krug also specifies that although "the virtual tourist is highly immobile, tied to his computer screen, his gaze seems to become not just mobile but *hyper*mobile—the utopian promise of digital technology is the unlimited access of the gaze," but this is actually an illusion because it is "even more of a managed, *programmed* commodity" (266–67).
5. Alison Booth writes, "While the hallucinations of author country derive from classical poetic convention, the tourist industry and the Internet have only increased the influence of literary personalities as *genii loci* haunting their homes and permeating their regions or cities, stamping their names on maps and characterizing the national culture." Alison Booth, "Author Country: Longfellow, the Brontës, and Anglophone Homes and Haunts," "Victorian Internationalisms," special issue, *Romanticism and Victorianism on the Net* 48 (November 2007), http://id.erudit.org/revue/ravon.
6. Whitman, *Poetry and Prose,* 223.
7. Ibid., 225.
8. University of St. Andrews Computer Human Interaction Research Group, "Summer School on Multimodal Systems for Digital Tourism," SACHI, http://sachi.cs.st-andrews.ac.uk/activities.
9. Whitman, *Poetry and Prose,* 241.
10. Aurélian Lacroix, "Digital Tourism," *JPG,* http://jpgmag.com (no longer available).
11. Whitman, *Poetry and Prose,* 223.

12. It is worth noting that technological and/or industrial development is frequently seen as antithetical to the preservation necessary for cultural tourism, even as it enables it. As James S. Miller says in his study of Colonial Williamsburg, "Where ethnographers and folklorists construed 'development' as the agent of a lamentable national amnesia, [the proponents of Williamsburg] posited these very same operations as the primary instruments through which America's indigenous past could most efficiently be resurrected." James S. Miller, "Mapping the Boosterist Imaginary: Colonial Williamsburg, Historical Tourism, and the Construction of Managerial Memory," *The Public Historian* 28, no. 4 (Fall 2006): 54. New tools intersect with a cultural or national past to preserve it and make it accessible and usable, but inevitably they change it as well. And it seems to me that there is an inherent, but productive, cognitive, narrative, and paradigmatic tension in using technologies typically cast as futuristic as a means to access the past.
13. In her essay in this collection, Erin Hazard helpfully uses Krzyzstof Pomian's theory of "the invisible," developed in his book *Collectors and Curiosities: Paris and Venice, 1500–1800*, to frame the intangible, even illogical, desire or satisfaction that marks our interaction with such artifacts or spaces.
14. Dean MacCannell says in his foundational study *The Tourist: A New Theory of the Leisure Class* (Berkeley: University of California Press, 1999) that the "touristic critique of tourism is based on a desire to go beyond the other 'mere' tourists to a more profound appreciation of society and culture. . . . All tourists desire this deeper involvement with society and culture to some degree; it is a basic component of their motivation to travel" (10).
15. Anne Trubek, *A Skeptic's Guide to Writers' Houses* (Philadelphia: University of Pennsylvania Press, 2011), 3, 19.
16. Thomas H. Benton (a pseudonym for scholar William Pannapacker), who describes the "spiritual feelings" that moved him when he was allowed to touch the beard on Whitman's death mask, says, "Scholars are supposed to 'interrogate' and 'problematize'; they are not supposed to feel anything or participate in so-called human experiences." Thomas H. Benton, "A Professor and a Pilgrim," *Chronicle of Higher Education* 52, no. 49 (August 11, 2006), http://chronicle.com. Alison Booth offers a helpful (and possibly exonerating) reflection on this tension, discussing "Benton's" confession: "That a tenured English professor allows himself to confess to going on pilgrimages under the veil of a pseudonym may reflect on our profession's disavowal of such commonplace motives. . . . It seems a little embarrassing that an academic should be excited by intimacy with the hairs of a poet's beard preserved in a plaster death mask. Yet I suggest that literature professors would have very little inheritance were it not for such things as death masks; professional critics descend from such forebears in literary trade as autograph-collectors, spirit-rappers, and pilgrims to Whitman's Camden haunts who wrote of their travels" ("Author Country"). Like Benton and Booth, I find this stance of analytical detachment to be somewhat disingenuous and restrictive; shedding it as a teacher was what enabled me to also crack the impartial mask of scholarship. Like Benton, "I find that my scholarly work gains momentum when I give myself over to the spiritual and emotional impulses that my rational self wants to dismiss."
17. Dot Creations, Confessions of an Armchair Tourist, http://confessions-of-an-armchair-tourist.blogspot.com/.
18. Krug also discusses this similarity, thinking of the CD-ROMs, computer games, screensavers and other products of "virtual tourism" in national parks and preserves as "armchair" tours evocative of "literary and visual traditions long before the advent of computers," even back to the travel books of the medieval period. Krug, "Virtual Tourism," 249–50.
19. Nicola J. Watson, *The Literary Tourist* (London: Palgrave Macmillan, 2006), 9. In this volume, Susann Bishop's extraordinary chapter on literary guidebooks also shows just how popular these publications were.
20. Ibid., 17.

21. Elizabeth Grubgeld, "Castleleslie.com: Autobiography, Heritage Tourism, and Digital Design," *New Hibernia Review* 10, no. 1 (Earrach/Spring 2006): 57.
22. This grant project was spearheaded by Matthew Gold of CUNY's New York City College of Technology. Its participants included Karen Karbiener of New York University, who added an unexpectedly international twist to the collaboration when she got a Fulbright to do research in Serbia and taught her class on Whitman at the University of Novi Sad; Carol Singley and Tyler Hoffman of Rutgers University–Camden; and, in addition to me, Brady Earnhart and instructional technology specialist James Groom of the University of Mary Washington.
23. Whitman, *Poetry and Prose,* 206.
24. Whitman is particularly appropriate for a discussion of digital tourism because of this rich, and long-standing, online presence. The Walt Whitman Archive, a model for work in the digital humanities, has been updating and growing since its inception in the mid-1990s (www.whitmanarchive.org). At the Library of Congress site, Whitman materials can be found in the exhibitions *Revising Himself: Walt Whitman and "Leaves of Grass"* (www.loc.gov/exhibits/whitman/) and the "American Memory" exhibit *Poet at Work: Recovered Notebooks from the Thomas Biggs Harned Walt Whitman Collection* (www.loc.gov/collection/walt-whitman-papers/about-this-collection/).
25. Adam Sweeting, in his analysis of literary house museums and the non-coincidental development of literary canonization and tourist attractiveness, remarks that despite the fact that not much was written in childhood or family homes, "efforts to preserve them suggest that physical spaces played an important role in the establishment and maintenance of reputation." Accepting house museums as important foundations of public memory, Sweeting writes that "a restored authorial home demonstrated that ephemeral qualities such as talent, taste, and introspection could be preserved for future generations as well. Like religious shrines—and the term shrine was tellingly applied to both literary and religious sites—a preserved author's home combined aspects of the spiritual with the physical." Adam Sweeting, "Preserving the Renaissance: Literature and Public Memory in the Homes of Longfellow, Hawthorne, and Poe," *American Studies* 46, no. 1 (Spring 2005): 23, 26.
26. The website for the Whitman house, which is maintained by the New Jersey Division of Parks and Forestry, offers "Links to Related Sites" not only for the Whitman Birthplace but also to the websites for house museums of other nineteenth-century American writers (Poe, Longfellow, Dickinson, Twain, Melville). State of New Jersey Division of Parks and Forestry, The Walt Whitman House: Camden, New Jersey, www.state.nj.us/dep/parksandforests/historic/whitman/.
27. For many discussions and insights vital to my thinking in this essay, I thank not only my co-teachers for Digital Whitman, James Groom and Brady Earnhart, but also, more than anyone else, the hardy band of Whitmaniacs who gave themselves to this experiment in digital pedagogy and to Walt Whitman: Samuel Krieg, Chelsea Newnum, Samuel Protich, Virginia Scott, Natalie Sayth, Erin Longbottom, Meghan Edwards, Allison Crerie, Brendon Bottle, Courtney Irvine, Sarah Lawless, Benjamin Brishcar, and Jessica Pike.
28. This tour, which was called Whitman's Wartime Washington, was developed by Washington's Rainbow History Project and led by poet and font of Whitman knowledge Kim Roberts. You can download an annotated map for this tour at http://rainbowhistory.org, under "Programs & Resources: Historic Walking Tours.
29. For this extraordinary access, we are indebted to historian and curator Barbara Bair of the Library of Congress Manuscript Division for her trust, patience, time, and enthusiasm.
30. MacCannell, *The Tourist,* 14.
31. Whitman, *Poetry and Prose,* 712.
32. Whitman is mentioned only in passing at Chatham, in a small display that also records the presence of another great American, Clara Barton, at the hospital camp.

33. Library of Congress, *Revising Himself: Walt Whitman and "Leaves of Grass."*
34. Whitman, *Poetry and Prose,* 189–90.
35. Mónica Risnicoff de Gorgas, "Reality as Illusion, the Historic Houses That Become Museums," *Museum International* 53 (2001): 14.
36. Grubgeld says of the Castle Leslie website: "This unusual and elaborate web site provides an opportunity to query the interrelationship of historical representation, literary tradition, web design, and marketing. As it constructs the interpretive frame for a private business that is nevertheless dependent on governmental and European Union restoration funding, it also raises fundamental questions about the ownership of memory in contemporary Ireland." Grubgeld, "Castleleslie.com," 46.
37. Krug, "Virtual Tourism," 257, quoting H. Lewis Ulman, "Beyond Nature Writing: Virtual Landscapes Online, in Print, and in 'Real Life,'" in *Beyond Nature Writing: Expanding the Boundaries of Ecocriticism,* ed. Karla Armbruster and Kathleen R. Wallace (Charlottesville: University of Virginia Press, 2001), 345.
38. Whitman, *Poetry and Prose,* 206.
39. Walt Whitman to Louisa Van Velsor Whitman, December 29, 1862, Life & Letters, Walt Whitman Archive, www.whitmanarchive.org.
40. "Poet at Work: Walt Whitman Notebooks 1850s–1860s," Library of Congress, American Memory, http://memory.loc.gov/ammem/collections/whitman/.
41. "Writers' house museums expose the heartbreaking gap between writers and readers. Part of the pull of the writer's house is the desire to get as close as possible to the precise, generative, 'Aha!' But we can never get there," says Trubek. "There was," she concludes in her chapter on the Whitman house in New Jersey, "is, and will be no reason to go to Camden to find Whitman." Trubek, *A Skeptic's Guide,* 5, 26.
42. Whitman, *Poetry and Prose,* 215.
43. Ibid., 611.
44. Whitman was one of the most photographed men of the nineteenth century. A full gallery of Whitman images, including several from the studio of famed war photographer Mathew Brady, is available in the Walt Whitman Archive.
45. Arguing that a "quest" for "historical verisimilitude" rather than "authenticity" is the point of restoration and heritage projects like house museums for artists and writers, Risnicoff de Gorgas says: "Each room is stage managed in order to portray a theme. This choice of scenography as the driving force of communication is aimed at surprising visitors in a framework of strong sensory impressions which are to accompany the viewing of the object and strengthen its impact and message. Objectivity does not exist in the exhibition given that each object is displayed as an interpreted object, with emphasis being placed, in some form or other, on certain aspects." Risnicoff de Gorgas, "Reality as Illusion," 11. Of course, authenticity is exactly what literary, or perhaps all, tourists most seek, even in such managed environments.
46. Ibid, 10.
47. This quotation is from an early Whitman poem, published in the *Long Island Democrat* on July 14, 1840, titled "We Shall All Rest at Last" ("Published Works: Periodicals," Walt Whitman Archive). Though the cemetery site does not indicate poetic line breaks, they are visible in the pattern of capitalization in this rhymed, metered, and highly un-Whitmanic poem.
48. Harleigh Cemetery Association, Harleigh Cemetery, www.harleighcemetery.org.
49. Whitman, *Poetry and Prose,* 611–12.
50. The phrase, used widely by theorists of tourism, is traced to Tobias Döring, "Travelling in Transience: The Semiotics of Necro-Tourism," in *The Making of Modern Tourism,* ed. Hartmut Berghoff, Christopher Harvie, Barbara Korte, and Ralf Schneider (New York: Palgrave Macmillan, 2002), 249–66.
51. Whitman, *Poetry and Prose,* 247.

# 6

# *Commemorating Writers' Workplaces*

## The Case of Mark Twain's Study and Quarry Farm

HILARY IRIS LOWE

*Following the last chapter's turn to the tourism of literary scholars, Hilary Iris Lowe takes a close look at the place where much of the Twain scholarship in the country happens: Quarry Farm, near Elmira, New York. What was once the home of Samuel Clemens's sister-in-law is now a private historic site owned and operated by a small liberal arts college, where Twain scholars often work, walking the same halls that Clemens walked for twenty-plus summers of family and writing retreats. Here, literary historians research and write about Clemens, his circle, and his work. Their work in turn informs many of the literary sites that celebrate Twain across the country, creating an unexplored feedback loop between scholars and their research and managed literary sites and their historic interpretation of Clemens.*

In early October 2012, on the night of a heated presidential debate, I gave a talk about Mark Twain and public history, tracing the preservation history and legacy of interpretation at the sites that are devoted to him. That the talk happened in a well-appointed barn at Quarry Farm, near Elmira, New York, was remarkable, but it wasn't the first time I'd visited there. While in the midst of the research I was reporting on, I'd spent two weeks there as a scholar-in-residence in the farmhouse, writing all day alone in the giant house, walking through the snowy woods to stretch my legs and mind between writing bursts. It was a near perfect writing experience. I was alone in an evocative world that wasn't my own; it was Mark Twain's.

If where we live tells us a great deal about who we are, then where we work and write likely tells us something important about our working and creative

FIGURE 6.1. Samuel Clemens in his study at Quarry Farm near Elmira, N.Y., ca. 1903, one of the many images of Clemens and his study that are framed and on display inside the scholars' quarters at the house today. *Photo by T. E. Marr. Courtesy of Library of Congress, Prints and Photographs Division.*

selves.[1] The most fetishized author spaces are undoubtedly the places—rooms, studies, desks, writing tables—where authors scrawled out or feverishly typed the works that we still read today. Part of the draw of visiting writers' adult homes is having the chance to see where they worked. Adam Sweeting has pointed out that admirers of Henry Wadsworth Longfellow occasionally broke into tears when he allowed them into his study. Today, when Stephen King opens his front door to trick-or-treaters, he has seen as many as 1,600 people excited just to make it to his front porch. Emily Dickinson's writing desk survives at Harvard's Houghton Library, far removed from her bedroom at the Dickinson Museum.[2] For fans of Mark Twain, the literary trail of homes, studies, workspaces, desks, and writing tables is vast—spanning from Virginia City, Nevada, to the Henry Ford Museum in Dearborn, Michigan, to Hartford, Connecticut, to Hannibal, Missouri. But biographers, scholars, and fans have come to see one place as distinctly important to the literary production of Sam Clemens: Elmira, New York.

Clemens's wife, Olivia Langdon Clemens, grew up in Elmira, and her family was based there throughout Clemens's very mobile life. This mobility is one reason why there are so many historic sites devoted to Twain, and one reason why the stability of Elmira is now seen as key to understanding Clemens's writing. All but one of the Clemens children were born in Elmira at Quarry Farm, a family home and occasional dairy which belonged to Olivia's sister Susan Langdon Crane and her husband, Theodore. In a way, it was the central location of the Clemenses' family life. While other Clemens homes were built, bought, or rented, the farmhouse—a house the Clemenses did not own but where they were always welcome—was their summer retreat for more than twenty years. People often think of Clemens writing in his house in Hartford—and he did. At Quarry Farm, however, he worked in his study during the hot summer months from eight in the morning till four in the afternoon (fig. 6.1).[3] Clemens was extremely productive in Elmira, in part because he and his wife had the support of an extended family and a relatively secure sense of isolation from the social life they were required to maintain elsewhere.

The study where Clemens worked was a gift from his devoted sister-in-law, Susan Langdon Crane, in 1874. She created it as a separate building on the grounds of her Quarry Farm, a little over 120 feet from the main house, on a perch overlooking the Chemung River Valley. Some say she wanted to ensure that he stayed on task with his writing; others have joked that she wanted to keep his cigars away from the main house. Over the years, the little octagonal study has been a much-sought site of pilgrimage.[4] During Clemens's life, fans tracked him down in Elmira and admired his study. After Clemens's death, his study and Quarry Farm stayed in his in-laws' family as a private residence, but they became sites for occasional pilgrimage by locals, scholars, and self-proclaimed Twainiacs. For instance, on Mountain Day, the young women at nearby Elmira College climbed up East Hill to Quarry Farm and picnicked at the study, and local boys sneaked onto the farm to see the famous study. Early pilgrims carved their names into the woodwork, asserting Mark Twain was here and so was I.[5]

The study became a site of local fascination and interest, but in 1952 it was moved off the farm after a trespasser burned furniture in its fireplace. The little building came down from the wooded hill on the back of a flatbed trailer and was placed on a new foundation at Elmira College.[6] Today thousands visit the study and tour it in the summer months.

That Clemens's study was moved is less remarkable than one might think. Mark Twain "stuff" is highly collectible and mobile, and sometimes inspires "authentic replicas." His study has become so associated with Elmira and Elmira College that it shows up on college logos and has inspired a near perfect replica on the grounds of Elmira's Eldridge Park.[7] Other buildings associated with Twain have been moved too; the building that spuriously claims to be his birthplace has been moved at least twice.[8] Canes made from timber salvaged from his birthplace were sold at at least two World's Fairs during Clemens's lifetime, and canes carved from trees on the grounds of his Hartford home have also become collector's items. His manuscripts and letters are among the most sought-after items of literary association and circulate worldwide, and three of his former houses are open to the public as museums—while countless other historic sites and historical markers dot the landscape, claiming Mark Twain slept here, lectured here, wrote here, and vacationed here. Not only has one house museum, described as the "Mark Twain Family Cabin," been relocated, but also it implies that it was the site of his conception.[9]

The places where authors wrote, and even the furniture on which they wrote, are of special interest both to collectors and to scholars—and the line between the two categories of literary enthusiasts is often blurry. Sam Clemens's desks and writing tables can be found at a number of museums across the country—and most are in places where he never wrote, or at least where he never wrote as an adult. You can find a writing table that Clemens used later in his life in the collection of the Henry Ford Museum. You can locate Twain desks at the Mark Twain Museum at the Territorial Enterprise Building in Virginia City, Nevada; at his birthplace museum near Florida, Missouri; encased in Plexiglas at the museum for the Mark Twain Boyhood Home in Hannibal, Missouri. And there are two in Hartford, Connecticut: one built into a display of his writing materials in the visitors' center and another a period table in his billiard room and study, both at the Mark Twain House and Museum.[10]

But of all the sites that celebrate Clemens, only two maintain the spaces where he lived and worked: the Mark Twain House and Museum in Hartford, Connecticut, a site open to the public that provides a remarkable view of him as a family man and as a public figure, and Quarry Farm, a site open only to scholars. It is this last site that is the subject of this chapter. Quarry Farm, and the literary tourism done there, reflects not just how scholars use spaces to understand literary figures, but how they create narratives of objects and place, and how they develop authors as historical characters *through* their scholarship. This chapter in many ways builds upon the unspoken argument of this collection—that the work of scholars is a kind of tourism as well as analysis. Mara Scanlon's chapter speaks most directly to this seeming crossover of purposes. Scholars are literary tourists as soon as they imagine the world and place a writer inhabited. A study of Quarry Farm allows an understanding of how scholars participate in literary tourism both by imagining literary spaces and by producing scholarship that is inspired by these places. Quarry Farm provides rare access to these specific touristic practices and the ways that managers of literary sites, even those open only to scholars, anticipate the scholar-tourist's needs, desires, and rituals of literary tourism.

## *Literary Places and Scholars*

Quarry Farm is not the only place where literary scholars can spend their time as "working tourists," as the other essays in this collection mightily attest. Literary scholar Diana Fuss, in her 2006 book *The Sense of an Interior: Four Writers and the Rooms That Shaped Them,* gets close to describing the scholarly impulse to be a literary pilgrim. Her scholarship draws upon authors' homes as she "attempt[s] to encounter these writers where they live, *to meet them,* to what extent possible, on their own ground and on their own terms."[11] Fuss, like the scholars who visit Quarry Farm, is interested in places where she can "meet" the writers she admires. She reflects, "It is not every day that one gets to sit in Emily Dickinson's cupola or to lie on Sigmund Freud's couch." For her and for many, "some research projects are pure wish fulfillment, intellectual enterprises that gratify both mind and fancy," and are the "culmination of a persistent desire to occupy, if only for a moment, the private lives of celebrated authors."[12] Fuss's desire to occupy the private spaces of authors shows that she, like many other readers and literary scholars, believes that a house, a living space, an office, or a desk can provide access to the actual "life" of an author.

Occupying the spaces of literary figures gives some scholars a kind of access to the origin of the literary mind, real or imagined. Fuss, while in Emily Dickinson's bedroom, analyzes the material detail of the poet's life—the doorjambs, window placement, and writing table. Dickinson's material traces help Fuss discover nuanced architectural readings of her poetry. While she is never terribly critical about the objects themselves or their curatorial arrangement in the house, these objects do help us understand "object relations" between the poet, her home, and the poet's object-infused poetry. When she visits the Emily Dickinson Museum, she finds Dickinson's poetry and the long history of its critical interpretation in every interior detail. Her account, to some extent, relies on the idea that Dickinson had really just left her desk exactly as it is today, next to the window. But Dickinson's desk sits safely at Harvard. She is able to ignore the anachronistic display of Dickinson's replica white dress within a glass cabinet, just outside the bedroom door and the replica desk. Fuss in many ways overlooks the difficulty in "meeting" an author at a historic site that is mediated by curators and managers.[13] The house has been owned by Amherst College since 1965, and opened formally to the public as the Emily Dickinson Museum in 2003. It was then that the museum staff began professionally interpreting Dickinson's home, her brother's house next door, and the three acres that unite the two houses to "educate diverse audiences about Emily Dickinson's life, family, creative work, times, and enduring relevance, and to preserve and interpret the Homestead and The Evergreens as historical resources for the benefit of scholars and the general public."[14] At the Dickinson Museum it is especially hard to ignore the intervention of preservationists and museum professionals, because Emily Dickinson's house has been restored while her brother's remains primarily undisturbed and in a state of arrested decay. Perhaps scholars must purposely overlook the curatorial elements of literary houses, in an act of imagination, to achieve an understanding of a literary figure through his or her house.

Kevin Kopelson, in *Neatness Counts: Essays on the Writer's Desk,* addresses a similar kind of literary tourism—although he does not define it as tourism. Kopelson re-creates, through photographs, poems, papers, and other sources, the desks of four writers. He ponders: "What do desks represent for writers? How do writers represent desks? For whom does the topography of the desk correspond to the topography of literary creation?" Although he is not always able to visit the studies, kitchens, and messy homes of those that he has singled out for study, he too is a literary pilgrim seeking, like Fuss, that thing (in this case the desk that reveals the habit) which connects reader to author, process to labor, and creative impulse to object.[15] While visiting Elmira, Twain scholar Shelley Fisher Fishkin did something similar as she wandered around the Quarry Farm family home, minutely interested in every chair, every book, and every nook that might hold clues about Clemens.[16] This particular variety of literary tourism is part of the *work* that goes on at literary sites. The evidence that scholars find in these settings comes from being able to see (or imagine) the house, objects, and landscapes as the writer saw them and, perhaps most important, to be able to *remake* the same connections that a writer made with his or her surroundings.

Other scholarly writers narrate a kind of modern-day anti-travelogue. Anne Trubek, in her book *A Skeptic's Guide to Writers' Houses,* epitomizes the postmodern literary scholar in terribly modernist literary museums.[17] Trubek is a skeptic, yawning at Norman Mailer's study and the historical inconsistencies of authors' homes. Unlike Fishkin and Fuss, Trubek sees these places as drenched in a nostalgia that evades the real work of writers and writing. Rather than spend the $100,000 necessary to museumify Langston Hughes's home in Cleveland (where he lived as a teenager and began writing), she would "buy every school kid a book of Hughes's poetry."[18] It is an understandable impulse. Ultimately, Trubek believes that we should stop memorializing long-dead authors and instead think about ways to support our living ones. Today, in a way, Quarry Farm does both, and shows how meaningful historical landscapes can be—if just to a very select group of tourists, writers, and readers.

## *Stalking Twain, Coveting His Objects, and Creating a Space for Reflection*

Popular interest in Clemens's things came early and during his lifetime. Just as relic seekers sought out pieces of his birthplace, others coveted his belongings, hoping that they held a key to his writing. Occasionally tourists and the press followed Clemens all the way to his "summer home," and eventually some of his most devout fans made their way there as well.[19] The writer Rudyard Kipling was one of these early literary pilgrims to Quarry Farm. He enjoyed telling people that he had traveled all the way from India to visit Clemens.[20] When Kipling arrived in the summer of 1889, he was not sure that Clemens was in Elmira, and if he was, where in Elmira he might be. The morning after he arrived, someone pointed him toward Quarry Farm, and Kipling hired a driver to take him up the "awful hill, where sunflowers blossomed by the roadside and crops waved." For Kipling, every detail of his visit to Quarry Farm set the scene for his article in *Harper's Magazine.* Even the local livestock stood "knee deep in clover, all ready to be transferred to photogravure." Well aware of the conventions of travel writing as well as religious and literary pilgrimage, Kipling wrote a compelling travelogue. Like all good pilgrims he was not the first to pursue Clemens up East Hill, and Kipling notes that "*the great man* must have been persecuted by outsiders aforetime and fled up the hill for refuge."[21]

Kipling's account, aside from being an entertaining piece about a young man's quest to find his literary hero, provides an important early description of Quarry Farm:

> It was a very pretty house . . . clothed with ivy, standing in a very big compound and fronted by a veranda full of all sorts of chairs and hammocks for lying in all sorts of positions. The roof of the veranda was a trellis work of creepers and the sun peeped through and moved on the shining boards below. Decidedly this remote place was an ideal one for working in if a man could work among these soft airs and the murmur of the longeared crops just across the stone wall.[22]

Kipling admired Quarry Farm as a workplace, but he portrayed it as if it belonged on the pages of a home design book by Andrew Jackson Downing.[23] Eventually he tracked Clemens down at another home—the Langdon house in downtown Elmira. Though Kipling was overjoyed and felt "blessed" to finally meet and have a conversation with Clemens, he found himself distracted by coveting a Clemens's memento. Kipling lamented that he "would have given much for nerve enough to demand the gift of" Clemens's pipe, for he had half-convinced himself that it would have given him "perhaps, a hint of [Clemens's] keen insight into the souls of men." But Clemens "never laid it aside within stealing reach." Likely Kipling restrained himself, or was dramatizing his awareness that even he desired something more than conversation with the writer he adored. He wanted a memento, a talisman of the man. Like a true religious pilgrim, he imagined magical powers in the "relic" that would be transferred to him upon his possession of it.[24] Kipling was not the only Clemens fan who wanted to have a piece of Twain: by 1905, relic seekers had already demolished at least one building believed to be his birthplace.[25] Museums and personal collections across the country hold everything from Clemens's white jackets to locks of his hair among their most prized items.

### *Scholars as Tourists at Quarry Farm*

Since Kipling's visit and Clemens's death, many others have made their way to Elmira to trace Clemens's time there, but few were granted access to Quarry Farm. Scholars occasionally discovered the location of Quarry Farm, and some were even welcomed by the Langdon family. Today Quarry Farm, like the relocated Clemens study, belongs to Elmira College and is part of its

Center for Mark Twain Studies. In 1982 Jervis Langdon Jr. donated Quarry Farm to the college, and the Center itself was founded in response to the gift. The Center is open to scholars who study Mark Twain and his world. And despite the fact that these scholars, and in effect the Center, have promoted the farm as one of the most important historical landscapes in Sam Clemens's life, the farm is not open to the public.[26]

The original gift agreement for Quarry Farm includes strict regulations about who can and cannot visit the house and under what circumstances. The house may be used only as a private residence for researchers interested in Mark Twain and his times. The farmhouse, barn, outbuildings, and more than six acres have been preserved as a place where scholars can live while working.[27] Flipping through the guest book at the house reveals that almost every Mark Twain scholar of note has spent at least a night or two at Quarry Farm since the Center was founded. When they visit, they walk the same floors that Sam Clemens and his family did and look out at the same view of the Chemung River Valley from the house's wide porch. Among them, Twain scholar Alan Gribben served as an influential adviser to the Center in its earliest days.[28] He guided Darryl Baskin, an early Center director, in creating a forum through which Twain scholars might share their work. Gribben and Baskin understood that scholars desired a place to learn about one another's research, a place where they might meet, study, and write, and a place where they might be at home with the subject of their scholarship.[29] Baskin promoted the Quarry Farm Fellowships and began an international conference on the "State of Mark Twain Studies."[30] The Center for Mark Twain Studies was designed to be, and ultimately became, the preeminent place for scholars to think about Clemens, his times, and his work.

In recent decades it seems that scholars have gained a great deal from Quarry Farm, and as a result, our collective understanding of Clemens has changed. Investigations into Clemens's relationships in Elmira have led scholars to believe that Elmira, and his circle of companions and in-laws there, changed the way Clemens understood the legacy of slavery in the United States. It was at Quarry Farm that Clemens both heard and wrote "A True Story," documenting Mary Ann Cord's life as a slave and the devastation she experienced as her children and husband were sold away from her.[31] It was also here that Clemens took up the tale of Huck Finn after many years and finished it.

The Center for Mark Twain Studies celebrated its twenty-fifth anniversary in 2008. The Center's then director, Barbara Snedecor, asked that scholars who had spent time at Quarry Farm reflect on their experiences for an anniversary edition of the Center's newsletter. Scholars from all over the world responded with much more than an accounting of their research time. One described Quarry Farm as a "mecca," another called it a "living memorial," and yet another repeated the popular sentiment that the residence provided a way to "meet" Sam Clemens through a "trip into the past."[32] The centerpiece of many scholars' commentaries was how their individual experiences at Quarry Farm changed the way they felt and thought about Clemens and his work. Many gushed that the experience of living in the space occupied by Clemens and his family made them feel as "at home at Quarry Farm—as Mark Twain did."[33] These scholars were "able to *meet* Sam Clemens on this very real common ground," and more than a few referred to the house as a "shrine."[34] In many ways, a visit to Quarry Farm is the ultimate experience for a devoted literary tourist. While many just imagine what it would be like to walk in the footsteps of their favorite writers, drink coffee on the same veranda, and commune with an author's home spaces, here they can.

Quarry Farm accommodates the kind of literary tourists that scholar Nicola J. Watson describes in her study of English literary tourism, those who seek out literary sites "to savour text, place and their interrelations."[35] And the research fellows who stay at the farm are exactly the kind of literary pilgrims that tourism studies scholar David Herbert identifies as a subset of tourists to sites like Chawton, those "well educated tourists, versed in the classics and with the cultural capital to appreciate and understand this form of heritage."[36] The scholars who visit Quarry Farm have made their business Sam Clemens, his writing, and the historical context of his times, and they are able to spend time in a domestic archive unlike any other in the world.

Among the most productive Twain scholars ever to visit Quarry Farm is no doubt Shelley Fisher Fishkin. Fishkin wrote about her experiences as a pilgrim to Mark Twain sites across the country in her 1996 book *Lighting Out for the Territory: Reflections on Mark Twain and American Culture.* She traces developments in Clemens's thinking about slavery, racism, and race through the geographic trajectory of his life and works. While she finds the motivation for *Tom Sawyer* and *Huckleberry Finn* in Hannibal, Missouri, she finds the roots of Clemens's anti-racism and anti-imperialism in Elmira, New York. Because Olivia Clemens's parents, Jervis and Olivia Langdon, were abolitionists, she credits Clemens's time in Elmira to his reevaluation of his ideas about race.[37] Much of Fishkin's book is a form of critical literary pilgrimage and speaks to what it is that literary scholars do when they visit these sites. They look for traces of the literary figure that they "know" through his or her work. Scholars find evidence of an author's work, whether it is in primary source materials or in the atmosphere of the place itself. Fishkin "savours" Clemens's texts in Elmira but also supplements them with a physical connection to a specific place and past time.[38] But even beyond this, scholars and writers-in-residence find inspiration of their own through their cohabitation with the past.[39]

In this way, Fishkin, and the many other scholars who visit Quarry Farm to find evidence of Sam Clemens, fit perfectly with literary historian Aaron Santesso's discussion of ideal literary tourism. The model that Santesso lays out in his article "The Birth of the Birthplace" sees the best tourists as those educated enough to understand an author's texts, times, politics, and the particulars of a literary place. But these ideal interactions can happen only when a literary site is relatively undeveloped, allowing each literary pilgrim to experience the author's place in relative seclusion. Places like Stratford and even The Mount, Orchard House, or The Wayside so mediate and shape the experiences of visitors that they can "feel" the management of the place. They see signage, visitors' centers, and official interpretation, and find that their paths through a site or even a whole town are carefully managed. Places like Quarry Farm, however, allow visitors to feel that the historic site is an undeveloped place, and this, in Santesso's estimate, evokes their best literary and scholarly imagination.[40]

Some visitors to Quarry Farm have gone so far as to say the place is "haunted" by the "spirit of Twain." While they hardly ever mean that the farm is actually haunted, they suggest the trope often enough that it deserves exploration. Guest books over the years provide a window into their sense of connection to the farm. One visitor mentions that time spent at the farm allowed the "turning back [of] the hands of time." Another observes that the "humane spirit of a great writer seems to inhabit this house." And as scholars have uncovered just how meaningful Elmira and his extended family were for Clemens and his writing, the cast of ghosts at the house has expanded. One such visitor finds "a mingling of presences, past *and* present: Auntie Cord [the subject of "A True Story"] is here in the kitchen, bending over an iron cookstove," while elsewhere she feels as if "Sue and Theodore [Olivia Clemens's sister and brother-in-law] speak low in their spacious bedroom lest others waken," and offers that there are "so *many* voices here!—And over all, the presence of Livy and her "Mr. Clemens," our Mark Twain. . . . They are in the front parlor, where he reads the day's creative output." While most visitors do not elaborate on these ghosts' activities, even in fun, many acknowledge that the elite group of tourists at Quarry Farm are the "apostles of St. Mark." These disciples sense "the shadows of the muses—when walking with the ghosts of Quarry Farm [and]—when in the presence of greatness."[41] If there ever were devoted literary tourists looking for a near religious experience with place, literary scholars, as these Twain experts show us, are the ones.

### *House as Evidence*

Ghosts are not all that scholars have found at Quarry Farm. Over the years, they have uncovered letters, marginalia, and even a long-lost traveling trunk that belonged to Clemens in the attic of the house. Every inch of the house and barn at Quarry Farm has been scoured for its Mark Twain treasures and for evidence of Clemens's life and work. And many find that "there is no amount of reading about Clemens that can quite equal a few nights spent in the guest room and sitting on the porch."[42] The place itself replaces other kinds of scholarly research and evidence—supplanting other critical approaches to Clemens's work with a profound domestic primary source. Quarry Farm is that source. Over the years, the works that have come out of research stints at the Center for Mark Twain Studies indicate that the farm has had a profound evidentiary influence on Twain scholars. The resulting scholarship is distinctly connected to the place. Scholars who visit other archives, like the Mark Twain Papers in the Bancroft Library at Berkeley, may declare their gratitude to the archivists and archive in their acknowledgments, but they almost never mention that the archive itself and its atmosphere contributed to their work. Here Quarry Farm seems to have lasting resonance.

For example, Twain scholar Susan K. Harris and others see the nearby Chemung River, visible from the farm's wide porch, as the inspiration for the Mississippi River that Huck and Jim travel on in *The Adventures of Huckleberry Finn.*[43] Joe Fulton found the subject for an entire book on the shelves of the Langdon family library at Quarry Farm. Though visiting for another Twain research project, he stumbled upon Clemens's notes in the margins of W. E. H. Lecky's *History of the Rise of the Spirit of Rationalism in Europe* and *A History of England in the Eighteenth Century.* These marginal notes, along with others in books that had belonged to Susan and Theodore Crane, led to Fulton's book *Mark Twain in the Margins.*[44] Studies such as his have promoted Clemens as a deliberate and careful researcher and writer, countering the long-popular conception that he was an author who largely drew upon wit-infused autobiography alone to craft his writing. Quarry Farm has, in the few decades since the founding of the Center, mattered a great deal in changing the way scholars think about Clemens.

Beyond the scholarly evidence that the farm provides, visiting the place itself has come to signify a meaningful step in a scholar's academic trajectory as a "Twain scholar." As one put it, "His presence is everywhere here, and I've never felt more like a Twain scholar (or more grateful to have chosen my course of study wisely)."[45] Quarry Farm has become essential not just as a gathering place, a source of evidence, and a refuge for scholars but as a vital marker of professional identity for Twain scholars. As the late preeminent Twain scholar Louis Budd put it succinctly, "Those of us even dimly in the know sign off with 'See you in Elmira.' "[46]

## *The House Designed for Scholars*

Today the house, like the other house museums discussed in this volume, provides evidence of site managers' intent to make the house what its visitors desire most. But uniquely, the house at Quarry Farm is designed to appeal to scholars, to evoke Twain, *and* to provide an excellent personal writing experience. This last design element creates a concrete way for visitors to connect with Clemens through their process *as writers* at Quarry Farm.[47] Some scholars come alone to work, and others bring their families. If they bring their families, they create a situation that replicates Clemens's own, in which they are surrounded by the people they care about *and* have support for scholarship, research, reading, and writing away from their primary residence. The house itself, with its workspace and library, its well-stocked kitchen, its comfortable reading chairs, computer, printer, and view, provides enough solitude and stimulus to make the act of writing in the space a form of literary touristic ritual. Like the literary tourists who stack stones in the cairn at the site of Thoreau's cabin, creating a ritual from Thoreau's retreat into the wilderness, literary scholars at Quarry Farm partake in a ritual of retreating to an environment that was so productive for Clemens more than 120 years ago.[48]

This ritual is made nearly perfect by the careful maintenance of the house at Quarry Farm. Though it appears as if the site is merely a family home thrown open for scholarly guests, all houses—in their decoration, design, and upkeep—present information about the people who live or lived in them. The house at Quarry Farm is such a marker of the Cranes, Langdons, and now the Center's and the scholars' time there. This house reveals something of the intentions of its current managers. The Center's directors have decorated the interior of the house over the years to maintain the Gilded Age divide between public and private spaces in the house. Downstairs, three rooms are maintained in near museum quality. Upstairs, private spaces are arranged for scholars. The more formal downstairs spaces, such as the parlor, dining room, and library, are outfitted with historic furnishings. Some date to the Clemens and Crane period, and some pieces have been acquired by the Center to flesh out the house with "Clemens period" essentials. The sofa where scholars sometimes pose for photos was donated by a local family and has no connection to the Cranes or the Langdons, but it fits the desired interior design. Staff members have placed original chairs throughout the main floor, which are carefully marked with paper signs requesting that visitors refrain from sitting on them—further signifying their relationship with the Clemens period.

### *Decorating with Photographs*

Susan Crane's tall secretary desk, where Clemens sometimes wrote, resides in the parlor, and on it sits a framed photograph of the parlor when the she lived there. Scholars can compare the photograph to the room as they experience it in the present day. Around the residence are other photographs of the house as it was during the Cranes' residence and pictures of Sam Clemens in various locales on the grounds. Though the house is not a museum that attempts to re-create the exact environment that Clemens would have encountered while summering there, the furnishings and arrangements do evoke that period. The photographs provide reinforcing evidence that scholars are in the "real" place. Authentic (or near authentic) objects surround them, even though the photographs of Clemens in various Quarry Farm locales likely would not have been placed around the house during his stays there.

Upstairs the house arrangement is less precisely historical. The bedrooms are arranged for the comfort of guests. The upstairs resembles a pared-down bed-and-breakfast more than a historic house museum. The furnishings are simple, the wallpaper and paint light and airy. The scholars' study, arranged to maximize space, provides a computer, printer, wireless Internet access, cable television, and a nearly complete collection of primary source material and international secondary scholarship on Twain.[49] Yet even upstairs there are carefully placed objects that are meant to evoke the house's status as a site of pilgrimage. In the scholars' study, for instance, there are several photographs of Clemens in his study and an illustration of the study's interior, which emphasize that writing is the way that visitors can connect with their subject. Although they cannot spend time writing in Clemens's study, because it was moved to Elmira College, they are surrounded by images of it.

Other ambiguously old objects are artfully distributed throughout the house. There is an early typewriter in one of the bedrooms, an old treadle Singer sewing machine, a dresser that is decorated with silk flowers in a vase and an old iron key, and rotary phones. Most of these items may not relate to the "Clemens era," but they are arranged carefully to evoke a sense of the past. Even the rotary phones, which clearly do not date to Clemens's or Susan Crane's time at the house, serve to remind scholars that they have stepped out of the present day and are occupying a third space between Clemens's time and their own. This careful staging of Quarry Farm as a historic house, a scholarly refuge, and a place that is in between times is effectively an interpretive schema as much as any at the other historic house museums discussed in this volume. Although no house museum curator has designed a formal interpretive plan, the staff at the Center for Mark Twain Studies have carefully assessed the needs and desires of their particular visitors and sought to meet them.

For instance, in the kitchen at Quarry Farm you can begin to tease out the Center's and the house's long relationship with Clemens. An enormous wood-burning and coal-burning stove set into the west wall dates to the Clemens period. It is an impressive appliance, a Richardson-Boynton & Co. iron stove that is marked "Our Favorite" across the top ovens and wood box. It is reported to be the stove over which Mary Ann Cord once cooked and warmed the bathwater for the Clemens daughters. It stands next to a more recent model (circa 1960s) that dates to Jervis Langdon Jr.'s last residency at the house, and this is where scholars heat the water for their tea and cook while they are visiting. In the cupboard someone has left a collector's set of Tom Sawyer–themed 1980s glassware. There was one glass drying in the dish rack when I arrived for my visit, and the oddness of the mass-produced keepsake glassware was striking at first. Catty-cornered from the cupboard is a little nook with a tiny photograph of Clemens and his family on the long eastern porch of their house in Hartford. The kitchen is the one room in the house, and perhaps of all the sites where Twain is celebrated, where the broadest continuum of Twain commemoration is displayed. The house is no longer a private home, and it is not quite a museum. It is an evocative gallery, littered with authentic objects that are meant to inspire visitors to think about Clemens in all his forms. But because the visitor can interact with these objects—from the collectable glasses to the decorative vases that were used at Sam and Olivia Clemens's wedding—the house provides scholars with both a commemorative and an authentic material experience.

The one decorating motif that stands out is the framed "snapshots" placed throughout the farmhouse of one of the most famously photographed men in American letters. Many Americans might not have read Sam Clemens's novels, short stories, or autobiographical pieces, but most will certainly recognize a photograph of him. Moreover, Twain scholars are not likely to forget what he looked like. At Quarry Farm there is a carefully displayed series of images that argue: here Sam Clemens lived among the people he loved, and he loved this place. Images of him in his study, or pausing on the stone steps leading up to the study, show him as a man relaxed among family, not posing for a profile portrait of an author.

It seems odd at first that the second-most pervasive photographic subject in the house is Twain's study itself. It has been missing from Quarry Farm for more than sixty years, and the removal has left a hole at the site. Alan

Gribben, as early as 1987, formally recommended that the study be moved back to Quarry Farm. In a letter to then director Darryl Baskin, he argued for a "reunion of the study with its environment."[50] The pictures of the study throughout the house, especially dominant in the researcher's office space, may be an attempt to account for its absence as much as to inspire scholars to write as Clemens did at the farm. After all, the farm would be able to recreate Clemens's ritual of writing more precisely by including the exact space where Clemens found refuge to write. If scholars had access to his study, the little table on which he wrote, and the view outside his windows, might they not come to understand even more about his writing and his process? Even a replica might lend perspective to the little ledge where the study once stood.

Adding a replica would, in effect, make the house an overt place of historical interpretation, bringing the farm perilously close to joining the ranks of commercialized Twain spots, from Mark Twain's Cave in Hannibal, Missouri, to Walt Disney's Mark Twain Riverboat. Quarry Farm and the Center for Mark Twain Studies seem unlikely to cross that delicate barrier between scholars' retreat and directly curated exhibition. As it is, the farmhouse remains largely as it was when the Langdons gave it to the college in 1982. The college has maintained the site, replaced the furnace, repaired chimneys, and started small restoration projects, but the place has not changed substantially from how the family would have seen it in the early 1980s.

In this way, although the house was changed to suit the Langdon family long after the "Clemens period," it is authentic. Founding tourism studies scholars like Dean MacCannell have argued that the authentic experience is almost always already out of reach, because the sites of tourism always present a commodified version of themselves to tourists.[51] Quarry Farm is not *just* a tourist site. Even it if was, other definitions of "authentic" that focus on existential authenticity might better fit the experiences that scholars have at the site. Since the mid-1990s, tourism and museum studies scholars have started to focus on the "existential authenticity" found in the personal experience of the tourist. Following MacCannell, some have begun to argue that the "real" work of the tourist is in defining a sense of self through experience—by testing what we see at museums, historic sites, or tourist destinations against those parts of ourselves that most need testing. This "identity-work" allows the tourist-scholar to measure himself or herself in the experience of place.[52] For a literary scholar there is no better professional or existential examination than to "face" the subject of one's biographical inquiry in the place where he or she worked.

Quarry Farm is certainly faithful to the Langdon family's own memories of Clemens, to their time there, and to the Langdons' plan to foster serious consideration of their Mark Twain. And now, after years as a site of pilgrimage and scholarship, it is authentic, or at least genuine, to the scholars who inhabit it. Recent calls for historic sites to expand their "period of significance" are not needed here. To adapt the language of the National Trust for Historic Preservation, at Quarry Farm the period of significance has always been now.[53] The farm allows the scholars who visit not only to become a part of the interpretive story by living with the "ghosts of Twain," but also to expand what is significant about the place to include Clemens's extended family and community, and even the work of the scholars who have come before. Though this place, like any other site that celebrates Mark Twain, is the result of decisions made over time, it now presents a narrative about the origin of Clemens's writing that has resonance with and comes directly from the work of literary scholars. The Langdon family's express desire in opening the site to scholars was that Quarry Farm could be used to "promote and encourage scholarship." It has done precisely that.

At the quadrennial conferences that the Center holds on the state of Mark Twain studies, there is often a "coming-together . . . on the site of Mark Twain's fabled octagonal study."[54] Here at the ledge and near the study's foundations, scholars share a drink, and some smoke cigars. At a conference in August 2009, the pilgrims on the hill all sang a rousing rendition of "Will the Circle Be Unbroken" with Hal Holbrook, and in 2013 they held an impromptu hootenanny on the front porch after gathering at the site of the study.[55] The rituals at Quarry Farm speak to the ways that scholars imagine themselves reenacting events in Clemens's spaces. Nearly every person who visits the farm goes to the site of the study and tries to imagine it when Clemens was there. So today, the fact that the study is missing heightens the absence of Clemens at the farm. At other house museums and literary sites where the author's desk is exhibited, curators set the scene as though the author had just stepped out, an open book, pen, papers, or glasses left behind. At Quarry Farm, Clemens hasn't just stepped out. But Twain scholars have. Each leaves his or her impression behind, a note in the guest book, an article or book in the library, and a ritual of literary and historical work that has become its own tradition. Even I left a short entry in the guest book, noting ghosts—literary and scholarly—that still haunt the halls.

## NOTES

1. Among recent investigations of how humans use and customize our workspaces is Uta Brandes and Michael Erlhoff's very useful *My Desk Is My Castle: Exploring Personalization Cultures* (Basel: Birkäuser, 2011). This chapter is in many ways a revision of my earlier investigations of Quarry Farm. Among the many people I have to thank for my original research and my never-ending questions about Quarry Farm are Susan K. Harris, who

encouraged me to apply for a Quarry Farm fellowship; Barbara Snedecor, who looked after my every need while I was there and has put up with my study of her and her predecessors at the Center with great kindness and humor; Mark Woodhouse, Elmira College's best human asset and former archivist; and Kevin Mac Donnell, whose collecting expertise was invaluable to me in beginning the process of tracking down Twain's writing tables, desks, and objects.

2. Adam Sweeting, "Preserving the Renaissance: Literature and Public Memory In the Homes of Longfellow, Hawthorne, and Poe," *American Studies* 46, no. 1 (Spring 2005): 29; FAQ, "Do you really have a haunted house at your home on Halloween?," Stephenking.com. For a description of Harvard's Emily Dickinson Collection, see http://hcl.harvard.edu/libraries/houghton/collections/modern/dickinson.cfm.
3. "Mark Twain's Summer Home: A Visit to His House and Study in the Suburbs," *New York Times,* September 10, 1882. In an interview with Rudyard Kipling, Clemens said of Hartford: "I spend nine months of the year at Hartford. I have long ago satisfied myself that there is no hope of doing much work during those nine months. People come in and call. They call at all hours, about everything in the world." "Rudyard Kipling on Mark Twain," *New York Herald,* August 17, 1890.
4. For an excellent overview of the site's architectural history, see Lorraine Welling Lanmon, *Quarry Farm: A Study of the "Picturesque,"* Quarry Farm Papers no. 3 (Elmira, N.Y.: Elmira College Center for Mark Twain Studies, 1991).
5. Elmira College's relationship to the Langdons predates the commemoration of Mark Twain. Jervis Langdon, Olivia Langdon Clemens's father, was one of the early trustees of the college in 1855. Olivia attended the college (which was then called the Elmira Female College) as a day student, and eventually Jean Clemens, Sam and Olivia Clemens's youngest daughter, attended the college briefly. Mark Woodhouse, interview by author, January 31, 2008.
6. This move happened despite the interest of the Henry Ford Museum in acquiring the study for its collection. Irene Langdon, conversation with the author, January 25, 2008.
7. See "Twain Study Moved to Eldridge," *Elmira Gazette,* April 4, 2010; and see also the Eldridge Park Carousel Preservation Society's website page "Moving the Mark Twain Study," which summarizes an account of the study's addition to the park grounds; www.eldridgepark.us. The local builders had support from Elmira College to build the study replica and used the original plans, held at the Mark Twain Archive, Gannett-Tripp Library, Elmira College.
8. Hilary Iris Lowe, "Persistence of Fiction: One Hundred Years of Tom Sawyer at the Mark Twain Boyhood Home," in *Destination Dixie: Tourism and Southern History,* ed. Karen L. Cox (Gainesville: University Press of Florida, 2012), 17–48.
9. You can find this house at the Museum of Appalachia near Norris, Tennessee.
10. In 2003 a desk with a minor association with Clemens sold at Sotheby's to a private collector for $48,000. "Mark Twain Collection Brings $1.4 Million at Sotheby's," press release, June 19, 2003, http://files.shareholder.com.
11. Diana Fuss, *The Sense of an Interior: Four Writers and the Rooms That Shaped Them* (New York: Routledge, 2004), 5, emphasis added.
12. Ibid., vii.
13. Ibid., 43–57.
14. The college purchased the Homestead in 1965 but used it as faculty housing and meeting space, with some limited public use until 2003. *Emily Dickinson Museum, Ten Years: 2003–2013* (Amherst, Mass., 2013), 5.
15. Kevin Kopelson, *Neatness Counts: Essays on the Writer's Desk.* (Minneapolis: University of Minnesota Press, 2004), xv.
16. Shelley Fisher Fishkin, *Lighting Out for the Territory: Reflections on Mark Twain and American Culture* (New York: Oxford University Press, 1996), 77–79.

17. Anne Trubek, *A Skeptic's Guide to Writers' Houses* (Philadelphia: University of Pennsylvania Press, 2010).
18. Anne Trubek, "Read My Book? Tour My House," *New York Times,* October 15, 2010.
19. For press coverage of Sam Clemens's time in Elmira, see "Interview with Mark Twain in His Mountain Studio in Chemung—Remarkable Declarations: A Remarkable Statement for a Literary Man," *Hartford Daily Courant,* August 30, 1876; "Mark Twain's Summer Home: A Visit to His House and Study in the Suburbs of Elmira," *New York Times,* September 10, 1882; "A Misunderstood Man," *Chicago Daily Tribune,* November 7, 1882; Edwin J. Park, "A Day with Mark Twain: The Genial Humorist at His Summer Home," *Chicago Daily Tribune,* September 19, 1886; and "Mark Twain: He Plays as Umpire at Game of Base-Ball at Elmira," *Los Angeles Times,* July 16, 1887.
20. "Rudyard Kipling on Mark Twain." First published in a Turkish newspaper, Kipling's account eventually appeared in the *New York Herald* and has since been collected and redistributed by Twain and Kipling scholars alike.
21. Ibid., emphasis added. Kipling complains of arriving in the middle of the night after having come all the way from Hartford. During the Clemenses' first years there, and even at the time Kipling visited, getting to Elmira was a longer journey for them than most wanted to make for a summer getaway. Jervis Langdon Jr. called upon his railroad expertise and researched the trip from Hartford to Elmira. The journey took two days; the last leg alone, from Manhattan to Elmira, took more than ten hours throughout most of the years when the Clemenses spent their summers there. Eventually rail service did improve. See Jervis Langdon, "Feature," *Dear Friends* 22 (1991): 2.
22. "Rudyard Kipling on Mark Twain."
23. Indeed the house may have belonged there. Lorraine Welling Lanmon explores the connection between Quarry Farm, Susan Crane, and Andrew Jackson Downing and others in *Quarry Farm: A Study of the "Picturesque,"* 5–7.
24. "Rudyard Kipling on Mark Twain."
25. Clifton Johnson, *Highways and Byways of the Mississippi Valley* (New York: Macmillan Company, 1906), 179.
26. See Jervis Langdon, Elmira College, Chemung County Historical Society and National Trust for Historic Preservation, Four (4)-Party Agreement Regarding Quarry Farm, Elmira, N.Y., December 31, 1982 (Elmira, N.Y., 1982), copy held at the Mark Twain Archive, Gannett-Tripp Library, Elmira College.
27. The barn at the farm has been converted into an excellent space for Center programming. Members of the public can visit for special events held there. By and large, however, the house itself is open only by invitation or special appointment.
28. Alan Gribben, *Mark Twain's Library: A Reconstruction* (Boston: G. K. Hall, 1980).
29. Alan Gribben, interview by author, February 29, 2008.
30. See "Announcements: The Elmira College Center for Mark Twain Studies at Quarry Farm," *American Literature* 59, no. 1 (1987): 115; "Announcements: Quarry Farm Fellowships," *American Literature* 63, no. 1 (1991): 113; and "Commentary," *Nineteenth-Century Literature* 43, no. 4 (1989): 561. Gretchen Sharlow, interview by author, January 29, 2008. For a brief summary of the Center's history, see *Dear Friends,* Twenty-fifth Anniversary edition, 1–3.
31. Mark Twain, "A True Story, Repeated Word for Word as I Hear it." *Atlantic Monthly,* November 1, 1874, 591–94.
32. Harold Bush, Shelley Fisher Fishkin, and Maria Zuppello in *Dear Friends,* Twenty-fifth Anniversary edition, 5, 7, 13.
33. Harold Bush in *Dear Friends,* Twenty-fifth Anniversary edition, 5.
34. Connie Anne Kirk, in *Dear Friends,* Twenty-fifth Anniversary edition, 9, emphasis added.
35. Nicola J. Watson, *The Literary Tourist: Readers and Places in Romantic and Victorian Britain* (New York: Palgrave Macmillan, 2006), 1.

36. David Herbert, "Literary Places, Tourism and the Heritage Experience," *Annals of Tourism Research* 28, no. 2 (2001): 313.
37. Fishkin and others have noted Jervis Langdon's important work with the Underground Railroad, especially as a contributor to Frederick Douglass's escape. See Fishkin, *Lighting Out for the Territory,* 80.
38. Fishkin builds upon this work in *Writing America: Literary Landmarks from Walden Pond to Wounded Knee* (New Brunswick: Rutgers University Press, 2015). In this book she takes the National Register of Historic Places (among other historic sites and districts) as a starting point to develop a diverse literary itinerary for the nation, including a chapter that expands on her Twain work. Ultimately she sees all historic landmarks as literary ones and contends that once we all do this we can more fully understand the past.
39. Fishkin's account was written for a popular audience. Her personal interactions and readings of Twain have led at least one scholar to point out that Sam Clemens has inspired many who study him to believe that they have a personal, autobiographical connection to him. Some scholars' works have crossed over into advocacy of Mark Twain. See Harold Bush, "Our Mark Twain? Or, Some Thoughts on the 'Autobiographical Critic,'" *New England Quarterly* 73, no. 1 (2000): 101–22.
40. Aaron Santesso, "The Birth of the Birthplace: Bread Street and Literary Tourism before Stratford," *English Literary History* 71, no. 2 (2004): 377–403, 386.
41. Quarry Farm Guest Book.
42. Quarry Farm Guest Book.
43. Susan K. Harris in *Dear Friends,* Twenty-fifth Anniversary edition, 5.
44. Joe B. Fulton, *Mark Twain in the Margins: The Quarry Farm Marginalia and a Connecticut Yankee in King Arthur's Court,* Studies in American Literary Realism and Naturalism (Tuscaloosa: University of Alabama Press, 2000).
45. Quarry Farm Guest Book.
46. Louis Budd, "Anniversay Edition," 5.
47. There are other literary homes set aside for scholarly or literary production. For instance, Middlebury College in Vermont owns the Robert Frost Farm and occasionally uses the house for the Bread Loaf Writers' Conference and other events. Norman Mailer's home in Provincetown served for a while as a home for writers-in-residence but has since returned to private hands. Melville's house Arrowhead serves as the home for the Berkshire Historical Society and has a long-serving writer-in-residence, and there are writer-in-residence opportunities at Jack Kerouac's cottage in Orlando and Edna St. Vincent Millay's estate at Steepletop in upstate New York, among others. Most of these sites, however, primarily serve creative or creative nonfiction writers rather than scholarly production.
48. See, for instance, Lawrence Buell, "The Thoreauvian Pilgrimage: The Structure of an American Cult," *American Literature* 61, no. 2 (1989): 175–99; see also Klara-Stephanie Szlezák's chapter in this collection.
49. The scholarly library at the house, especially now that it includes the late Michael Kiskis's collection, is second to none. Even the impressive Mark Twain Papers at Berkeley's Bancroft Library, which holds the largest collection of Clemens's original correspondence, can't rival the unmitigated 24-hour access to both facsimiles of these letters and the research library. In addition, Elmira College's nearby Gannett Tripp Library Special Collections has a significant collection of Clemens's manuscript materials available to scholars on campus.
50. Alan Gribben to Darryl Baskin, August 4, 1987, Mark Twain Archive, Gannett-Tripp Library, Elmira College.
51. Dean MacCannell, *The Tourist: A New Theory of the Leisure Class* (Berkeley: University of California Press, 1976), 1–16.
52. See Ning Wang, "Rethinking Authenticity in Tourism Experience," *Annals of Tourism Research* 26, no. 2 (1999): 349–70; John H. Falk, "An Identity-Centered Approach to Understanding Museum Learning," *Curator* 49, no. 2 (2006): 151–66; and Jay Rounds, "Doing Identity Work in Museums," *Curator* 49, no. 2 (2006): 129–49.

53. Erin Carlson Mast, Morris J. Vogel, and Lisa Junkin Lopez, "The Period of Significance Is Now," *National Trust for Historic Preservation Forum Journal,* 24, no. 4 (2014): 43–51.
54. Jim Leonard, "Re: Unbroken Indeed," email to Mark Twain Forum, August 11, 2009.
55. For a fuller picture of conference events, see Mark Twain Forum discussion archives (Twain-L) from August 2009 and August 2013, https://listserv.yorku.ca/archives/twain-l.html.

# 7

# "Shut not your doors to me, proud libraries!"

## The Repatriation of Edith Wharton's Library

CAROLINE HELLMAN

*As Mark Twain's desks, writing tables, and even studies have been mobile and traveled all over, so, too, has Edith Wharton's library. Touring Wharton's library not only allows the active literary tourist to see Wharton's house, The Mount, for the remarkable literary place it was but also facilitates a "tour" of what Caroline Hellman argues is Wharton's most intimate autobiography. Hellman's work helps scholars and public historians engaged in maintaining literary homes understand how valuable an author's books and marginalia are. She suggests that this moving library's life mirrors Wharton's own and argues that, like the house Wharton designed, the library has a great deal to tell the literary tourist and scholar about the past.*

One January day found me in the sewing room of The Mount, Edith Wharton's home in Lenox, Massachusetts, overlooking the snow-covered gardens and grounds, the Berkshire hills in the distance. The Mount's librarian, Nynke Dorhout, had kindly squared me away on the second floor of the home in the old service wing. In Wharton's day, the space contained an adjacent closet for the author's dresses; instead of gowns, I sat flanked by volumes from Wharton's library. Around me lay Emerson's collected poems and essays (heavily annotated), two editions of *Moby-Dick* (unmarked), two editions of *Leaves of Grass* (one marked, one not), and many of Wharton's own books (corrected). I had been to The Mount innumerable times before, initially as a visitor delighting in historic houses, subsequently as an academic exploring the personal domestic practices of authors alongside those of their fictional characters. But The Mount's acquisition of Wharton's library in 2006 means that a visit to the house offers a new, more comprehensive understanding of the author. As the repatriation of the author's library to The Mount represents a spiritual reunion of two significant pieces of Wharton's autobiography—her house and her books—and a wonderful opportunity for scholars and scholarly tourists, the library is a significant acquisition for the Edith Wharton Restoration, the organization that owns The Mount. My chapter examines the history of the house, what the library illuminates about Wharton herself, and how the library offers visitors a new understanding of Wharton's erstwhile home.

Today, a visit to The Mount includes a tour of the home and an overview of the author's life. Rooms are decorated by twenty-first-century interior designers, as the original furnishings are long gone, and the majority of the operating budget is dedicated to educational programs and preservation of the house. Visitors may enjoy lunch on the terrace and peruse the bookstore, which occupies the old laundry room. Wharton's suitcases, emblazoned with *EW,* fill the elevator. To welcome more visitors to The Mount and acquaint them with the wealth of the library, as well as to raise funds, The Mount offers gift packages that include membership, private tours of the library, admission and a tour of the house, and a (new) copy of a Wharton book.

If historic houses are concerned with a loss of the past and the attempt to recover that past, the repatriation of Wharton's library goes a long way toward redeeming the loss of the author. Just as the books' homecoming connotes her long absence—her divorce, her permanent move to France, and, finally, her death—the return of the library suggests an alternative life story for Wharton, one in which she and her books remained in Lenox at The Mount, never departing the Berkshires, and the United States, for good. More than a beloved piece of furniture or a teacup, Wharton's library is a form of autobiography, encompassing inscriptions and dedications from literary and political acquaintances, notes on American literature, corrections to errata, and objections to illustrations added to her texts by publishers. While The Mount is Wharton's story in design, the library is her story in letters, suggesting that Wharton's true home was actually portable, moving with her books.[1]

Edith Wharton wrote in her autobiography *A Backward Glance* (1933) that her life after she moved to France was characterized by a variety of pleasures, human and literary: "These new friendships, and many others, added much to my enjoyment of Paris; but the core of my life was under my own roof, among my books and my intimate friends."[2] It is a rare privilege to examine some of the books she mentions here, books that traveled from Wharton's successive residences in New York, Newport, and Lenox before crossing the ocean to France. Through the years, of course, Wharton's library evolved, and by the end of her life she had been given books and had given books away.[3] She also had duplicates of some works in different editions, housed at different residences. In thinking about Wharton's library, one can consider the geographic trajectory of the collection as well as the implications of its contents. To trace this trajectory back to the last time the books were at The Mount, it is useful to revisit the history of The Mount itself.

Setting and interior were extremely important to Wharton. This is evident in her nonfiction: her co-authorship with architect Ogden Codman Jr. of *The Decoration of Houses* (1897); her books *Italian Villas and Their Gardens* (1904), *Italian Backgrounds* (1905), *A Motor Flight through France* (1908), *Fighting France* (1915), *French Ways and Their Meaning* (1919), and *In Morocco* (1920); her fictional settings, whether a moneyed New York residence, a snowy New England evening, or the battlefields of war; and her life, during which she occupied eleven distinct residences, the majority of whose interiors she designed. The author believed that setting was central to understanding how people—and characters—crafted their lives and their selves. Interior design and architecture were a single language, she argued, a language that spoke volumes about inhabitants. Her most often quoted insight into interiors comes from "The Fullness of Life," a short story published in the December 1893 issue of *Scribner's Magazine,* in which she describes a woman's backward glance at life with her husband:

> I have sometimes thought that a woman's nature is like a great house full of rooms: there is the hall, through which everyone passes in going in and out; the drawing-room, where one receives formal visits; the sitting-room, where the members of the family come and go as they list; but beyond that, far beyond, are other rooms, the handles of whose doors perhaps are never turned; no one knows the way to them, no one knows whither they lead; and in the innermost room, the holy of holies, the soul sits alone and waits for a footstep that never comes.[4]

The library is not mentioned here, but it was in fact her innermost room. Indeed, as Carol Singley has argued in a portrait of the author, we "have looked for Edith Wharton in the drawing room; we must also seek her in the library, voraciously consuming volumes of philosophy, history, art, science, and religion, as well as literature."[5] Let us look for her, then, beginning with her ideas about interiors, as well as how they were applied to objects to which she was extremely attached.

Wharton first outlined her design philosophies in her book with Codman, *The Decoration of Houses,* an interior design manual influential in the creation of ideal domestic spaces for the upper class. Most important, the authors advocated for interior design and architecture to be considered in tandem, rather than independently. Wharton and Codman discussed the importance of order, reason, and simplicity for the American interior. Proportion and symmetry were essential. Doors were important, as differentiating between spaces established proper patterns of domestic life; so did boundaries between public and private areas. Rooms were supposed to have distinctive functions. A library's primary decoration should be books, the authors declared, set into recessed shelves. The Mount's library adheres to this prescription, with the only ornament an inset tapestry on one wall.[6]

Wharton was able to implement her other philosophies, too, at The Mount.[7] On its 113-acre lot in the Berkshires overlooking Laurel Lake, the author worked with its initial architect, Codman, and with later addition Francis Hoppin, on the home, which was influenced by English country houses as well as neoclassical French and Italian designs. Construction took place in 1901 and 1902. The Mount's interior floor plans underscore boundaries—between public and private, between genders, and between classes. In a transition from the landscape into the home, visitors enter the house through a grotto-like space with rusticated stucco walls and mirrors on the doors. The forecourt and entrance hall, which Wharton treated as outside rooms, facilitate the separation of public and private space, keeping unwanted visitors at bay.

The majority of servant spaces, including the kitchen, scullery, and laundry, occupied the ground floor. One floor above are spaces for social interaction, including the den, library, drawing room, and dining room. All of these open onto the terrace and afford views of extensive terraced Italian gardens. The grand first-floor rooms, built for public use, are distinct from the second floor's smaller private spaces, comprising Wharton's suite, Mr. Wharton's bedroom and bath, and three guest rooms. The author allotted herself a much larger study and bedroom suite than she did Teddy, her husband, suggesting her influence on the design of the house, as well as the importance of space to her writing. Wharton typically wrote in her bedroom, as opposed to her study or library. Consequently, the most elaborately decorated room in the entire home was not one for public use but Wharton's boudoir, where eight floral still-life paintings are set into wooden paneling. The Mount's interior was the antithesis of crowded Victorian parlors "crammed . . . with artificial plants, wobbly velvet-covered tables littered with gewgaws and festoons of lace on mantelpieces and dressing tables," which Wharton and Codman decried in their design handbook.[8]

During Wharton's residence at The Mount, she was prolific, publishing the novels *Sanctuary* (1903), *The House of Mirth* (1905), *Madame de Treymes* (1907) *The Fruit of the Tree* (1907), and *Ethan Frome* (1911), set in the Berkshires, in addition to a book of poetry and several short story collections. Yet she declared her design efforts superior to her literary ones. In a July 1911 letter to W. Morton Fullerton, she reported, "Decidedly, I'm a better landscape gardener than novelist, and this place, every line of which is my own work, far surpasses the House of Mirth."[9]

In 1911, after a separation from Teddy that followed a period of increasing discord, Wharton moved abroad permanently to France, and The Mount was sold. Despite her departure, the house remained extremely important to Wharton throughout her life. In her autobiography *A Backward Glance* (1934), Wharton wrote: "There for over ten years I lived and gardened and wrote contentedly, and should doubtless have ended my days there had not a grave change in my husband's health made the burden of the property too heavy. . . . The Mount was my first real home, and though it is nearly twenty years since I last saw it (for I was too happy there ever to want to revisit it as a stranger) its blessed influence still lives in me."[10]

The sizable twenty-by-twenty-five-foot wood-paneled library on the main floor was a significant attribute of the house, and its contents moved with her. That the library was in effect the only part of the home that was mobile—and that she planned for a library at all—indicates its importance. The collection of books was clearly more significant to her than the room the books occupied in the house. Wharton was well aware that the history of such rooms lay with men. In *A Backward Glance* she noted:

> In my grand-parents' day every gentleman had what was called "a gentleman's library." In my father's day, these libraries still existed, though they were often only a background; but in our case Macaulay, Prescott, Motley, Sainte-Beuve, Augustin Thierry, Victor Hugo, the Brontës, Mrs. Gaskell, Ruskin, Coleridge, had been added to the French and English classics in their stately calf bindings. Were these latter ever read? Not often, I imagine; but they were there; they represented a standard; and perhaps some mysterious emanation disengaged itself from them, obscurely fighting for the protection of the languages they had illustrated.[11]

She characterizes her father's library as aligned with those of her male ancestors and also as a dying breed in contemporary interior design. Yet it was a room in which she spent many memorable days of her childhood, exploring: "I have wandered far from my father's library. . . . But the library calls me back, and I pause on its threshold."[12] Her declaration here attests to the influence of her early education from the books in his library, and the distance she traveled beyond these formative first steps.

After her death in 1937, the contents of her library were divided; Wharton bequeathed the majority of her books to two men, William Royall Tyler, the son of Elisina and Royall Tyler, who worked with Wharton on her charity

FIGURE 7.1. The Library at The Mount, 2012. *Photo by David Dashiell. Courtesy of The Mount, Lenox, Mass.*

relief efforts during World War I, and Colin Clark, the son of the British art historian Kenneth Clark, and Wharton's godson. The books in Tyler's possession, accounting for a third of Wharton's collection, were placed in storage in England and later destroyed by fire during the Blitz, in 1940.[13] The books that Clark inherited he ultimately sold to the London booksellers Maggs Brothers, who then sold them to George Ramsden, a book dealer in York, England. Ramsden, after laboring for two decades to reassemble Wharton's library and purchasing six hundred more volumes from the Clark family (stray books were found in the libraries of Colin, Colette, and Alan Clark), eventually sold the library to The Mount in 2005 for £1.5 million (roughly $2.6 million).[14] The collection arrived in 2006.

The library at The Mount does not encompass the author's entire collection but only the volumes that survived World War II.[15] Of the 2,700 tomes now residing at Wharton's former home in Lenox, Massachusetts, 1,800 are in storage and 900 grace the recessed bookshelves of her library, the only room at The Mount to boast its original contents (fig. 7.1). When the books first came home, Ramsden dressed the library, deciding which texts to display on the basis of the condition of the books; historical accuracy, indicated by photographs of the library from Wharton's time; representation of a cross-section of the author's interests; and aesthetic concerns.[16]

The library shelves showcase French philosophy, Russian, German, Italian, French, and American literature, and drama; theology and classics; history; gardening and architecture; poetry; and Wharton's own volumes. Wharton's signature on the flyleaf—either "Edith Newbold Jones" or "Edith Wharton"—clarifies which books she acquired as a child and young adult, and which after marriage. The author's bookplates are from Land's End, her home in Newport, Rhode Island, prior to her residence at The Mount; Pavillon Colombe, her home north of Paris; and Hyères, her home on the French Riviera (fig. 7.2). The oldest book on display is a 1546 edition of Baldesar Castiglione's *Il Cortegiano* (The Courtier), almost four centuries senior to the newest books from the 1930s, acquired just before her death. Stephen McKenna's *Dermotts Rampant* (1931) bears the inscription "For Edith Wharton, with the author's homage and in the hope that by sending her this book hot from the press, he may secure it a place in the Sainte-Claire library before the last shelf is filled."[17] Just as the contents of the library are far-ranging in subject matter, so too is the biographical information gleaned about Edith Wharton from the collection.

Immediately apparent from the titles, ranging from Baudelaire's *Fleurs du Mal,* to Giovanni Bocaccio's *La Fiammetta con la lettera consolatoria a M. Pino de' Rossi,* to *Richard Wagner an Mathilde Wesendonk: Tagebuchblätter und Briefe, 1853–1871,* is Wharton's multilingual prowess. Though she received no formal education, she read widely and spoke fluently in English, French, Italian, and German, and even attempted to translate Anglo-Saxon.[18] In Friedrich Schiller's poetry collection, *Gedichte,* in a section titled "Parables and Riddles," there is a riddle in German, translated here:

> A bridge weaves its arch with pearls
> High over the tranquil sea;
> In a moment it unfurls
> Its span, unbounded, free.
>
> The tallest ship with swelling sail
> May pass beneath its arch with ease;
> It carries no burden, 'tis too frail,
> And with your quick approach it flees.
>
> With the flood it comes, with the rain it goes;
> What it is made of nobody knows?[19]

At the foot of the page, Wharton scrawled her answer in German, *Regenbogen?* (Rainbow?).

FIGURE 7.2. Wharton's bookplates. *Courtesy of The Mount, Lenox, Mass.*

There is not only a range of languages represented but also a range of subject matter. Readers acquainted with her collection *The Descent of Man and Other Stories* (1904) will be unsurprised that two editions of Darwin's *Origin of Species* (1895 and 1900), in addition to *The Descent of Man* (1895) and *Journal of Researches into the Natural History and Geology of the Countries Visited during the Voyage of H.M.S. Beagle Round the World, under the Command of Capt. Fitz Roy, R.N.* (1912), grace one shelf. Books on evolution, astronomy, and science abut tomes on religion, history, and philosophy, the secular and the sacred sharing space. Perusing only a few selected titles gives the visitor a sense of the breadth of Wharton's reading habits: Robert Browning's *Dramatic Idylls,* William Conant Church's *Ulysses S. Grant,* Chang Tzu's *Musings of a Chinese Mystic,* Professor Asa Gray's *How Plants Grow,* and George Santayana's *Skepticism and Animal Faith.* Wharton's catholic taste in reading extended beyond her library at home to the books she took with her on the road. Writing from a 1911 vacation in Salsomaggiore, Italy, to her lover W. Morton Fullerton, she reported:

> The rest of my library (snatched up at haphazard) consists of Hugo's Postscriptum, Renan's Averroes, which I've never read, Flaubert's Novembre, Lewes's History of Philosophy, which I love & haven't read for years, Emerson, Reynolds's Discourses on Art—such a mixture of drivel & insight, (as when he says of Poussin that he was "naturalized in antiquity")—Doestoievsky's "Idiot," Melville's "Moby Dick" (do you share my taste for Melville? I like him almost as well, & and in the same way, as Borrow), Woltmann's "Die Germanen in Frankreich," —& Bazalgette's translation of "Leaves of Grass," which Walter sent me a titre de curiosite & which is a tour de force!!"[20]

The library reveals the evolution of Wharton's reading practices, as well as the personalities who contributed to this growth. While her family was most influential in constructing her literary taste, other notable figures contributed to her collection. Henry James gave her a copy of *The Golden Bowl,* inscribed "To Edith Wharton / in sympathy—Henry James / November 1904." (This coincided with James's first visit to The Mount; he could have been alluding to the disintegration of Wharton's marriage.) Theodore Roosevelt gave Wharton a copy of his 1915 *America and the World War,* inscribed with the words "To Edith Wharton from an American-American!"[21]

During her childhood, Wharton's parents strictly monitored her literary exposure. "My mother herself so little a reader was exaggeratedly scrupulous about the books I read; not so much the 'grown-up' books as those written for children. I was never allowed to read the popular American children's books of my day because, as my mother said, the children spoke bad English without the author's knowing."[22] Her mother finally let her read Louisa May Alcott's *Little Women* and *Little Men* when Wharton pleaded that all the other children were reading then. Yet, like her mother, the adult Wharton, too, was skeptical of popular literature, expressing this in a 1903 essay, "The Vice of Reading," which deplored the literary tastes of the masses.[23] She applied the same principles of taste to literature that she applied to interior design, lamenting what she perceived as thoughtless, common trends. Today, in addition to the volumes Wharton inherited from her father's mid-nineteenth-century library—philosophy, classics, and poetry—one can peruse volumes of Keats and Shelley that George Frederic Jones and Lucretia Stevens Rhinelander, Wharton's parents, gave their daughter.

The author's reading proclivities were different from her writing ones. Wharton-as-writer penned texts such as *The House of Mirth, The Age of Innocence, The Custom of the Country,* and *Glimpses of the Moon,* among others, that offer a critical examination of rigid class politics and social contracts, along with conflicts regarding the old world and the new, Europe and America, romantic versus conservative visions of life, and the constant consumption of modern existence. Wharton characterized many relationships, romantic and otherwise, in terms of the marketplace, consumption, and exchange. Wharton-as-reader bracketed, checked, and underlined Transcendentalist ideals.[24] In Whitman's "Starting from Paumanok," she marked the sixth section, "The soul, / Forever and forever—longer than soil is brown solid—longer than water ebbs and flows."[25] In Emerson's essay "The Over-Soul," Wharton's checkmarks appear next to the lines "As with events, so is it with thoughts. When I watch that flowing river, which, out of regions I see not, pours for a season its streams into me, I see that I am a pensioner; not a cause, but a surprised spectator of this ethereal water; that I desire and look up, and put myself in the attitude of reception, but from some alien energy the visions come." One can trace Wharton's interest from the Romantics to the Transcendentalists and see a potential disjunction between the material concerns of her own texts and the alternative visions of the world in the texts in her library. Yet, in poring over passages Wharton annotated, I began to notice familiar themes from her works, and even her life. In Emerson's essay "Love" (1884), Wharton's marks surround "Not always can flowers, pearls, poetry, protestations, nor even home in another heart, content the awful soul that dwells in clay."[26] The yearning for contentment and the uncertainty over how to achieve it permeates many of her works. Another passage Wharton marked underscores her interest in distinguishing classes of people from one another. In Emerson's essay "Prudence," she bracketed the passage reading:

> There are all degrees of proficiency in knowledge of the world. It is sufficient, to our present purpose, to indicate three. One class live to the utility of the symbol; esteeming health and wealth a final good. Another class live above this mark to the beauty of the symbol; as the poet, and artist, and the naturalist, and man of science. A third class live above the beauty of the symbol to the beauty of the thing signified; these are wise men. The first class have common sense; the second, taste; and the third, spiritual perception.[27]

Like Wharton, Emerson wrote about classes of people, though he offered different systems of classification from the social strata of Wharton's New

York. His philosophies and his words resonated deeply with Wharton; she advised a friend who was having trouble writing to read Emerson again and ground himself.[28]

Emerson's essays and poems are marked heavily, but it is Whitman's *Leaves of Grass* whose influence seems to have radiated outward for the author.[29] As a child, Wharton was not allowed to read Whitman; as an adult, Wharton hailed the Brooklyn bard. Wharton's markings in the volume offer insight into a lifelong friendship, her autobiography, and her interest in a democratic vision very different from the socially constricting vision in her texts.[30] In a July 7, 1908, letter to her friend Sarah Norton, Wharton lauded Whitman. "He has no system, & not much logic, but wonderful flashes of insight, & a power of breaking through conventions that is most exhilarating, & clears the air as our thunderstorms just now do—not! I think it salutary, now & then, to be made to realize what he calls 'die Undwerthung aller Werthe,' & really get back to a wholesome basis of naked instinct."[31] She owned more than one copy of *Leaves of Grass,* but it is her 1897 edition, a gift from Walter Berry, that contains pencil markings throughout. Bearing two bookplates—from Land's End, her home in Newport, and from Pavillon Colombe, her home in Saint-Brice-sous-Forêt, the volume also contains Berry's inscription, excerpted from "Song of Myself" (sec. 47, ll. 11–12): "Who can stray from me? / I follow you whoever you are from the present hour." Follow each other they did, at home and then abroad, through World War I, until Berry's death in 1927.

Because Wharton left checkmarks but few notes in her books, the reader can only surmise her thoughts. In the table of contents for *Leaves of Grass,* Wharton marked the poem "Shut Not Your Doors": "Shut not your doors to me, proud libraries, / "For that which was lacking on all your well-fill'd shelves, yet needed most, I bring / Forth from the army, the war emerging—a book I have made" (ll. 1–3). Depending on when Wharton marked this particular poem, perhaps she discussed it with Henry James, who wrote a memorable 1865 review of Whitman's "Drum-Taps."[32] Perhaps she was thinking of her own books to come out of her experience of World War I, *The Book of the Homeless* (1915) and *A Son at the Front* (1923). Less ambiguous is that the poem "A Backward Glance O'er Traveled Roads," the last preface to *Leaves of Grass,* was the source for the title of Wharton's autobiography *A Backward Glance.* The notion of a backward glance appears again in another relevant line she marked in "Song of Myself": "Backward I see in my own days where I sweated through fog with linguists and contenders" (sec. 4, ll. 15–16). Explaining the name of her Lenox residence, Wharton wrote in *A Backward Glance,* "On a slope overlooking the dark waters and densely wooded shores of Laurel Lake we built a spacious and dignified house, to which we gave the name of my great-grandfather's place, The Mount."[33] One could also think its name came from its setting. Another way to think of the house relates to a Whitman passage that Wharton marked in "Song of Myself": "My feet strike an apex of the apices of the stairs / On every step bunches of ages, and larger bunches between the step, / All below duly travel'd, and still I mount and mount" (sec. 44, ll. 16–18).

Also interesting to read are Wharton's responses to editions of her works. Like her friend Henry James, who resented the pictorial representations in *Portrait of a Lady,* Wharton objected vehemently to the illustrations in *The House of Mirth* and excised them from her own copy of the book, along with the list of illustrations. She annotated the chronicle of war in *Fighting France* with specific dates. She kept lists of errata and edited printed copies of her texts, indicating her attention to detail with frustrated annotations. Her copy of *A Backward Glance* chronicles sixteen misprints encompassing missing commas and accent marks for French words, repeated adjectives, incorrect prepositions, and misspelled names of characters. She clearly read closely and with care, establishing a list of errors as she read, her work ethic evident. These errors were not always rectified in later editions, however; Wharton's copies of *A Mother's Recompense* and *Summer* contain many corrections, but current editions retain the original mistakes. Readers of *Summer* will understand Charity Royal's growing belief about Harney that she has chosen poorly in love with the words "At any rate it began to loom against the rainy dawn" instead of the correct version, "At any rate it began to loom in her now as it loomed against the rainy dawn," the latter iteration articulating the burden of thought. While the average visitor to The Mount may not be captivated by this linguistic shift, Wharton scholars will be interested to observe these distinctions firsthand.

The copies of her own works also contain pasted ephemera. Inside *A Backward Glance* is "News and Views of Literary London," a summary of British reviews of the autobiography, with Wharton's penciled date, "June 24, 1934." One critic was fascinated by her description of the development of the literary mind. Tucked into *The Writing of Fiction* is a letter from Villa Medici in Fiesole, dated "1 November 1925," from the critic and essayist Percy Lubbock. "Well it is very clear to me," he writes in response to receiving the book, "that my pen in your hand is a good deal sharper than yours in mine—I do like this book." Wharton saved other correspondence in her volumes as well. When Lavinia Davis sent along her book *A Bibliography of the Writings of Edith Wharton,* Wharton pasted into the book Davis's kind note about the pleasure of cataloging Wharton's work. Awareness of one side of correspondence can lead to other findings; Lavinia Davis's son recently shared Wharton's response to his mother's missive. In the note, Wharton apologized for her delayed reply, mentioning the difficult succession of her longtime maid's illness and death, her housekeeper's mental breakdown, and her secretary's illness as reasons for her tardiness. She noted, "I am delighted to have within reach this excellent genealogy of my books, for I am often asked questions about dates and publishers and am unable to answer them without a guide."[34] While the curator of the library has removed Wharton's letters for preservation reasons, copies exist for the visitor to peruse.

Also curious is what is missing from this record. Wharton owned a copy of *The Scarlet Letter,* for example, but did not annotate it. Her edition was published in 1920, and I cannot help but wonder, thinking of *The Age of Innocence,* if she had reread Hawthorne around that time. The work of some of Wharton's best-known contemporaries—Cather, Fitzgerald, Woolf, and Hemingway, among others—is strikingly absent. Of course, the library cannot tell the entire story of Wharton's reading practices because some books were destroyed while others were scattered. *The Great Gatsby* is an example of one of many absent texts that Wharton certainly read, as her response to Fitzgerald is well documented.[35] And in a letter to a friend, Wharton alludes to a British journalist's dual review of *The Mother's Recompense* and "Mrs. Woolf's latest," referring to *Mrs. Dalloway.*[36] While Wharton's collection of George Eliot can be found at The Mount (Eliot's collected essays contain an inscription to Wharton from Charles Scribner: "For the George Eliot of her time. C.S. Aug. 17 '08."), one might wonder about the absence of other female literary forebears—the Brontës, for example. But the fact that *Wuthering Heights* is missing does not mean that Wharton did not own it. In fact, Wharton's copy of *Jane Eyre* is a fairly recent acquisition by The Mount, donated in 2012 by a British woman whose aunt had purchased the book years before as a fourteenth birthday present for her niece. The name on the Pavillon Colombe bookplate was initially unfamiliar to both women, until they realized that the owner was one of the most famous names in American letters. *Jane Eyre* is the second of Wharton's seven-volume set of *The Life and Work of the Brontë Sisters* to return to The Mount. In the meantime, the stray book garnered another reader of Wharton. "I didn't know anything about Edith Wharton until now," Susan Middleston, the former owner of the book, marveled. "I hadn't even read her works, but I am now, starting with *The Age of Innocence.*"[37] Books of Wharton's remain at large; the librarian is approached from time to time by people in possession of books that somehow wandered off, which has sparked the mission to return them to what I feel is their rightful place.

In *A Skeptic's Guide to Writers' Houses,* Anne Trubek explores the holy grails of these storied homesteads: "[Writers' houses] aim to do the impossible: to make physical—to make real—acts of literary imagination. Going to a writer's house is a fool's errand. We will never find our favorite characters or admired techniques within these houses; we can't join Huck on the raft or experience Faulkner's stream of consciousness. We can only walk through empty rooms full of pitchers and paintings and stoves."[38] Because Wharton participated in the design of The Mount, there is already reason enough to visit the home. While the furnishings are not original, the literary tourist can glimpse modern equivalents of Wharton's philosophies from *The Decoration of Houses* at work. Though a visitor cannot sit in a Louis XV chair that Wharton owned, she can hold in her hand a volume that the author pored over and annotated (or corrected, in the case of her own works).

Trubek invokes poststructuralist theory and Roland Barthes's essay "The Death of the Author," which argues for the reader's dismissal of the author's presence altogether, encouraging the disregard of authorial intention and biography in particular. She concurs: "Those who believe otherwise, those who worship at the shrine of the 'great man,' who are fascinated by trivialities like Shakespeare's mistress, Shelley's early death, or Hemingway's drinking, have it all wrong. They are unsophisticated readers mired in a middlebrow concept of individuality and celebrity gossip, a realm of literature loving that Barthes calls "ordinary culture."[39] There is a false hierarchy here: the notion that the interest in the life of an author beyond understanding words on a page is "middlebrow" or unsophisticated posits that any aspect of so-called ordinary life is unsophisticated—residences, relationships, lives, deaths—and prevents access to the work.[40] Not everyone is a writer, but everyone lives somewhere—and can potentially better understand an author through her or his home.

That the library is at the house and not in the Beinecke Collection at Yale or in private hands makes it accessible to more readers of Wharton, who are more likely to visit her home than to make an appointment to peruse the Yale archives, suiting Wharton's admiration of Whitman's democratic vision. In "Song of Myself," Wharton left a checkmark next to the line "Not words of routine this song of mine" (line 42). In "Song of the Open Road," she bracketed the line "To know the universe itself as a road, as many roads, as roads for traveling souls," underlining the last four words. Whitman's words resonated for Wharton; readers of Wharton's books and of her life know that the lines are apt descriptions of her courageous legacy. The posthumous history of Wharton's books, dispersed to a number of libraries, some destroyed, some intact, mirrors Wharton's personal trajectory: lives built in a variety of places, some destroyed while others survived.

In 1971, The Mount was one of the first National Historic Landmarks dedicated to women. Today, Wharton's legacy lives on in both academic and popular culture. As 2012 was the 150th anniversary of her birth, the author and her work have lately been celebrated in exhibits, academic conferences, articles, and books. But the reconstruction of her legacy that is perhaps most meaningful is the return of the contents of her library to The Mount. The library constitutes much more than a design of yesteryear's upper class, or a room to tour. There are books to open, lines to consider, pencil marks to ponder. The books also have lives beyond the house; as Ramsden notes in his introduction to the catalog of the library, Wharton gave cameo roles to her own books in her novels. In *The House of Mirth,* Lily Bart picks up a first edition of La Bruyère's *Les Caractères* (1688) during both her first and last visits to Selden's library. Wharton's writings, in her novels and in her war reportage, tell one story about her; her reading habits, in multiple languages, across a spectrum of subjects and disciplines, tell another. It is fitting that both these stories are once again housed in a structure of her design.

## NOTES

I would like to thank The Mount's librarian, Nynke Dorhout, for her generous guidance and assistance.

1. As is evident in other chapters in this volume, many literary sites had other existences before they were made into museums, whether authors died or moved away, or furnishings were dispersed long before preservation efforts began.
2. Edith Wharton, *A Backward Glance* (1934; repr., New York: Scribner, 1964), 294.
3. Books in the library came from the libraries of Walter Berry, Morton Fullerton, Charles Eliot Norton, Henry James, Bernard Berenson, and Theodore Roosevelt.
4. Edith Wharton, "The Fullness of Life," *Scribner's Magazine* 14, no. 6 (December 1893): 700.
5. Carol Singley, *Edith Wharton: Matters of Mind and Spirit* (New York: Cambridge University Press, 1998), xi.
6. Ogden Codman and Edith Wharton, *The Decoration of Houses* (New York: Scribner's, 1897).
7. Wharton built a summer home in Lenox, Massachusetts, a town whose prior literary residents included Nathaniel Hawthorne, Herman Melville, and Fanny Kemble.
8. Wharton, *Backward Glance,* 106.
9. *The Letters of Edith Wharton,* ed. R. W. B. Lewis and Nancy Lewis (New York: Macmillan, 1988), 242.
10. Wharton, *Backward Glance,* 125.
11. Ibid., 52. Wharton's father borrowed books from the New York Society Library. In an essay accompanying the library's exhibit of Wharton's father's borrowing practices, Harriet Shapiro notes that both sides of Wharton's family had used the library for generations, with Wharton's maternal great-grandfather listed in the earliest surviving ledger from 1789–1792. See Harriet Shapiro, "Keeping Up with the Joneses at the New York Society Library," in *Edith Wharton's New York City: A Backward Glance,* exh. cat. (New York: New York Society Library, 2012), 16.
12. Wharton, *Backward Glance,* 64.
13. Some of the Wharton books in Kenneth Clark's collection (before they were passed on to his son Colin) were destroyed by a fire in his London home, while others became

damp-stained in his Saltwood Castle library. See George Ramsden, *Edith Wharton's Library: A Catalogue Compiled by George Ramsden* (Settrington: Stone Trough Books, 1999), xvi.

14. See Alan Cowell, "After a Century, an American Writer's Library Will Go to America," *New York Times,* December 15, 2005. Some of Wharton's books still have "Saltwood Castle" (the name of Sir Kenneth Clark's residence) penciled inside.
15. During the First World War, Wharton labored to assist those displaced from their homes in France and Belgium. She established various relief organizations and refugee housing, and was appalled by images she saw firsthand at the front of houses reduced to rubble and lives exposed. See Edith Wharton, *French Ways and Their Meaning* (New York: D. Appleton and Company, 1919). The next war, of course, would destroy some of her own prized possessions.
16. Ramsden published a limited-edition run of a catalog of the library that includes the condition of each book, the provenance and donor information (if known), highlights of markings, and connections to Wharton's texts and letters.
17. Today, the Sainte-Claire home in Hyères houses government offices.
18. In *A Backward Glance* she wrote: "I used to say that I had been taught only two things in my childhood: the modern languages and good manners. Now that I have lived to see both these branches of culture dispensed with, I perceive that there are worse systems of education." Wharton, *A Backward Glance,* 48.
19. Friedrich Schiller, *Gedichte* (Whitefish, Mont.: Kessinger Publishing, 2010).
20. *Letters of Edith Wharton,* 238.
21. Wharton was a cousin of Theodore Roosevelt's second wife, Edith. Roosevelt provided the introduction to *The Book of the Homeless,* a collection of art and letters that Wharton assembled to raise funds for refugees during the First World War. In the introduction he wrote: "We owe to Mrs. Wharton all the assistance we can give. We owe this assistance to the good name of America, and above all for the cause of humanity we owe it to the children, the women and the old men who have suffered such dreadful wrong for absolutely no fault of theirs." Theodore Roosevelt, introduction to *The Book of the Homeless* (New York: Charles Scribner, 1916), x. Wharton included a eulogy to him in her 1926 volume *Twelve Poems.*
22. Wharton, *A Backward Glance,* 51.
23. Barbara Hochman links these perceptions of high and low literary cultures to Wharton's magazine piece. See Edith Wharton, "The Vice of Reading," *North American Review* 177, no. 563 (October 1903): 513–21.
24. In light of Wharton's interest in Transcendentalism, the seal on Lily Bart's stationery in *The House of Mirth* ("Beyond!") takes on a different connotation.
25. Walt Whitman, *Leaves of Grass* (Boston: Small, Maynard, and Company, 1897), 1–2.
26. Ralph Waldo Emerson, "The Over-Soul," in *Essays: First Series* (New York: Riverside, 1884), 221, and "Love," ibid., 139. See also Emerson's *Poems* (New York: Riverside, 1884).
27. Ralph Waldo Emerson, "Prudence," in *Essays,* 47.
28. In a letter to W. Morton Fullerton in October 1912, Wharton advised, "You've read too much French & too much Times. I can't too strongly urge you to drop both tongues for a few weeks, & go back to English—to what Arnold called 'prose of the centre.' Read Emerson, read Tyndall, read Froud[e] even, read Arnold—get away from authors of your own métier, from all the scientific-politico-economic charabia of your own specialists into the clear air of the born writers." *Letters of Edith Wharton,* 281.
29. Wharton's notes for an unfinished essay on Whitman are with her papers at Yale's Beinecke Library. In her outline she wrote that Whitman offered the best examples of (1) description of nature, (2) human sympathy, and (3) cosmic philosophy. See "Whitman, Walt, Sketch of an Essay on, with notes, holograph manuscript," box 19, folder 615, Edith Wharton Collection. Yale Collection of American Literature, Beinecke Rare Book and Manuscript Library, Yale University.

30. Wharton was so fascinated by the poet that she made him a character in her New York novella *The Spark* (1924).
31. *Letters of Edith Wharton,* 159.
32. Henry James, "Mr. Walt Whitman," *The Nation* 1 (November 16, 1865): 625–26.
33. *Letters of Edith Wharton,* 125.
34. Edith Wharton to Lavinia Davis, 1933, The Mount.
35. In a June 8, 1925, letter to Fitzgerald, she wrote: "I have been wandering for the last weeks and found your novel—with its friendly dedication—awaiting me on my arrival here a few days ago. . . . Meanwhile, let me say at once how much I like Gatsby, or rather His Book, & how great a leap I think you have taken this time—in advance upon your pervious work. My present quarrel with you is only this: that to make Gatsby really Great, you ought to have given us his early career (not from the cradle—but from his first visit to the yacht, if not before) instead of a short résumé of it. That would have situated him & made his final tragedy a tragedy instead of a 'fait divers' for the morning papers." *Letters of Edith Wharton,* 481–82.
36. Ibid., 480.
37. Quoted in Claire Cox, "Edith Wharton's Copy of Jane Eyre Returns to The Mount in Lenox," *Berkshire Eagle* (Pittsfield, Mass.), November 11, 2012.
38. Anne Trubek, *A Skeptic's Guide to Writers' Houses* (Philadelphia: University of Pennsylvania Press, 2010), 5.
39. Ibid., 16.
40. Relatedly, and ironically, Trubek's objection to Walt Whitman's home in Camden, New Jersey, is that it is ordinary. But of course Whitman celebrated the ordinary in his poetry. Ibid., 20.

# 8

# *Making a Little House*

## Literary Tourism at Rocky Ridge Farm

MICHELLE McCLELLAN

---

*Historic sites that are devoted to celebrating the homes and haunts of women are exceedingly rare. Writers like the Warners, Wharton, and Laura Ingalls Wilder are among the few female figures who dot this historic landscape. In this chapter, Michelle McClellan takes on the many sites that celebrate Laura Ingalls Wilder, whose "Little House" books made a series of rough-hewn midwestern domestic scenes part of the American imaginary. But what of the house that Wilder lived in as an adult when she wrote her semi-autobiographical tales? A comfortable, well-equipped early twentieth-century Missouri farmhouse, it does not always live up to the log cabin myth that Wilder helped popularize among her readers. Exploring how this house, called Rocky Ridge, has become part of the Wilder tourism circuit, and providing meaningful interpretation about Wilder's adult life and work as farmer and writer, McClellan reminds us of the connections and divergences between the author's labor and her literary creations.*

---

Few American homes are as familiar today as the "Little House," the iconic emblem of the enormously popular series of books in which Laura Ingalls Wilder recounts her childhood in the Upper Midwest and Great Plains during the 1870s and 1880s. Selling millions of copies in dozens of languages since publication in the 1930s and 1940s, the eight-volume series has epitomized the American pioneer experience for generations of readers in the United States and around the world. Transcending their status as classics of children's literature, the books have become a cultural and marketing phenomenon. A popular television program loosely based on the books ran on NBC during the 1970s and 1980s, and a myriad of spin-off products, including picture books, paper dolls, and prequels purporting to recount the lives of Wilder's mother and grandmother, appeared in the 1990s. The "Little House" idiom has become widely used in popular culture, even among those who are relatively unfamiliar with the original book series.

Generations of readers have affirmed that much of the power of the books comes from their presumed factual accuracy. Furthermore, as the titles of the books suggest (*Little House in the Big Woods, Little House on the Prairie, On the Banks of Plum Creek,* and so forth), location and setting shape the stories in crucial ways. It is no accident that "Little House" serves as the brand of the series; making and remaking home is a central theme as the Ingalls family repeatedly moves on in search of a better life. Readers have delighted in the detailed descriptions Wilder provides of home construction techniques and household tasks of the late nineteenth century. Given the well-defined sense of place in these texts, it is not surprising that fans began to seek out the locations so described, as well as visiting Wilder herself at her home in Mansfield, Missouri.

Following Wilder's death in 1957, organized commemorative efforts began in Mansfield and in De Smet, South Dakota, the setting of four of her books. Through the 1960s and 1970s, tourism increased in these communities and elsewhere, as other towns realized their Little House connections and the television show brought additional attention. There are now Little House destinations in Wisconsin, Minnesota, Kansas, and upstate New York, as well as South Dakota and Missouri. Even places with a relatively tangential relationship to the series have marked (and marketed) themselves as Little House sites, such as Burr Oak, Iowa (an interlude that Wilder left out of her books), and Spring Valley, Minnesota (where the Wilder family lived only briefly with Almanzo Wilder's parents). The *Little House Guidebook* lists eight developed sites, along with other locations associated with the Ingalls and Wilder families, such as the school for the blind in Iowa that Laura's sister Mary attended during the 1880s, and the home in San Francisco where Laura's daughter Rose lived in the early twentieth century.[1]

Today, the established sites attract more than ten thousand visitors each year, with many fans traveling to all or at least most of the Little House locations. Tourists document their journeys on blogs and in memoirs such as *The Wilder Life: My Adventures in the Lost World of "Little House on the Prairie"* by Wendy McClure (2011) and *My Life as Laura: How I Searched for Laura Ingalls Wilder and Found Myself* (2011), in which Kelly Kathleen Ferguson recounts how she completed a Little House circuit while wearing nineteenth-century prairie attire.[2] All of these accounts help build networks of like-minded fans. The recently formed Laura Ingalls Wilder Legacy and Research Association (beyondlittlehouse.com) promotes interest in and financial support for the

FIGURE 8.1. Rocky Ridge farmhouse during the 1930s, when Wilder began the *Little House* series of books. *Photo by Kucker Studio. Courtesy of the Herbert Hoover Presidential Library–Museum, National Archives and Records Administration.*

sites; its conference event, "Laurapalooza," included a trip to Walnut Grove, Minnesota, the locale of *On the Banks of Plum Creek.*

In most of the locations described in the books, few structures remain that are directly associated with the Ingalls family, who tended to move on after only a few years in each place. A first task for civic groups in those communities that seek to remake themselves into Little House destinations is to identify and restore any extant structures that can be connected with the Ingalls family. Those locations that lack such resources must rely on reconstructions and plaques to indicate where buildings used to be or mark other points of interest to Little House readers.[3]

In contrast to the transience of the Ingalls family and the small and temporary qualities of many of their homes as described in the Little House books, Wilder spent the majority of her adult life in a comfortable farmhouse that she and her husband built in the Missouri Ozarks (fig. 8.1). Wilder did not mention this property, which she christened Rocky Ridge Farm, in any of the Little House books published during her lifetime, because the series concluded with her marriage in the Dakota Territory.[4] Ironically, Rocky Ridge

Farm is by far the most intact site associated with the Ingalls and Wilder families, and the one with the closest connection to the lived experience of the historical person Laura Ingalls Wilder. Rocky Ridge Farm represents the ultimate success of Laura and Almanzo Wilder in their lives, but it is beyond the narrative arc of the Little House series. The very existence of the site could invite visitors to consider an inherent tension between the youthful protagonist of the books and the elderly author behind them. It also provides important clues to the complex relationship between Wilder and her daughter Rose Wilder Lane, a well-known writer during the 1920s and 1930s and, later, an influential theorist in the development of the Libertarian movement in the United States.[5] As an adult, Lane lived on the farm with her parents, remaking the landscape just as she edited her mother's manuscripts. Wilder and Lane understood both homemaking and writing to be creative processes, intertwined in many ways, since the two women drew on pioneering and farming as subjects for journalism and literature, while income earned from writing enabled them to pay for improvements to the property.[6]

The integration of Rocky Ridge Farm into the Little House cultural narrative demonstrates how literary tourism has the potential to reify or destabilize complicated connections among fiction, biography, history, and community identity. Literary tourists seeking to understand Laura Ingalls Wilder can draw on overlapping and potentially contradictory forms of evidence: the published books, including both the original series and volumes added after Wilder's death; the historical record and recent research, including major biographies of Wilder and Lane; and the historic sites themselves. Rocky Ridge Farm was understood by the Wilders as a self-consciously modern project, one that conveyed particular messages about country life in an era of rapid urbanization and industrialization. It also had a regional specificity that served as the setting for some of Lane's writing, a geographical identity quite different from the prairies and plains of the upper Midwest. Today, however, the cultural resonance and nostalgic appeal of the Little House books—and the interpretive choices at Rocky Ridge Farm that link the property primarily to that series—obscure the complex meanings the house and farm once had, flattening out distinctions between different historical periods and places. The immense popularity of the Little House books and the tangible landscape of Rocky Ridge Farm work together here, and the powerful fusion of literary and place-based evidence elevates some narratives while effacing others.

Laura Ingalls was born in Wisconsin in 1867 and then traveled with her family through Kansas and Minnesota, as her parents sought to make a living on a series of marginal farms. They finally settled in De Smet, Dakota Territory, where Laura married Almanzo Wilder in 1885 and gave birth to their daughter Rose the following year. After years of drought and crop failures, along with severe illness and the death of an infant son, the young family moved to Missouri in 1894, settling just outside the small town of Mansfield in the southwestern part of the state.[7] By one measure, Wilder's career as a writer began with this trip. She kept a travel diary and sent an account of the journey back to the local paper in De Smet, which printed it. Wilder saved the clipping in her scrapbook with the notation "First I ever had published."[8] Soon after their arrival in Missouri, the Wilders purchased forty acres. They lived at first in a log cabin on the farm, then moved to town so both Laura and Almanzo could earn wages. As they established themselves, they gradually added more acreage to the farm and constructed a farmhouse over a period of more than fifteen years, from 1896 to 1913.[9]

Wilder began a career as a writer as well. Although her formal education had ended with high school (from which she did not even graduate), she grew up in a family in which reading and writing were very important. Like her mother before her, Wilder taught school prior to her marriage, and the family worked and sacrificed so that her older sister Mary could attend a college for the blind. The few books they owned, and other reading material they acquired occasionally such as church youth magazines, were treasured objects for the Ingalls family, to be enjoyed communally as they were read aloud. Similarly, Lane recalled a cherished ritual from her own childhood, when Wilder would read aloud from books Lane brought home from the school library for an hour after supper to her husband and child gathered around the fire. Despite—or because of—their poverty, both the Ingalls and Wilder families considered such reading practices to be important for self-improvement as well as pleasure and family intimacy.

Such recognition of the power of reading no doubt informed Wilder's ambitions as a writer as well. While the Little House books are the most well known of her publications, and their appearance when she was in her sixties and seventies gave rise to the notion that she produced these books effortlessly from a faultless memory combined with a previously untapped literary talent, Wilder actually wrote extensively for regional, and occasionally national, publications in a genre that might be characterized as "farm journalism." When the editor of the regional publication *The Missouri Ruralist* learned of Wilder's expertise in poultry raising and her ability to articulate issues of concern to rural women, as she was increasingly demonstrating through civic involvement, he encouraged her writing, which eventually led to a regular column called "As a Farm Woman Thinks."[10] In feature articles and in her column, Wilder presented Rocky Ridge Farm as an idealized model of progressive rural living, one that was especially resonant in light of Americans' increasing anxiety about the fate of rural families during the rapid urbanization and economic dislocations of the early twentieth century.[11] Wilder intended her writings to be a counterpoint to that anxiety. You don't need to move to the city for modern conveniences, she insisted to her readers, and staying in the country allows freedom, independence, and self-sufficiency that are impossible in the city.[12]

Feature articles, including a few with the byline A. J. (Almanzo) Wilder, introduced readers to Rocky Ridge Farm, recounting the Wilders' move from South Dakota, their acquisition of the property, and their tireless efforts at improvement ever since. In one such profile, ostensibly written by Almanzo, he recalled that the farm looked "unpromising enough" initially, contrasting sharply with the level prairies he had left behind. But, he explained, his wife had "taken violent fancy to this particular piece of land"; the couple then set to work to realize the farm's potential. Details about crops, acreage, and net profits communicated accomplishment and success, made possible through expertise and dedication. By 1911, when this article was written and the farmhouse was near completion, the farm was no longer rocky, but the name served as a constant reminder of how much had been accomplished, of "the battles we have fought and won," and conveyed "a touch of sentiment and an added value to the place."[13]

As the resonance attached to the name of the farm suggests, financial security, while important, was not the whole story. Country life brought many advantages over city living, from the opportunity to be outdoors and enjoy better health, to a contentedness that came from self-knowledge and emotional independence.[14] While the Wilder farm comprised one hundred acres at the time these articles were published, Laura Wilder insisted that the same way of life could be achieved on much smaller properties, even as little as five acres. She explained how labor-saving devices had fundamentally altered farm work, especially for women, and described ingenious schemes for bringing running water (both hot and cold) into the kitchen, bathroom, cellar, and barnyard. Other technological and social improvements, such as telephones and circulating libraries, eroded the isolation that once may have characterized rural life. In short, Wilder proclaimed that the rural-to-urban migration of this period in American history should be reversed, and would soon be. "There is a movement in the United States today," she informed readers, one that is "widespread, and very far reaching in its consequences. People are seeking after a freer, healthier, happier life. They are tired of the noise and dirt, bad air and crowds of the cities and are turning longing eyes toward the green slopes, wooded hills, pure running water and health giving breezes of the country." This did not mean going backward, Wilder emphasized. Indeed, she admonished her readers, "Keep up with the march of progress for the time is coming when the cities will be the workshops of the world and abandoned to the workers, while the real cultured, social and intellectual life will be in the country."[15]

Just as Rocky Ridge Farm expanded in acreage, so was the house gradually transformed from a rude log cabin to an impressive showplace. Large by local standards, the farmhouse at Rocky Ridge boasted modern conveniences and unique design elements. This home represented an exceptional achievement, one that gave Wilder the authority to dispense advice to other farm women even as she reminded readers that she shared their interests and concerns.[16] As with modern-day coffee table books about authors' homes, Wilder's domestic, design, and writing skills were linked. But if the exquisite taste of famous writers is considered to be an "effortless byproduct of their artistic genius," as Ben De Bruyn writes in his chapter in this volume, Wilder's trajectory was the opposite. Her success as a farm woman gave her license to write.

For aesthetic and ideological as well as practical reasons, the Wilders constructed the home using natural materials from the farm itself. As Wilder explained in a 1920 column, "I have a fancy that the farm home should seem to be a product of the soil where it is reared, a permanent growth, as it were, of conditions surrounding it wherever this is possible."[17] The Wilders' fireplace was formed by three large rocks found on the property, while the beams and extensive woodwork in the parlor and other areas of the house were milled from trees on the farm. Later observers have speculated that Wilder may have been influenced by the Arts and Crafts movement and the designs of Frank Lloyd Wright (an almost exact contemporary of hers), as suggested especially by the square columns and woodwork in the parlor.[18] The use of materials from the farm also comported with self-sufficiency, a value that the Wilders frequently expressed.

The organization and use of interior spaces also provided lessons in how to live. Wilder was especially proud of a library nook off the parlor, and the acquisition of enough books to fill it—rather than reliance on a lending library—marked an economic, even more than an intellectual, achievement. Detailed articles with extensive illustrations appeared in the national magazine *The Country Gentleman* in 1925 describing the kitchen and dining room. The kitchen was portrayed as a modern workshop for the up-to-date farm wife, while the dining room piece presented an image of gracious living.[19] Wilder's own home thus served as evidence for her assertions about the satisfactions of rural life.

As these depictions of domestic spaces indicate, Wilder's columns and articles also communicated messages about gender roles in country life. Although she eschewed the term "feminism," Wilder insisted that farms provided particular advantages for women. For farms to succeed, she insisted, women must be true partners with their husbands. But because a farm was also a home, a farm woman's ambitions and financial contributions did not compete with her family commitments, as women's paid work could often do in cities, but rather strengthened them.[20] In addition to strong marriages and a sense of achievement, farm women enjoyed active social lives and maintained community networks, countering the stereotype of rural women as isolated and ignorant. Well known as an active clubwoman and gracious hostess, Wilder urged other women to seize the advantages inherent in country life: "I must say if there are any country women who are wasting their time envying their sisters in the city—don't do it. Such an attitude is out of date."[21] In all these writings, Wilder brilliantly combined the self-consciously traditional—and supposedly timeless—values of hard work, perseverance, and ingenuity with a celebration of progress, all realized in the achievement of Rocky Ridge Farm and the self-sufficient lifestyle it seemed to represent.

These connections between writing and home intensified with the return of Rose Wilder Lane to Rocky Ridge Farm during the 1920s. Lane had left home at an early age, completing high school with her aunt Eliza Jane Wilder in Louisiana, training in telegraphy in Kansas City, and then moving to San Francisco, where she embarked on a career in real estate and, ultimately, journalism. In turn, her writing career allowed her to move to New York and to travel extensively in Europe. Throughout, she fostered her mother's writing efforts, editing her mother's work and using her own contacts to place some of Wilder's pieces in national magazines.[22] Both women viewed Wilder's venture into writing as a way to augment farm income, even as the content of her publications celebrated agricultural self-sufficiency. Now back at Rocky Ridge Farm, Lane launched two projects: constructing a new home for her parents on the property, and urging her mother to pursue publication for her autobiographical manuscript "Pioneer Girl."

One of the highest-paid writers in the United States during the 1920s, Lane spared no expense in the design and construction of the Rock House, as it has become known, embellishing a Sears plan home so that it resembled an English stone cottage. Lane's stated intent was to provide her parents with a more stylish and convenient home. Yet her desire to move her parents out of the farmhouse they had created and into a home she built suggests that family relationships, especially between mother and daughter, were complex, as other scholars have discussed at some length.[23] Lane immersed herself in construction details, hiring contractors and professionals and purchasing materials from the nearby city of Springfield, Missouri, in contrast to the origin story of the farmhouse, which celebrates self-sufficiency. Over the Christmas holiday in 1928, Laura and Almanzo moved into the Rock House, and Lane took over the farmhouse for her own use and that of her friends, other writers who came to stay with her for months, even years, at a time.[24]

Although Wilder no longer wrote for *The Missouri Ruralist,* she remained interested in writing and composed her memoir, "Pioneer Girl." The 1929 stock market crash (which erased much of the savings accumulated by Lane and the Wilders) and the ongoing economic pressures of the Great Depression provided further motivation to pursue publication. In a collaborative process that was obscured at the time, but has since been scrutinized by scholars and debated by fans, Wilder, with Lane's editorial help and publishing connections, embarked on the first volume of what would become the Little House books.[25] *Little House in the Big Woods* was published by Harper and Brothers in 1932. Subsequent volumes followed, as the two women passed ideas and manuscript pages between the Rock House and the farmhouse. Lane also continued with her own writing during this period, some of it featuring local Ozark characters and settings, while other stories and novels were set in the Great Plains, drawing on her parents' experiences.[26] Given her literary celebrity and wide-ranging travel, Lane was a frequent guest speaker at her mother's club meetings and other community events. During these years, Lane also battled depression and ambivalent feelings toward her mother, which she documented at length in her journal.[27] By the mid-1930s, Lane resolved to leave Rocky Ridge Farm. When she moved away, first to Columbia, Missouri, for a writing project and then to New York City, Laura and Almanzo moved back into the farmhouse.[28] The Rock House was later sold.

As the Little House book series was completed in 1943 and then reissued with illustrations by Garth Williams in 1953, it became enormously popular.[29] The books were translated into other languages, used extensively in schools, and adapted for the radio. Wilder received considerable recognition both locally and nationally. The Mansfield public library was named in her honor, and she was a frequent guest of honor at area club meetings and events. She received large amounts of fan mail from readers, especially children, and she was invited to address the Detroit Book Fair in 1937. Several of the books in the series were designated Newberry Honor titles, and a new award in children's literature was established in her name. The children's rooms at public libraries in Detroit and Pomona, California, were named for her. Through all this, Lane's role in the production of the Little House books received no attention, furthering the idea that Wilder had crafted them herself, basing them only on her childhood memories.

Wilder's death in 1957 allowed, even seemed to require, a fresh assessment of her legacy, especially by residents of the places where she had lived. In Mansfield and in De Smet, citizens simultaneously paid tribute to Wilder and to the Little House books and asserted particular claims to her in the context of their current community identity. Laura and Almanzo had not lived in De Smet for over sixty years, only returning a few times late in their lives, and by 1957 almost no structures remained that had any direct connection with them—certainly no clear focal point like Rocky Ridge Farm. Yet De Smet had been the longtime home of much of the rest of the Ingalls family, particularly Charles and Caroline Ingalls (Pa and Ma) and Laura's sister Mary, and it was the setting of four of the Little House books. These factors made it relatively easy to integrate the texts into community history; after all, Wilder's books described events that had occurred in that place, during the founding era of the town. So seamless is the identification that today, De Smet bills itself (borrowing the title of one of the books) as "THE Little Town on the Prairie." The local scale intersects with the national here, since Wilder, like Henry David Thoreau, discussed elsewhere in this volume, became closely associated with a particular place that stood for larger, inherently "American" qualities. The Little House books are quintessential pioneer stories, and so their setting—the prairie as the frontier West—is fundamental, reinforced by the very titles and "brand" of the series.

Meanwhile in Mansfield, Rocky Ridge Farm loomed large as a possible memorial, but the situation was complicated. The Wilders had sold the property, retaining only a life lease, which allowed them to live in the house and receive an income of $50 per month from the buyer.[30] Almanzo died in 1949, and at Laura's death in February 1957, the buyer was free to assume control of the entire property. Local residents formed a committee to manage the Wilder legacy in and for the community, inspired in large measure by the depth of interest expressed in letters and inquiries they received from fans outside Mansfield. "Realizing the national renown of its late authoress, Mrs. Laura Ingalls Wilder, Mansfield citizens have started a movement to make a shrine of her home, which is located east of Mansfield on Highway 60," reported a local paper.[31] Citizens consulted Lane, who had inherited her mother's literary estate though not the farm itself. Lane proposed that the Mansfield public library move into the house, thus combining the functions of museum and library, with living quarters for the librarian on the second floor. Others expressed concern that the home was located too far out of town to serve as a library or any kind of attraction or memorial.[32] Local women's clubs organized an open house at Rocky Ridge, which was announced in the local newspaper. Although the home was identified as that of "the late authoress," her literary renown was not the only appeal. "This will be an opportunity for many in the Ozarks to see the interior of the Wilder farm home," the notice announced.[33] This phrasing suggests that, at this time, the house itself represented a local attraction independent of the books, shaped by Wilder's regional renown as a farm woman and hostess, and perhaps by curiosity over how the Wilders might have spent their book royalties on furnishings and décor.

Attendance at the open house numbered five hundred people, which may have convinced those who had been skeptical of the practicality of Rocky Ridge Farm as a memorial. Local citizens formed a nonprofit association, fund-raising began in earnest, and Lane contributed $7,500 for the association to purchase the farmhouse and three acres from the couple who had bought it from her parents and who continued to farm the remainder of the property.[34] Furnishing the home was another matter, since Wilder had bequeathed much of the contents of the house to a younger couple who had helped care for her and Almanzo in their later years. Lane continued to correspond with this couple regarding the disposition of some of the Wilder belongings for several years, even after the home had been opened to visitors. Having long since moved away from Missouri herself, Lane attempted to manage these affairs from a distance, reassuring the couple that of course her mother had wanted them to have these items, but asking them to consider whether the objects might be better in the farmhouse, now open to the public.[35] Volunteers converted the Wilders' bedroom into an exhibit space for artifacts, provided maintenance, and led tours for visitors. A continuous need for funds led to the development of a gift shop, and visitation increased. Lane arranged for a local couple, L. D. and Irene Lichty, to become curators of the site. In 1963 she built a home for them on the property, near the farmhouse, thus institutionalizing their role and altering the landscape significantly.[36]

Although the nonprofit association officially oversaw the home and property, Lane clearly retained considerable influence in shaping her mother's legacy. Her actions illuminate, even as they created, some of the interpretive challenges that face Rocky Ridge Farm as a literary tourism destination even today. In 1962 Lane published *On the Way Home,* in which she provides retrospective framing essays for the concise travel diary that Wilder kept during the family's 1894 journey to Missouri. This juxtaposition can make the book an unsettling text for devoted Little House fans who come to it after reading the original series but without knowledge of the Wilders' later life. While Lane's introduction provides some measure of transition, explaining how and why the family moved to Missouri, even the title can be confusing, because Laura and Almanzo seem fully rooted in the Dakota Territory at the end of the series, whether the hopeful ending of *These Happy Golden Years,* the original capstone title, or even *The First Four Years,* published posthumously in 1971. Although the latter book chronicles the hardships and tragedies that, in reality, drove the young family away from Dakota and ultimately to Missouri, the text itself concludes with Wilder's determination to succeed where they are, despite the obstacles they face. "Home" would therefore seem to be the prairie, not the Missouri Ozarks.

*On the Way Home* thus offers fascinating connections across place and time, and between the authorial voices of mother and daughter. Its publication also reflects the literary, domestic, and financial concerns that animated the careers of Wilder and Lane, as well as the relationship between the two women. In the epilogue she wrote for this volume, almost exactly fifty years after the farmhouse was completed, Lane recalled her mother's vision: "It would be a white house, she said, all built from our farm. Everything we needed to build it was on the land: good oak beams and boards, stones for the foundation and the fireplace," and so on for two paragraphs, including plans for built-in bookcases. The language here echoes Wilder's farm journalism, and of course it perfectly matches the house as it was ultimately built. In case the message was not clear, the lengthy description is adjacent to a photograph of the house, with the caption "Laura's dream realized."[37] The fulfillment of Wilder's goals for the farm thus takes on an air of inevitability through the feedback loop of textual description (even if only retrospective) and tangible structure. Lane's masterly alignment of literary with architectural evidence reinforces the notion that all the Little House books are historically accurate and shapes the interpretive options available at Rocky Ridge Farm. The fact that Lane published *On the Way Home* in large part to help raise money for the museum only highlights the continuing links between writing and home, even if "home" was now a literary site open to tourists.

The complications of reacquiring the house and artifacts, and the self-consciousness with which Lane at least approached the presentation of Rocky Ridge Farm, have been minimized in the interpretation of the home for visitors. Although the Wilders' bedroom was initially given over to display cases, those were later removed to foster the impression that everything remains exactly as it was at the time of Wilder's death. Even the kitchen calendar is still turned to February 1957, the month she died.[38] The decision to interpret the home to the moment of 1957 obscures Lane's presence, including the changes she made to the home while she lived in it during the 1920s and 1930s. Her role is rendered even less visible because the second floor, where she wrote and slept, is not open to visitors. On guided tours, which is the only way tourists can view the interior of the house, docents emphasize Laura and Almanzo's hard work and ingenuity, repeating that they built this home with their own hands, using materials from the farm, and lived here for more than half a century. In these ways, the tour echoes many of the themes that Wilder explored in *The Missouri Ruralist,* even though those writings are not nearly as well known as the Little House books.

Outside the farmhouse, the landscape has also changed over the years, enriching but also complicating visitors' understanding of the relationship between the Laura in the books and the lived experience of Wilder and her family. Rose Wilder Lane, who died in 1968, had no surviving children. In 1971 her legal heir provided funds to build a separate museum on the grounds, and, significantly, he donated many of Lane's personal effects as well. For more than four decades, this museum offered a treasure trove of Ingalls-Wilder memorabilia, but the museum building was squeezed between Rocky Ridge farmhouse and the ranch-style home that Lane had built for the Lichtys as longtime curators. This constellation of buildings created a profoundly different cultural landscape from that experienced by the Wilders when they lived on the farm. When Laura and Almanzo walked out of their farmhouse, they did not confront the museum on their very doorstep. Recognizing that this building arrangement detracted from the setting and contradicted the expectations of many visitors to see an isolated farmhouse amidst bucolic scenery, the stewards of Rocky Ridge Farm launched a new master plan in the 2010s to return the landscape more closely to what the Wilders would have known. A new museum building opened in April 2016, farther away from the historic farmhouse. At this writing, the curators' home and the 1971 museum building were still standing, but ultimately they will likely be removed.

Moving the museum protected the integrity of the farmhouse as an artifact but it did not solve fundamental challenges in historic site interpretation, particularly those associated with writers. In the original museum, objects were presented chronologically, with one section devoted to Lane's career. Yet there was no overarching interpretation or even designation of items as more or less important. The lack of labels or clear exhibit organization meant that visitors depended on their existing knowledge to assign meaning to what they saw, creating a hierarchy among tourists, as discussed in Hilary Iris Lowe's essay in this volume. The most salient objects in the museum for most viewers were those that Wilder mentioned in the Little House books, leaving casual fans familiar only with the television show confused, especially by family photographs. In the new museum, there are fewer artifacts and more interpretive labels, but the focus on the Little House books remains central; if anything, Lane's role is reduced even more.

For devoted fans who have read the books many times, the experience of seeing items described in the books in three-dimensional reality remains emotionally powerful, a reaction that brings strong interpretive consequences. The most famous artifact is "Pa's fiddle," which some fans consider a relic of near sacred proportions because of its rich symbolic role in the books. This instrument, which belonged to Laura's father, Charles Ingalls, retains pride of place in the new museum. The fiddle and other items that can be recognized from the texts reinforce the notion that the Little House series is not fiction but history, and that the books and the site are eminently accurate and trustworthy.

Even as the presence of these artifacts reassures visitors that the stories are real, the fact that there is both a house and a museum, and the very different forms of display within them, can be jarring to tourists.[39] Although the objects in the house are not reproductions as in the cabin at Walden Pond, this division between the house as a museum and an adjunct facility filled with objects creates some of the same ambiguity as in Concord, where Thoreau artifacts are not in the replica cabin but in a museum across town.

This tension between a young heroine and the elderly author behind her is not unique to the Little House books, of course. The slippage between Louisa May Alcott and the character Jo from *Little Women* at Orchard House, and between Mark Twain and Huck Finn in Hannibal, Missouri, raise very similar constellations of issues.[40] Other Little House sites can address this dilemma in part by translating the Little House books into local history, an interpretive approach which also means that they can portray Laura at whatever age she lived in that place.[41] Since none of the books in the original series is set in Missouri, those who shape interpretation at Rocky Ridge Farm must choose a different strategy. For neighbors and visitors who knew Wilder or were familiar with her columns in *The Missouri Ruralist,* the home and her early writings went together; though separate genres, they could be understood as related accomplishments of a highly competent farm woman. But these days, tourists are much more likely to be visiting because of their affection for the Little House books or even the television show. Accordingly, this site has adopted the tagline "Where the Little House Books were Written." Visitors want to know where and how Wilder wrote, as is a common theme in literary tourism, as we see in other essays in this volume.[42]

Yet even this branding is not as straightforward as one might imagine. For decades, guides in the farmhouse informed tourists that Wilder had written the books in the small study off her bedroom. Docents encouraged visitors to imagine Wilder awaking in the early morning with an idea or memory and creeping into her study (so as not to wake Almanzo) to take advantage of her inspiration and jot it down. In fact, however, Wilder composed the first several books in the series while she was living in the Rock House. Once the Rock House, too, was acquired by the memorial society and opened to the public, the narrative had to change. Today a sign outside the Rock House proclaims, "The Little House Books Began Here."

However these slogans are allocated across the buildings on the property, they signal that the importance of Rocky Ridge Farm comes from its association with the Little House books, even though the site could be an attraction for other reasons: as an example of regional vernacular architecture, for its role in community history, and as a kind of informal "demonstration home" linked to Wilder's earlier writing.[43] The priority accorded the Little House books means that other interpretive possibilities are effaced, including a more nuanced attention to Lane's life and career. Unlike her parents, who moved to Mansfield as adults and were always outsiders to some degree, Lane arrived when she was a young girl and grew up in the community. She also used the Ozarks as a setting for some of her published work, and she returned to Rocky Ridge Farm as an adult, literally remaking the landscape both during her parents' lives and after their deaths. For all these reasons, Lane might have emerged as the central attraction in literary tourism at Rocky Ridge Farm. But Lane's position in Mansfield was generally more complicated than that of her parents, despite—or because of—the fact that she had grown up there. After all, she moved away repeatedly and embraced a cosmopolitan style of life that was radically different from Mansfield's ways. Moreover, the stories she wrote about such small towns were not always complimentary, while the Little House books were situated at a comfortable distance in place and time, even as they articulated traditional values that could be recognized and embraced by most Mansfield residents. Finally, the ways in which Wilder and Lane obscured Lane's role in the creation of the Little House books mean that the focus on those texts as the central meaning of Rocky Ridge Farm as a literary site leaves no obvious or straightforward place for Lane.[44]

Concentrating on Wilder as the author of the Little House books as the major interpretive framework for Rocky Ridge Farm could prompt visitors to confront a perpetual tension between the author and the character, between Wilder's twentieth-century life here and her nineteenth-century life on the prairie. Yet the more time passes, the less necessary such analysis seems to be, at least for most tourists. More than fifty years after her death, the elderly Laura Ingalls Wilder seems to be telescoping with the young Laura, as both recede into the past. The nostalgia that we can now feel for both iterations of Laura fundamentally distorts the claims that Wilder herself made about her home. She did not treat it as a frozen icon of a pioneer past but instead held it out as a dynamic symbol of modern progress. Yet it grows increasingly difficult for twenty-first-century visitors to see Rocky Ridge Farm as state-of-the-art and progressive; from our vantage point, it looks almost as quaint and primitive as a little house on the prairie. Furthermore, even as the solidity and permanence of this structure may contrast with the log cabins and claim shanties of the Little House books, the values associated with it are largely consistent: hard work, self-sufficiency, family loyalty, self-improvement through reading and writing. Such an alignment means that Rocky Ridge Farm can be assimilated into, in fact represent the culmination of, the Little House cultural framework.[45]

## NOTES

1. William Anderson, *The Little House Guidebook* (New York: HarperTrophy, 1996), includes detailed descriptions of the sites as well as brief overviews of how each was established and early tourism. Anderson is widely acknowledged as the leading expert on the history of the Ingalls and Wilder families, having conducted research and written on these topics for decades. A museum volunteer and tour guide in De Smet during the late 1960s and early 1970s, he was also centrally involved in the development of tourism there. He has served on the board of directors for the Laura Ingalls Wilder Home Association in Mansfield, which oversees Rocky Ridge Farm, and has been consulted by staff and volunteers at many other sites. William Anderson in discussion with the author, January 2009.
2. Wendy McClure, *The Wilder Life: My Adventures in the Lost World of "Little House on the Prairie"* (New York: Riverhead Books, 2011); Kelly Kathleen Ferguson, *My Life as Laura: How I Searched for Laura Ingalls Wilder and Found Myself* (Winston-Salem, N.C.: Press 53, 2011).
3. For example, the Laura Ingalls Wilder Memorial Society in De Smet, South Dakota, has restored the Surveyors' House, described in *By the Shores of Silver Lake,* and the Ingalls family home, among other structures, while the *Little House on the Prairie* site in Kansas has built a replica of the Ingalls family's log cabin as depicted in that book.
4. *The First Four Years,* Wilder's chronicle of the early years of the Wilder marriage, and *On the Way Home,* an account of the family's journey to Missouri, were published after Wilder's death.
5. The most detailed account of Lane's life and career is William Holtz, *The Ghost in the Little House: A Life of Rose Wilder Lane* (Columbia: University of Missouri Press, 1993).
6. John E. Miller discusses this connection in "The Place of 'Little Houses' in the Lives and Imaginations of Laura Ingalls Wilder and Rose Wilder Lane," in *Laura Ingalls Wilder and Rose Wilder Lane: Authorship, Place, Time and Culture* (Columbia: University of Missouri Press, 2008), 47–70.
7. A number of biographies of Laura Ingalls Wilder have appeared since the 1990s, some for young readers. The most thoroughly contextualized is John E. Miller, *Becoming Laura Ingalls Wilder: The Woman behind the Legend* (Columbia: University of Missouri Press, 1998).
8. William Anderson, ed., *A Little House Sampler* (New York: Harper and Row, 1988), 87.
9. Miller, *Becoming Laura Ingalls Wilder,* chap. 4.
10. Ibid., chap. 5; Anderson, *Sampler,* 96–97.
11. Many of these writings have now been collected and published. The discussion in the text relies on several such compilations, including Anderson, *Sampler;* and Stephen W. Hines, ed., *Little House in the Ozarks* (Nashville: Thomas Nelson, 1991).
12. Wilder was not alone during this era in articulating the appeal of the country in counterpoint to the city. See William L. Bowers, *The Country Life Movement in America, 1900–1920* (Port Washington, N.Y.: Kennikat Press, 1974). It is not clear to me how consciously Wilder identified with this movement, and it was diffuse rather than centrally organized in any case. Her vocabulary suggests that she was very familiar with the concerns that other writers and reformers articulated as part of the movement.
13. "Rocky Ridge Farm" (June 1911), in Hines, *Little House in the Ozarks,* 38–40. Although the byline reads A. J. Wilder, most scholars attribute it to Laura.

14. "Going after the Cows" (April 1923), in Hines, *Little House in the Ozarks,* 119, and "Compensation" (November 1919), ibid., 79–80.
15. Anderson, *Sampler,* 99–103. Anderson uses the title "Favors the Small Farm Home," while Hines includes a slightly different version of the same article under the title "The March of Progress" (February 1911); see Hines, *Little House in the Ozarks,* 30–33.
16. See Hines, *Little House in the Ozarks,* 173, for a short piece by John F. Case, editor of *The Missouri Ruralist,* in which he highlights Wilder's qualifications to advise other farm women.
17. "My Dream House" (March 1920), in Hines, *Little House in the Ozarks,* 34.
18. Anderson, *Guidebook,* 73.
19. Both "My Ozark Kitchen" and "The Farm Dining Room" are reprinted in Anderson, *Sampler,* 136–48.
20. "A Day Off Now and Then" (February 1914), and "Dear Farm Women" (January 1921), in Hines, *Little House in the Ozarks,* 174–76 and 183–98; "Whom Will You Marry?," *McCall's,* June 1919.
21. "March of Progress" (February 1911), in Hines, *Little House in the Ozarks,* 30–33, quotation on 32.
22. Holtz, *Ghost in the Little House,* chaps. 1–7; Miller, *Becoming Laura Ingalls Wilder,* chaps. 4–5.
23. This relationship is a central theme in the Holtz biography, *Ghost in the Little House;* on the Rock House in particular, see especially 194–96. Miller covers the same period in *Becoming Laura Ingalls Wilder,* chap. 6; see especially 176–78.
24. Holtz, *Ghost in the Little House,* especially chap. 10. Today, tour guides explain that Laura Ingalls Wilder did not like the Rock House at all but acquiesced to living there while Lane occupied the farmhouse.
25. This debate, which has been heated among scholars and especially among fans for decades now, goes beyond the scope of this chapter. As his title suggests (*Ghost in the Little House*), Holtz argues that Lane essentially ghostwrote the Little House books. Most Little House fans angrily rejected Holtz's thesis, although it is important to note that other scholars have addressed similar questions even though they do not generally agree with the extent of his conclusions. The matter of Lane's role had been raised earlier, by some of the first scholars to work with manuscript materials. See, for example, Rosa Ann Moore, "Laura Ingalls Wilder and Rose Wilder Lane: The Chemistry of Collaboration," *Children's Literature in Education* 11, no. 3 (1980): 101–9; William Anderson, "Laura Ingalls Wilder and Rose Wilder Lane: The Continuing Collaboration," *South Dakota History* 16.2 (1986): 89–143; and Anita Clair Fellman, "Laura Ingalls Wilder and Rose Wilder Lane: The Politics of a Mother-Daughter Relationship," *Signs: Journal of Women in Culture and Society* 15, no. 3 (1990): 535–61. As these titles indicate, most scholars agree that there was considerable collaboration between the two women; the question often seems to founder on distinctions between "ghostwriting" and "editing." It is important to note that during their lives, Wilder and Lane downplayed Lane's role, even disingenuously so. Pamela Smith Hill provides a nuanced analysis of the relationship between the two women, Wilder's development as a writer, and Wilder's understanding of the connection between fiction and history in her books in *Laura Ingalls Wilder: A Writer's Life* (Pierre, S.D.: South Dakota State Historical Society Press, 2007).
26. Lane could be a prolific writer, producing magazine articles and short stories with great frequency. She collected some of her Ozark stories, which had appeared in the *Saturday Evening Post* and *Ladies' Home Journal,* in *Old Home Town* (London: Longmans, Green and Company, 1935). See Holtz, *Ghost in the Little House,* 254–57, for discussion and analysis of this collection. Lane also wrote *Let the Hurricane Roar,* based to some degree on her parents' homesteading experience but using the names Charles and Caroline for the protagonists; it was published as a serial in the *Saturday Evening Post* in 1932, and later released as a novel.

27. Holtz, *Ghost in the Little House,* especially chaps. 11–13.
28. Ibid., 264–65.
29. Anita Clair Fellman, *Little House, Long Shadow: Laura Ingalls Wilder's Impact on American Culture* (Columbia: University of Missouri Press, 2008), traces how the books have circulated through various domains, including schools, home reading practices, popular culture, and political discourse; see 203–4 for the details regarding translations, awards, and recognition. For details on the trip to Detroit, see Miller, *Becoming Laura Ingalls Wilder,* 19.
30. Interestingly, this transaction was reported in the paper, although not the monthly rental figure. "The Wilder's Farm Home" explains that the Wilders had sold their farm to Mr. and Mrs. H. L. Shorter, retaining "the privilege of remaining in their home place their remaining years." This short article, really a caption to a photograph of the house, also explains that "most of the materials" to build the house "came from their farm." "The Wilder's Farm Home," undated newspaper clipping, Laura Ingalls Wilder scrapbook, Mansfield Public Library (Laura Ingalls Wilder Library), Mansfield, Mo. See also Miller, *Becoming Laura Ingalls Wilder,* 250.
31. "Citizens Form Group to Get Court Charter," undated newspaper clipping, Laura Ingalls Wilder scrapbook, Mansfield Public Library. See also "Author's Renown Shown in Scores of Letters Received," and "Mansfield Would Establish Shrine to Preserve Mrs. Wilder's Memories," the latter of which states, "The feeling seems to prevail that it would not be a requisite to maintain the Wilder home east of the city as a shrine." Clippings in Wilder scrapbook, Mansfield Public Library.
32. [William Anderson], "The Story of the Laura Ingalls Wilder Home Association, 1957–2007," *Rocky Ridge Review* (Summer 2007), 1–4.
33. "Open House Set for May 19," undated newspaper clipping, Laura Ingalls Wilder scrapbook, Mansfield Public Library.
34. [Anderson], "Story of the Laura Ingalls Wilder Home Association."
35. Rose Wilder Lane to Neta Seal, March 1957, April 1957, January 1958, May 1958, and February 1962. Transcripts of letters provided by Laura Ingalls Wilder Memorial Society, De Smet, S.D.
36. [Anderson], "Story of the Laura Ingalls Wilder Home Association."
37. Laura Ingalls Wilder, with a setting by Rose Wilder Lane, *On the Way Home* (New York: Harper and Row), 117–20.
38. The description and analysis of Rocky Ridge Farm are based on a series of visits from the 1990s to the 2010s. For more on the new master plan and the transformation of the landscape, see www.lauraingallswilderhome.com.
39. In *Destination Culture: Tourism, Museums, and Heritage* (Berkeley: University of California Press, 1998), 3, Barbara Kirshenblatt-Gimblett distinguishes between "in situ displays" such as period rooms and "in context displays," in which a taxonomy or other conceptual framework determines how objects are arranged. While this typology may not map perfectly onto Rocky Ridge Farm, it is helpful in understanding why the juxtaposition of the home and museum can be disorienting, even with the museum in a new location. The presence of Lane's artifacts in the original museum building almost suggested that she lived in the museum rather than in the house.
40. See Patricia West, *Domesticating History: The Political Origins of America's House Museums* (Washington, D.C.: Smithsonian Institution Press, 1999), on Alcott; and Hilary Iris Lowe, *Mark Twain's Homes and Literary Tourism* (Columbia: University of Missouri Press, 2012).
41. While this orientation avoids the precise complications at Rocky Ridge Farm, it can bring its own problems. At some of the other sites, there is no interpretive room for the adult Laura. For example, when one little boy was shown a picture of the elderly Mrs. Wilder while visiting the *Little House on the Prairie* site in Kansas, he burst into tears, crying, "That can't be Laura! Laura is a little girl!" Author's interview with site manager, Little House on the Prairie, Independence, Kans., June 2006.

42. At this writing there were unfortunately no plans for a Quarry Farm–like facility for Wilder scholars.
43. The National Historic Landmark nomination form for Rocky Ridge Farm (1990; NPS ref. no. 70000353) similarly privileges the Little House books: "The Laura Ingalls Wilder House is historically significant as the residence of Laura Ingalls Wilder, famous children's literature author, who began writing at the age of sixty-five while living in this modest homestead."
44. The interpretation has become more open to acknowledging Lane's contribution to the Little House books, as noted on the website for the organization, but it remains a controversial topic for many guides and visitors alike.
45. My thanks to volume editors Jennifer Harris and Hilary Iris Lowe for their comments on an earlier version of this chapter which contributed to this insight.

# 9

# *Author Homes in Coffee Table Books*

## Half-Reading, Literary Décor, and the Good Life

BEN DE BRUYN

*Building upon the exploration of libraries within historic house museums, and alternative paths for literary tourists of all stripes, Ben De Bruyn argues that today's literary house museums and oft-photographed authors' homes have provided a vibrant decorating and aspirational model for many readers. Writing at the nexus of the discussion of armchair tourism, digital literary tourism, literary guidebooks, and coffee table books on authors' private spaces, De Bruyn takes on "imaginary travel" as literary tourism.*

Literary tourism and its academic interpretation involve a turn to the author as well as a turn to those real-life items that he or she used and curators feel should be presented to the public. Where did Walter Scott live, for example? What did he wear? Which items of his rich collection of antiquities are displayed? Although these heritage sites are famous for allowing us to see the writing spaces and nonliterary objects used by the revered author, we should not forget that most writers are also avid readers, that these sites also contain many books, and that they therefore present an implicit picture of what the ideal reader's home looks like. From this perspective, these spaces teach their visitors unspoken lessons about the display of books and the design of reading nooks. The role of books and reading spaces in such sites becomes particularly clear, as I show, if we consider contemporary coffee table books about author homes and about interior design.

These books have a bad reputation, as the succinct definition by the *OED* already suggests: too big for a bookshelf, full of beautiful pictures, costing a lot.[1] Just as many people might be tempted to contrast literary tourism with proper reading, in fact, gaudy coffee table books ("gift books" or "furniture books" in older idioms) might compare unfavorably with proper *literary* books. In both cases, the former is imagined to be an explicitly visual, material, and commercial affair, the latter a deeper textual, imaginative and cultural one. One is superficial and tasteless, the other spiritual and tasteful. Such prejudices may explain why literary tourism and coffee table books have only recently attracted sustained academic attention, despite the fact that visits to literary (historical and/or fictional) sites and the use of books for display purposes have a history leading back to the nineteenth century and beyond. In contrast to common and critical prejudices, scholars like Nicola Watson and Leah Price have actually shown that each of these practices is already an interesting starting point for a more detailed investigation of the interplay between literature and material culture.[2] Yet, although many publications on literary tourism draw on gift books, among other things, to trace the changing representations of authors' homes and related sites, the existing literature does not offer a systematic discussion of such books about authors' homes and the resulting interplay between cultural memory and book history.[3]

In this chapter I focus on one instance of that interplay, namely, the contemporary conjunction of literary tourism and coffee table books, and use it to reflect on lifestyle, the display of books in writers' houses, and what I call "half-reading." What do these decorative books teach us about tourism, reading, and literary history in the early twenty-first century? To use John Urry's phrase, what sort of "imaginative travel" is involved here?[4]

## *Literary Tourism, Book History, and Half-Reading*

In recent years, many "literary" coffee table books have appeared, and I am not able to discuss all of them here, let alone in detail. As my argument revolves around books and libraries in literary sites, this chapter focuses on publications in which images of houses and interiors (rather than people and landscapes) occupy center stage, especially J. D. McClatchy and Erica Lennards's *American Writers at Home* (2004) and Leah Price's *Unpacking My Library* (2011), paying special attention to their shared features and the ways in which they participate in a broader discourse about literature and popular culture.[5] In taking their readers to the homes of living and deceased authors, these books function as props, one might say, for a sort of vicarious literary tourism. In reading them, we therefore encounter all the issues associated with this topic: the search for a more intimate relation with the author, the tension between proper pilgrims and tasteless tourists, the clash between highbrow aspirations and middlebrow concerns, the mix of recognition and disappointment upon visiting a literary site, the emphasis on the autobiographical and regional dimensions of literary works, the elision of the commercial dimensions of writing and reading, and so on.[6] Although these issues reemerge in what follows, my primary focus is on the specific questions raised by literary tourism in the context of early twenty-first-century coffee table books: questions about reading and nonreading, literature and lifestyle, authenticity and its commodification.

Before turning to these books, however, we should consider an important methodological question: How do you read a coffee table book? To put things even more succinctly: *Do* you read a coffee table book? Although, in what follows, I analyze the words as well as the images inside these books, it may be argued that such a procedure goes against the ways in which they are actually used. For, the objection might go, is it not more accurate to say that we only look at the photographs or even the cover of such books? Are they not furniture rather than literature? Do those who *have* such books actually *read* them, or are they indeed prime examples, as reputation has it, of unread books and the peculiar phenomenon of "nonreading"? As Leah Price has pointed out in a study of Victorian print culture, the deep-rooted preference for spiritual texts over superficial books has steered many literary critics away from situations in which books (and other print artifacts) are not read but used in different ways, namely, to wrap food, wipe excrement, hit children, hide from unwelcome gazes, or strike up a conversation with the as yet unconverted. Investigating these forms of "nonreading" inevitably leads one to consider coffee table books, as this reflection indicates: "Is it legitimate to hide behind the newspaper, use an encyclopedia as a doorstop, turn a newspaper into fish wrapping, match the binding of your bible to your dress, fill a study wall with hollowed-out books, *decorate a living-room table with intact ones that you have no intention of opening*?"[7] If many people spontaneously answer no to this last question, she continues, that is because "the logic that exalts reading copies while mocking coffee-table volumes shares its structure with contrasts between showy and serviceable clothing, or even between food addressed to the palate and that designed to please the eye."[8]

Price's argument about nonreading and its cultural representations is thought-provoking, and her study provides a useful template for further research on the literary and nonliterary uses of books.[9] Yet the binary distinction between reading and nonreading implies that her book provides few clues about how we "read"—browse, peruse, dip into, skim?—coffee table books. What does it mean to use books that call for something less than rapt reading but something more than thoughtless skimming? In a humorous little book that nevertheless raises serious questions, Pierre Bayard has reflected on various kinds of "nonreading" as well, noting that we often skim instead of read books: "Rather than read in an orderly fashion, the reader takes a stroll through the work, sometimes beginning at the end." As he points out, such behavior unsettles the difference between reading and nonreading: "In which category do we place the behavior of those who have spent a certain amount of time on a book—hours, even—without reading it completely?"[10] Although Bayard is mainly thinking of novels, this problem is even more acute in the case of coffee table books. Maybe a better term for our activity in this case would be something like "half-reading," a term, moreover, that may be fruitful in thinking about literary tourism as well. For another way of "half-reading" a literary oeuvre, of course, consists in visiting the houses of writers or other sites associated with their work.[11] Like the coffee table books discussed in this chapter, such houses create the impression that a partial encounter with a literary oeuvre suffices to understand its import or at least its place in cultural history.

Even though I do not offer a detailed theory of half-reading, I nevertheless want to preface my analysis by drawing attention to three features of coffee table book reading. In my view, these books are made and used in ways that encourage three effects with regard to their contents: trivialization, aestheticization, and homogenization. By talking about their trivialization effect, I do not mean to say that coffee table books are trivial; rather, I mean that including a certain topic in such books inevitably recategorizes it as a subject for leisurely and noncommittal conversation rather than specialized or animated debate. These books are made to be browsed and put down again by owners and guests alike without readers feeling that they have missed anything vital or that their personal sensibilities have been challenged, let alone offended. Eschewing scientific, religious, or political debates as well as narrative tension, these books are, in contrast to objects of great urgency, highly "put-downable." This trivialization should not be equated with simple popularization, moreover, for whatever subject is included in the pages of a coffee table book thereby also acquires (the semblance of) additional value and beauty. This aestheticization effect is established not only by its stylish cover and glossy images (which may be beautiful or stylish in various ways) but also by its format. A coffee table book may sit on a lowly table rather than a pedestal, but its size, weight, and hardcover format spell out that it is not, like the paperback, a cheap and accessible mass market product. Like the nineteenth-century annual, you might say, it has upper-class connotations.[12]

And since these books are designed to be opened and browsed at will, their contents should finally also be relatively homogeneous. That is, readers should encounter approximately the same content at whatever point they happen to open the book in question. In books like *American Writers at Home* and *A Journey through Literary America,* different pages obviously yield information on different authors, houses, and regions, but for the purposes of the ideal coffee table reader, these differences are less important than the shared qualities. More like a dictionary or an anthology in this respect than a novel or a traditional literary history, these books are metonymy writ large; in principle, each part should be equally important and should also encapsulate every message of the book as a whole in extended *pars pro toto* fashion.[13] Not only does the narrative, therefore, show little urgency, but also the relation between words and images is unambiguous, with captions duplicating the information conveyed by the body of the text and photos placed close to the associated commentary, often merely illustrating and localizing textual information rather than evoking less readily apparent meanings.

The first two effects are central to the present discussion, for they concern the interplay between the trivialization and aestheticization of literature and history, one might say, in contemporary coffee table books. Here, however, I want to consider homogenization briefly in more detail. Upon closer inspection, after all, Annie Leibovitz's *Pilgrimage* (2011), another coffee table book, appears to disrupt standard homogenizing strategies. For one thing, her book contains photos that have little or no accompanying text. The reader finds photographs of Elvis's Graceland and Jefferson's Monticello (the book does not deal solely with literary writers like Dickinson and Thoreau), for example, but gets no more information apart from short captions. When locations are both photographed and explicitly discussed in the body of the text, even more strikingly, photographs and discussion are occasionally placed very far apart in the book. The visit to the location of Thoreau's cabin is described early on, on page 53, for instance, but the relevant photos do not appear until much later, on pages 178 and 180–81. Some photos are also introduced without captions or accompanying narrative, making it impossible for the reader to (immediately) identify and locate the sights in question.[14] One can readily imagine many reasons for these loose ties between words and images (the size or color scheme of certain photos might have been factors, for instance), but the net result is that it is often difficult to find the text that goes with a photo, especially if the book is read in the leisurely fashion most people would associate with coffee table books. By disconnecting words and images, it might be argued, Leibovitz resists the homogenizing strategies of standard coffee table books. And yet it could be objected that this confusing juxtaposition of photos and short narratives actually reinforces the homogenization effect; if *any* picture can accompany the story of *any* literary or artistic "pilgrimage" and vice versa, these different words and images are ultimately collapsed into a broader narrative of general (American) creativity and inspirational settings that erases the specific traits of the figures and locations portrayed even as it highlights the unique contribution of the artist who shot the pictures. In half-reading such books, what matters is not the specific genius of a certain writer or the *genius loci* of her birthplace, but the generalized notion of creativity celebrated by these equally creative pictures. Visiting a literary site might be considered a similar exercise in half-reading a story of creativity, as I mentioned; to literalize Bayard's metaphor, walking through the home of a writer is akin to *taking a stroll* through the work.

## *Author Homes and the Good Life*

Another striking aspect of coffee table books on writers' houses is their explicit "lifestyle" dimension. This dimension might seem unremarkable, for many critics have observed that writers' houses provide clues not just about the authors' aesthetic views but also about their particular "lifestyles." Critics note, for instance, that the Frankfurt Goethe house "represents the young Goethe, his education, studies and the *lifestyle* of the wealthy and educated middle class at that time" and that Walter Scott's ill-fated pseudo-castle is seen to express "his *lifestyle* as 'Laird of Abbotsford.'"[15] In both instances, this term refers to the ways in which an author's choice of house and interior reveals a certain individual or group identity (as in "bohemian lifestyle"). Yet it is clear that the term "lifestyle" cannot be used just for referring to such personal idiosyncrasies but also captures "everything from exercise regimens to home décor," that is, the whole set of consumerist practices encouraged by modern advertising as well as lifestyle shows and magazines.[16] Choice forms of consumerism are frequently portrayed as the ideal strategy for exhibiting supposedly unique personalities, of course; yet it is still important to disentangle these two meanings of the term "lifestyle," as contemporary coffee table books not only try to exhibit the unique traits of certain authors and homes but also simultaneously smooth over such differences—the homogenization effect again—to conjure up a broader and vaguer image of the "good life." They evoke not merely the specific lifestyles of writers like Ernest Hemingway or artists like Georgia O'Keeffe but also the supposedly more general pleasures of leisure travel, delectable food, and fine clothes. (Although they are alleged to appeal to everyone, it goes without saying that these things are not available to all and hence reveal the lifestyle of a particular well-to-do class.) Just consider the lavish illustrations of pools, gardens, dinner tables, kitchens, and bathrooms in *American Writers at Home*.[17] Literary reading has always been tied, arguably, to specific lifestyle practices, but what does this connection look like in contemporary coffee table books? Why are authors' homes pictured, packaged, and sold as if they were the ideal locations not just for writing and reading, but also for indulging in more material pleasures? They often look like hotels rather than museums, after all, with their coffee, tables, and books.

If we want to understand the current, intensified connection between literature and lifestyle, a good place to start is Jim Collins's analysis of the contemporary literary landscape in *Bring on the Books for Everybody* (2010). Taking issue with familiar jeremiads about the decline of reading, he argues that the advent of new media and concomitant changes in literary taste and infrastructure have actually led to a renewed popularization of literary culture as well as an implicit "literarization" of popular culture. Neither development is in itself new, Collins demonstrates in an extended analysis of Henry James's work (and many other examples from the nineteenth century could be adduced), but the mass-mediated and hyper-commodified character of the early twenty-first century has nonetheless created new possibilities in terms of the visual repackaging of the literary experience and what we might call the literary repackaging of the shopping experience.[18] In our contemporary "convergence culture," we not only encounter literature between the covers of a book but also listen to song versions of Cormac McCarthy's *The Road*, watch Don Draper recite Frank O'Hara's poetry on *Mad Men*, and go online to discuss the merits of Robert Pattinson's performance in David Cronenberg's version of *Cosmopolis* with other DeLillo fans. Additionally, we come across books in the photographs of interior decoration magazines, get our advice about wine from literary figures like Jay McInerney, and stay in "literary" hotels like New York's Library Hotel, with its complimentary reading room and non-complimentary "literary inspired cocktails" like The Hemingway and The Great Gatsby.[19] Even though Gary Shteyngart's dystopian novel *Super Sad True Love Story* (2010) laments that future Americans will frown upon the smell of books, the reverse may be true, as Karl Lagerfeld's perfume Paper Passion and its endorsement by Nobel Prize winner Günther Grass indicate.[20]

What makes this argument especially compelling for my purposes is that Jim Collins, in analyzing the ways in which contemporary literature is marketed, frequently refers to the display of books and the deliberate creation of a literary *mise-en-scène*. The Sundance home décor and clothing catalog, for instance, puts books in the hands of fashion models—turning the book into the ultimate "accessory" (another form of nonreading)—and provides "expert" reading advice while identifying the necessary furnishings for avid readers: "a leather club chair, tripod library lamp, Cornell bookcase, serape rug." Additionally, Collins points out that bookstores like Barnes & Noble are designed to downplay their commercial character by establishing a friendly "library effect." Appealing to nostalgic fantasies about a pure (and clearly fictitious) literary past, these stores explicitly signal their "literariness" by using architectural styles that were in vogue when print was supposedly the only medium of cultural life, evoking "the neoclassicism [of] the not-for-profit cultural establishments of the Gilded Age and the more streamlined, but nonetheless vividly antique look of a transatlantic Arts and Crafts style." In the café area of such stores, we again encounter a seemingly ideal reading nook: "leather club chairs and couches . . . matched with Mission-style lamps." In such settings, we can truly enjoy the contemporary novel of manners, which—like its predecessors in earlier periods—implicitly offers taste advice to its readers and teaches them to distinguish "quality consumerism" from "chaotic consumerism." This systematic attention to taste cultivation also explains why modern literature draws on rather than simply debunks the discourse of lifestyle magazines. In the contemporary literary best seller, as in earlier versions of the novel of manners, "a taste for things literary and [a desire for] things of a more material nature (furniture, houses, clothing)" are not mutually exclusive but "wholly interdependent pleasures." And in each of these cases—bookshops, décor catalogs, best-selling novels—literary reading and associated forms of shopping are seen as deeply personal and *personalizing* experiences.[21]

As I have mentioned, many photographs from books like *American Writers at Home* hint at material as well as literary pleasures. If we go on to look at the text accompanying these photos, we encounter a similar message. Apparently, authors' homes from the nineteenth to the twentieth century are sources not just of good writing but also of lasting inspiration for consumers looking for the good life. For *American Writers at Home,* like many of these books, not only contains photos of clothes, antiques, pools, and fresh flowers but explicitly notes as well that authors and texts hold important lessons for contemporary readers interested in food, fashion, gardening, and decoration.[22] In terms of food, we hear of "the famous Alcott hospitality," of Faulkner's "venison and quail" hunting breakfasts, of Hemingway's love for a "raw conch salad with Key lime and salt brine sauce," and of Longfellow's "well-stocked wine cellar."[23] We also encounter an elaborate menu including ice cream served at the Twain house, and a photo with a candlelit wooden table where bread, cheese, and other foodstuffs are displayed, revealingly, next to an open book.[24] Regarding fashion, the book speaks of Edna St. Vincent Millay's beautiful "peacock cloche" and her "evening bags with exquisite Art Deco initialed clasps," of the elegant dresses worn by Eugene O'Neill's wife and the Hermès raincoat for their Dalmatian. It further reminds its readers of Edith Wharton's emphatic assertion that, despite what crass people think, it is possible to be both "fashionable" and "intelligent."[25]

Turning to gardening, the reader learns that Emerson was "an avid purveyor of pears," that Hawthorne "loved to garden," that Sarah Orne Jewett and Eudora Welty were likewise "avid gardener[s]," and that Robinson Jeffers and his family preferred "a wild garden, with old-style roses and fragrant plants like lavender," an image that is once again connected to literary reading: "After supper, [husband and wife] would sit in their parlor reading poetry and sipping their homemade orange wine."[26] As far as interior decoration is concerned, finally, we read descriptions of a "dresser with inlaid Minton tiles," of a "wall-to-wall Brussels-weave carpet," of the "Spanish antiques and hand-blown Venetian glass" provided by Hemingway's wife, Pauline (who later started an interior decorating company, the book adds), of a library "painted Pompeian red, with . . . matching bookcases," of the "state-of-the-art kitchen" given to Millay as a publicity stunt by *Ladies' Home Journal,* and of *The Decoration of Houses* (1897), the "handbook on design" co-written by Edith Wharton.[27] Again, the text connects this domain of lifestyle culture explicitly to writing, not only by recalling Twain's claim that his extravagant house was like a "*poem*" but also by juxtaposing, on a single page, photographs of Hemingway's typewriter and his tropical resort–like pool.[28] These literary museums, in short, appear suspiciously like hotels or restaurants or, more accurately, like more authentic literary retreats and eateries.

Despite (or because of) this systematic association of literature and lifestyle, the makers of *American Writers at Home* are keen to minimize the interest of these classic authors in luxurious accoutrements. To avoid being connected to the tasteless consumerism of nonliterary publications, perhaps, they aspire to an alternative, elevated, *literary* form of lifestyle. They set these authors up as consumers of modern luxuries, but portray them as coming to these things not through a slavish, unthinking submission to merchandising but through an inherent taste and distinction that we associate with their literary sensibility, thus naturalizing their taste in the fields of design, food, and fashion as an effortless byproduct of their artistic genius.[29] Sanitizing these acts of consumerism (not to mention the lavish illustrations) requires a lot of exposition, however. The book's introduction notes, for instance, that "most authors could not afford, *and even more would not want,* the sumptuous scale of Wharton's The Mount or the custom-made detail of Twain's interiors, because the larger the home, the greater the distractions."[30] What is more, the stories of these two writers with their extravagant houses "ended in sorrow." Somewhat at odds with the words and images I have been examining, then, the introduction maintains that American authors want "protected privacy," not luxury.[31]

This cautionary, deflationary moral returns in the later discussion of Faulkner and Wharton, where the author notes that the former may have aspired to be a country squire, "but without undue pretension," and that the latter had a "snobbish side" but nevertheless refused the tasteless "ostentation" of rich industrialist families.[32] Yet these elegant photos and reconstructed houses cannot but confirm claims about the contemporary connection between literary and material pleasures. Even for those settings encountered in the book that were originally bereft of modern comforts, the photos suggest otherwise. Originally, the home of Robinson Jeffers may have had "no electricity, gas, or telephone," but the photo of his wife's reading nook nonetheless shows an elegant and functioning lamp.[33] Ultimately, coffee table books about authors' homes indicate that our experience of these museum-like spaces is filtered, at least in part, through the lens of a distinctly commercial aesthetic.

## *Library Effects*

If it is true that recent literary publications are inextricably linked to lifestyle culture, the reverse is also true; as Collins suggests, recent lifestyle magazines are remarkably interested in literature and books. A good example of this trend is *Decorating with Books* (2006); a coffee table book on interior design which is associated with the shelter magazine *House Beautiful,* it provides decoration advice to bibliophiles of a modern as well as a traditional persuasion.[34] Covering "the basics of book display in the home," it invites us to use books as props in displays that will please the eye and prompt conversations with guests. As is readily apparent from the book's lavish illustrations, its readers are taken on an elegant tour of various exclusive locations, including "a Parisian apartment," a "fourteenth-century castle in Northern Italy," "a Manhattan penthouse," a "Hamptons hideaway," and a "seaside home in California."[35] Upon closer inspection, we find that these readers simultaneously encounter a series of unmistakably literary books, other photos showing the spines of David Foster Wallace's *Infinite Jest,* Antonio Gramsci's *Prison Notebooks,* the letters of Evelyn Waugh, and even Wayne Booth's *Rhetoric of Fiction* and Gilbert and Gubar's *Madwoman in the Attic.*[36] By now this broad association of luxury and the literary should be familiar. Here I take a closer look at one aspect of this association, namely, the ways in which the photos of books in coffee table books about interior design on the one hand and about authors' homes on the other establish a similar vision of the ideal reader's home. As I show, decorators and curators of literary sites, despite their different agendas and sensibilities, use and display books in strikingly parallel ways.

Let us consider some tips from *Decorating with Books* before returning to the heritage sites portrayed in *American Writers at Home.* Apart from cautioning us about the potential dangers of light and dust, *Decorating with Books* teaches us that a library—a rule, or so we are assured, established by none other than Edith Wharton—ideally functions as a backdrop for the books it contains; that the idea of the home library has returned in "the past decade," but that this should not stop us from displaying books throughout the house;[37] and that placing a stack of books near the foyer enables you to immediately signal your literary passion to visitors. Furthermore, we are instructed that single books are versatile items for creating "small still lifes"; that shelves and spines can complement the colors of their surroundings, and that if they do not do so of their own accord, we can use white paper "book covers" to unify them; that books can function as "sidetables, telephone tables, and even pedestals for pieces of sculpture"; and that we can hide our "entertainment center" and "movies" with cabinets or sliding panels.[38] Continuing, we are advised that an inviting reading nook requires two things, namely, "a comfortable chair and a good source of light"; that we can create "a tapestry effect" by filling shelves from end to end with books or, alternatively, that we can add "visual interest" and "offer the eye a place to rest" if we break up these monotone rows of books by incorporating family photos and valued possessions, by "alternating horizontal and vertical placement" of the books on the shelves, or by artfully juxtaposing books of varying heights, thereby creating "playful sloping patterns."[39] Finally, and tellingly, the book notes that visually appealing books may be bought in the same places where you buy vintage furniture, such as "antiques shops" and "flea markets."[40] This advice leads the reader to two broad conclusions. First, decorating your library is not only important but also intensely personal: "The possibilities for personal expression are endless." And second, books are invariably "stylish." Time and again, *Decorating with Books* teaches us that we must learn to see books as artworks in their own right, "three-dimensional objects [with specific] colors, sizes, and textures."[41] At times, the non-material dimension of books is acknowledged—"Books can *also* be appreciated on a purely aesthetic level"—while at other times it drops out of sight altogether: "Homeowners are now using books as decorative accessories . . . *without any intention of ever reading them.*[42] *Decorating with Books,* in sum, offers lessons in nonreading.

Examining some of these lessons more closely, let us compare this decoration advice with the setups we find in coffee table books on authors' homes, especially *American Writers at Home.* My argument is not just that the photos in these books participate in a general "literarization" of lifestyle and vice versa, but that they offer highly specific and remarkably similar advice about how to use books in our interiors. How can we make sense of this photographic form of bibliophilia, and what does it tell us about books, reading, and literary décor in the context of writers' homes and other literary sites?[43] To answer that question, we should look at some of these images in more detail. For this comparison, I begin by focusing on four photos from *American Writers at Home* and four from *Decorating with Books.* The first four photos were taken in the houses of Eudora Welty (fig. 9.1), Herman

Melville (fig. 9.2), and Robinson Jeffers, and there are important differences among these three sites in terms of style, period, and authenticity.[44] Though we should bear these in mind, I am more interested here in how these homes and their visual representations provide implicit lessons in interior design. For if we juxtapose them with four photographs of similar setups in *Decorating with Books*—a living room, a reading nook, a corner library, and a bookcase, the photos from *American Writers at Home* illustrate four lessons about how books can be used in home interiors according to contemporary decorators—and according to seemingly noncommercial literary sites.

Starting with the living room images, the photographs from *American Writers at Home* and *Decorating with Books* demonstrate that scattered books are less of a design mistake than one might imagine.[45] Even though this goes against common sense, both of them suggest that stacking books on the couch, on a chair, or even on the floor adds a tasteful finishing touch. In earlier times, we read in *Decorating with Books,* books were confined to libraries and bookcases and were usually not left "on a side chair . . . on a coffee table or along a bench in a hallway."[46] Now, however, books create elegant still-lifes throughout the house when "stacked on an ottoman, piled on the floor [or] lined up on a bench."[47] As the author of this coffee table book notes about a similar scene, "four groupings of relatively equal height work well with the round table, and the slight disorder of the arrangement complements the home's casual elegance."[48] Turning to the pictures of the reading nooks in *American Writers at Home* and *Decorating with Books,* we again encounter a highly similar *mise-en-scène.* In both cases, we find inviting ottomans located next to sources of light and stacks of books placed on open as well as enclosed shelves.[49] As *Decorating with Books*—and, implicitly, *American Writers at Home*—inform us, a reading nook requires a good chair and a good source of light, with a "bright window . . . for daytime reading [and] a lamp . . . at the ready for evenings and overcast days."[50] In both cases, moreover, valuable books—"special editions" or "antiquarian volumes"—are kept in a secretary behind glass doors.[51] The ideal reading nook is also placed in a quieter part of the house, we learn, preferably close to "a garden view."[52] The fact that we can discern the outline of greenery through the window therefore completes the "ideal reading nook" character of both pictures. The fireside libraries from *American Writers at Home* and *Decorating with Books* illustrate a third lesson, namely, that "no corner of the house is too humble to harbor a display of books."[53] Be it a built-in nook for firewood or an uninteresting corner in Melville's study—typical of the "corner[s] you've never known what to do with"—the addition of a "miniature library" transforms them into attractive parts of the room (another "library effect," if you will).[54] The final set of photos in this initial comparison consists of two images of bookcases from

FIGURE 9.1. A circular arrangement of books on a coffee table at the Eudora Welty site. *Photo by Erica Lennard.*

FIGURE 9.2. A corner library at the Arrowhead museum. *Photo by Erica Lennard.*

*American Writers at Home* and *Decorating with Books.* In these cases, the images show, books are placed both horizontally and vertically and are interspersed with prized possessions, travel mementos, and family photos, illustrating how well-chosen breaks in homogeneous rows of books may pique the interest of viewers.[55] Once again, then, the book still-lifes in these photos function as implicit design advice. If you want to live an elegant, literary life, then this is what you do with your books. Such lessons may be provided by lifestyle magazines, but they are also intimated by authors' homes, be they actively restored or lovingly maintained. Differently put, writers' houses show us not only how a specific author lived but also how an ideal reader should live. They are not just author homes but also *reader* homes.[56]

To show that this overlap is not limited to the two books mentioned earlier and that the homes of living authors may function in similar ways, let us turn to the decorating lessons and photographs in books dealing with the libraries of contemporary authors (a form of literary tourism that can take place only via artifacts like coffee table books, for obvious reasons). In these pictures from *Unpacking My Library* (2011), after all, we again encounter bohemian exuberance, well-lit, quiet, intrusive books and artistic book stacking (and it goes without saying that these scenes are as "staged," in their own way, as the other pictures we have seen). Let us consider these photos in more detail, bearing in mind the decorating lessons we encountered earlier.). The first photo, from Edmund White's house, exhibits a sprawling library, where the volumes are crowded on top of and next to the bookcases, creating a casual feel that is reflected in the cracked leather of the comfortable chair on the left. The bookcases in Jonathan Lethem's reading nook are more geometrical (a modern "tapestry effect," you might say), but the inviting reading chairs next to the lamp and window (with another tree just visible) nevertheless establish a relaxed setting for rest and reflection. The picture from Junot Díaz's kitchen reveals once again how an outsized book collection can successfully claim unusual spaces. Here we even find books *on* if not *in* the refrigerator, as the magnet featuring the cover of *The Brief Wondrous Life of Oscar Wao* indicates (second row from the top, third item from the right). Finally, the wall-size bookcase in Claire Messud and James Wood's home demonstrates the eye-catching use of varying shelf use, with tightly packed cubicles alternating with more spare rows—a strategy that contributes to an "artistic feeling," according to *Decorating with Books*—souvenirs and mementos breaking up the rows and alternating use of horizontal and vertical stacking. Here as well, a visit to a writer's home provides us with the information we need to establish a literary atmosphere and a tasteful interior. All you need is good coffee, a stylish table, and lots of books.[57]

As these comparisons show, "literary" coffee table books and "design" coffee table books offer similar advice about how to decorate our homes and libraries. Yet their implicit recommendations do not fully overlap. There are some things you can do with your volumes in *Decorating with Books* that you cannot do in *American Writers at Home* or even *Unpacking My Library.* These latter publications would undoubtedly agree that your choice of books and bookcases is a highly personal matter, but some modes of display and nonreading are nevertheless considered unacceptable. In these author-cum-reader homes, books are never used as coasters or tables, they are never covered with a white slipcover to harmonize their colors, they never face pages-outward to maximize their display function, they are never hidden from sight by suspending small paintings over the shelves of bookcases, there is no extreme color matching, there are few coffee table books altogether, and the shelves of bookcases are almost inevitably brimming with books, limiting the number of additional mementos and photos and causing the volumes, as *Decorating with Books* says, to "dominate the other furnishings in the room"[58] Ultimately, these photos of classic and contemporary writers' homes reveal the unspoken assumption that books are first and foremost texts and second if at all material objects (though I will return to manuscripts). This assumption surfaces most explicitly in *Unpacking My Library* when novelist Rebecca Goldstein is asked if she feels comfortable using books to prop up other things or to serve as a coaster: "Kant tells us that a person can never be used as a means to an end, but must be viewed as an end in itself. This is one of the formulations of his famous categorical imperative. Well, that pretty much sums up my attitude toward books. I would *never* use a book as a coaster or to prop up something else, any more than I'd use a person toward that end."[59]

Books are not lifeless objects, in other words; they are *people.* As such remarks drive home, these authors resist the instrumental use of books, the decorator's impulse to turn them into furniture. Here, hollowed-out books are traded in for literary manuscripts, fetishized objects that return the reader's gaze to literature even if their tasteful halo simultaneously envelops the surrounding tables, chairs, beds, and lamps, and elevates their beauty.[60] These differences between literary coffee table books and explicit lifestyle publications ensure that they finally appeal to different taste communities, even if a closer analysis suggests that they nevertheless provide surprisingly similar advice about how to create a literary home.

## *Staged Antiquity*

Apart from their format and mode of reading, their evocation of the good life, and their implicit decorating advice, there is one last dimension of these coffee table books that requires our attention, namely, their emphasis on the historical, "vintage" character of literary sites (particularly clear in the case of Leibovitz's seemingly low-fidelity photos). A good starting point is this passage from Nicole Krauss's novel *Great House* (2010), a scene in which one of the main characters visits the explicitly "literary" apartment of a would-be poet:

> So I turned my attention to the furniture, or what I could see of it under the mess—a sofa, a large wooden desk with lots of drawers, . . . a pair of bookshelves crammed with volumes in Spanish, French, and English, and the nicest piece, a kind of chest or trunk with iron braces that looked as if it had been rescued from a sunken ship and put to use as a coffee table. He must have acquired everything secondhand, none of it looked new, but all the pieces shared a kind of sympathy, and the fact that they were suffocating under papers and books made them more attractive than less.[61]

At first sight, this fictional location would not make a good addition to *Decorating with Books,* given the mess and the unconventional, artistic atmosphere evoked by the furnishings of its occupant. This scene, like many scenes from *American Writers at Home,* ultimately evokes a lived, *bohemian* quality that seems to differ from the more sanitized, *bourgeois* character of the setups in *Decorating with Books.*[62] Yet the scene from *Great House* also indicates that these differences may be subtle rather than essential (and that the decoration advice we have been examining plays a role in contemporary novels as well); the passage trains the reader's eye to notice individual items of furniture and points out their contributions to the tasteful effect of the interior, paying particular attention to books, papers, and weathered items of furniture. This overlap between literary culture and lifestyle publications can be seen not only in their treatment of books and luxurious settings but also in their use of *old* objects. Like the objects in the literary sites I have been examining, none of the items from this apartment "looked new"; everything appears as if it were acquired secondhand or even rescued from a sunken ship. In conclusion, I examine this emphasis on old objects in literary interiors and coffee table books, arguing that literary sites, because of their historical aura, are well suited to function as implicit decoration manuals at a time when houses with a true history have become increasingly rare.

In an age of cultural mobility, critics have noted, the modern house often lacks a prehistory that links it indelibly to its owners. The ensuing psychological discomfort explains the success of the commercial aesthetic of "quaintness," Daniel Harris has observed, with its celebration of baroque clutter, pre-electricity chiaroscuro, artificial imperfections (to simulate affectionate use), and soulful heirlooms, and its simultaneous rejection of minimalist emptiness, glamorous advertising, flawless plastics, and impersonal commodities.[63] This aesthetic is illusory, for it overlooks the fact that the historical middle class lacked the money to create clutter, that contemporary "quaint" artifacts are *artificially* aged and hence equally impersonal, and that the acts of consumption it inspires are not about salvaging the past but, simply, about shopping. Consumers nonetheless subscribe to this aesthetic because it compensates for the obligatory newness of our possessions (scuffed or obsolete appliances and clothes have to be replaced as soon as possible) as well as for the sense of uprootedness created by our frequent relocation. In other words, "quaint" commodities compensate for the fact that our homes lack a sense of "personal history" and a "look of permanence"; nowadays, we no longer live in "domestic museums . . . full of the heirlooms of the entire clan."[64]

That is why many consumers try to reclaim this sense of history by exhibiting objects that look old or that expose the owner's prehistory. As soon as the home was presented as something that "might be created through careful shopping," Elizabeth Outka has noted in her analysis of early twentieth-century "neo-nostalgic homes," "the value of having personal ties to a particular place was recognized and re-created as a product that might be packaged and sold."[65] New homes could acquire a sense of history through the use of "objects that in themselves imply the passage of time—such as a weathered piece of furniture—or a new home that, through a combination of . . . styles from different periods, offered a sense of time's flow." Additionally, this sense of history could be evoked by objects that alluded to "a (potentially fictitious) personal history." Via these strategies, designers and owners could make sure that their new homes evoked a rich "temporal density," while simultaneously avoiding "bogus antiquity" and outdated technology (Jazz Age style, for instance, being one thing, Jazz Age amenities quite another).[66] Via this manipulation of personal as well as historical time—Outka speaks of "time-play" here—homeowners could engage in "fantasy time travel" and take "an almost cinematographic tour of their own history," ultimately allowing them to satisfy (or almost satisfy) the frustrated desire of living in an ancestral home furnished with authentic heirlooms.[67] If modern tourist sites often trade in "staged authenticity," to use Dean MacCannell's famous phrase, modern homes frequently reveal what one might call a form of "staged antiquity."[68]

These ideas shed light on a final important dimension of literary coffee table books. As I have demonstrated, these publications implicitly function as taste primers and decoration manuals, stimulating their readers to display books in certain ways and to aspire to the consumerist fantasy of the good life. That does not mean that either these books or the literary sites they portray can be reduced to strictly commercial undertakings. Clearly, these sites are also *museums,* featuring authentic objects and furnishings that are not indifferent "objects" of consumption but valuable "things" that have often played an important role in American literary history.[69] Yet the irony is that these sites and their verbal and visual reproductions may actually be even more successful at functioning like luminous ideals in terms of interior design because they are museums—unique, quasi-religious spaces that seem to connect their visitors (and readers) almost directly to a fabled time when the ancestral homestead had not yet been traded in for the prefabricated home and when books and literary culture were supposedly not yet relegated to the sidelines by an encroaching commercial and visual culture. In other words, the commercial dimension of these sites may actually derive its force from their noncommercial, museum-like character. Commercial and historical imperatives are hard to disentangle, in short.

A scene from *Decorating with Books,* for instance, exhibits a dressing-area-turned-library where the color scheme of the walls and shelves was deliberately harmonized with "the warm brown tones of the books from yesteryear," and a collection of prized possessions including a black-and-white "portrait of the owner's great-grandfather" rests on an antique table.[70] Along the shelves, moreover, books are interspersed with other photos and mementos. Combining a more or less genuine heirloom with deliberate reconstructions of old furnishings, this scene clearly captures the commercial aesthetic of the quaint. We encounter something similar in *Unpacking My Library.* In the contemporary study of authors Lev Grossman and Sophie Gee, as one shot shows, we not only find a sleek laptop and stylish cell phone but also a weathered desk and, if you pardon the pleonasm, a rustic rake. This startling juxtaposition is again typical of the quaint, which "delight[s] in visual paradoxes, placing the ultra-feminine next to the unpolished and the coarse: [as in] a china cup resting on a roughhewn beam."[71] As a later detail shows, moreover, an antique set of books sits next to a hardcover copy of Grossman's own book *The Magicians* (2009), the recent date of which is downplayed by its jacketless appearance, which neatly integrates it into its leather-bound surroundings.[72] Apparently, time-play is a matter not just of weathered furniture but also of weathered books. Bearing these pictures in mind, who is to say that we don't bring a similar framework to bear on the shots of Longfellow's nineteenth-century study in *American Writers at Home,* for example, with their dark chiaroscuro quality, a visual marker that is typical of the quaint, according to Daniel Harris, as it hints at a world before "diffused electric lighting and central heating" ended the idealized, fireplace-centered togetherness of the nineteenth century. Real and staged antiquity, like real and staged authenticity, interpenetrate here, and reveal the tension between historical and commercial mindsets.[73] Longfellow's study may be an actual historical site, but its visual representation stresses its bygone quality in a way that may remind visitors of quaint commodities rather than historical realities. Via the colors and textures of photos, books, and other furniture, these pictures of libraries evoke different periods, in an authentic or quasi-authentic fashion, and thereby conjure up a rich sense of personal, familial, and indeed *literary* history.

Again, the crucial thing here is not, or not only, that authors construct a certain sense of who they are by decorating their homes in a certain way and thereby engaging in a deliberate form of time-play, but rather that the maintenance or reconstruction of this time-play in authors' homes implicitly functions as authoritative advice to reader-visitors, telling them how they themselves can create a literary home and the concomitant illusion of a (literally as well as metaphorically) *storied* life. And this is something that scholars, curators, visitors, and readers should bear in mind. How should we deal with the fact that literary sites may be experienced through the commercial lenses of the quaint and the good life? And how should we use and display books in such sites? In thinking about these practices in more detail, we should also consider another aspect of the time-play performed by these coffee table books. They do not just record the decorating strategies of authors (and their curators) or implicitly create an ideal of the reader's home, to my mind, but also *function as time-structuring devices themselves.* Like the books in the photographs I have been discussing, coffee table books themselves can be used as quaint props and quasi-authentic finishing touches. Putting a book like *American Authors at Home* on your coffee table is a form of time-play in and of itself, which functions almost like a piece of weathered furniture. And it is able to fulfill that function without being read—or fully read. Like visitors to literary homes, in other words, half-readers of coffee table books participate in a form of memorialization that popularizes literature even as it elevates our everyday surroundings and connects our coffee, tables, and books to the ongoing project of American literary history.

## NOTES

1. Earlier terms for related types of books include annuals, furniture books, gift books, and grand piano books. "Coffee table books" was "a 1962-vintage replacement for 'grand-piano books.'" Leah Price, "The Subconscious Shelf," *New York Times Book Review,* November 13, 2011. Critics have written on earlier incarnations of the coffee table book and its peculiar place in the nineteenth-century print ecology. See Vanessa Warne, "Thackeray among the Annuals: Morality, Cultural Authority and the Literary Annual Genre," *Victorian Periodicals Review* 39, no. 2 (2006): 158–78; and Alexandra Urakova, "'The Purloined Letter' in the Gift Book: Reading Poe in a Contemporary Context," *Nineteenth-Century Literature* 64, no. 3 (2009): 323–46.

2. Nicola J. Watson, *The Literary Tourist: Readers and Places in Romantic and Victorian Britain* (Houndmills: Palgrave Macmillan, 2006); Leah Price, *How to Do Things with Books in Victorian Britain* (Princeton: Princeton University Press, 2012).
3. Watson mentions "souvenir publication[s]," "souvenir photographs," and guidebooks which, like contemporary coffee table books (but with a stronger emphasis on practical advice), "would relieve visitors of the necessity of rereading [a] poem *in situ* by garnishing their suggested itinerary with the essential extracts, serving at once as guidebook and souvenir." Watson, *The Literary Tourist,* 84, 113, 162.
4. See John Urry, *The Tourist Gaze,* 2nd ed. (Thousand Oaks, Calif.: Sage, 2002), 142.
5. Limiting ourselves to recent books in nonstandard sizes that juxtapose words and images and deal with different authors, we can delineate four rough types of "literary coffee table book" on the basis of the genre they approximate: the author portrait gallery, the literary photography book, the illustrated interview, and the accessible literary history. Examples include, in the first category, Lynda Koolish, *African American Writers: Portraits and Visions* (Jackson: University Press of Mississippi, 2001); Annie Leibovitz, *Pilgrimage* (New York: Random House, 2011), in the second; Leah Price, ed., *Unpacking My Library: Writers and Their Books* (New Haven: Yale University Press, 2011), and Dan Crowe and Philip Oltermann, eds., *How I Write: The Secret Lives of Authors* (New York: Rizzoli, 2007), in the third; and J. D. McClatchy and Erica Lennard, *American Writers at Home* (New York: Vendome Press, 2004), and Thomas R. Hummel and Tamra Dempsey, *A Journey through Literary America* (Napa, Calif.: Val de Grâce Books, 2009), in the fourth. For additional examples of these "often lavishly illustrated guidebooks," see Harald Hendrix's list in "Writers' Houses as Media of Expression and Remembrance: From Self-Fashioning to Cultural Memory," in *Writers' Houses and the Making of Memory,* ed. Harald Hendrix (London: Routledge, 2008), 2 and 10n5.
6. For detailed discussions of these topics, I refer to Nicola Watson and Andrea Zemgulys, *Modernism and the Locations of Literary Heritage* (Cambridge: Cambridge University Press, 2008); and Hendrix, "Writers' Houses."
7. Price, *How to Do Things with Books,* 6, emphasis added.
8. Ibid., 35–36.
9. For more on Price, see my review of *How to Do Things with Books* in *Reception: Texts, Readers, Audiences, History* 5 (2013): 100–103. In a 2013 piece, she examines coffee table books and their place in our digital culture in more detail. Especially interesting for my analysis are her observations that such books celebrate the "glamor" of print "in the digital age" and that the joys of reading are increasingly interwoven with things like "wine and cheese." See Leah Price, "Books on Books," *Public Books,* June 5, 2013, Publicbooks.org.
10. Pierre Bayard, *How to Talk about Books You Haven't Read,* trans. Jeffrey Mehlman (2007; repr., New York: Bloomsbury, 2009), 30.
11. I am grateful to the editors for pushing my analysis further in this respect.
12. The popularity of annuals in the early nineteenth century has been linked to "middle-class interest in aristocratic culture," as Vanessa Warne observes. "Featuring portraits of lords and ladies, as well as poems by them, many annuals celebrated aristocrats, their lifestyles and their values" Warne, "Thackeray among the Annuals," 160. These books looked like aristocratic items as well, with their ornate bindings and costly engravings.
13. Roland Barthes argued that some sections of a literary text are easier to penetrate than others, but the same does not apply, in my view, to coffee table books. In his term, such books are "isotropic": because they are often opened at random, every part should have roughly the same overall effect. See Roland Barthes, *The Pleasure of the Text* (1973; repr., New York: Hill and Wang, 1975), 36–37.
14. Leibovitz, *Pilgrimage,* 136–37, 138–39.
15. See Bodo Plachta, "Remembrance and Revision: Goethe's Houses in Weimar and Frankfurt," 54, and Anne Rigney, "Abbotsford: Dislocation and Cultural Remembrance," 80, both in Hendrix, *Writers' Houses and the Making of Memory,* emphasis added.

16. See Eric O. Clarke, "Kant's Kiss: Reflections on the Philosophy of Lifestyle," *boundary 2,* 38, no. 2 (2011), 204. To return to the *OED,* "lifestyle" refers not just to "the characteristic manner in which a person lives his or her life" but also to "a product etc. which is designed to appeal to consumers by association with a lifestyle regarded as desirable."
17. McClatchy and Lennard, *American Writers at Home,* 106, 185 (pools); 42, 63, 167, 184, 205 (gardens); 32, 100, 115–16, 119, 158, 205 (dinner tables); 211 (kitchens); and 172 (bathrooms).
18. For further details, see Jim Collins, *Bring on the Books for Everybody: How Literary Culture Became Popular Culture* (Durham: Duke University Press, 2010); and Ben De Bruyn, "E-readers, Deconvergence Culture and McSweeney's Circle: An Interview with Jim Collins," *Image and Narrative* 14, no. 3 (2013): 193–206. That many of the developments singled out by Collins have predecessors in earlier periods is amply shown, for instance, in Joan Shelley Rubin's *Songs of Ourselves: The Uses of Poetry in America* (Cambridge: Harvard University Press, 2007).
19. See Library Hotel, Library Hotel Services, www.libraryhotel.com, and the Bookmarks Lounge description on the New York City tourist website nyctourist.com, Bookmarks Lounge, www.nyctourist.com/bookmarks-lounge.
20. See Gary Shteyngart, *Super Sad True Love Story* (New York: Random House, 2010); and the description of 'Paper Passion' on the Steidl website, "Paper Passion," http://steidlville.com/books.
21. Collins, *Bring on the Books for Everybody,* 228, 61, 64, 65, 12, 245, 236.
22. A similar argument might be made about *Pilgrimage* and *A Journey through Literary America.* Consider the irrelevant photo of the beach chairs in the latter book (268–69) or the remark by Leibovitz that Emily Dickinson "must have spent as much time gardening as writing" (*Pilgrimage,* 52). It's also interesting to see that the photographer of *American Writers at Home* has published many books on gardens and that the publisher of *A Journey through Literary America* is related to various wineries. See Val de Grâce Books, "Our Books," www.valdegracebooks.com.
23. McClatchy and Lennard, *American Writers at Home,* 14, 80, 106, 147.
24. Ibid., 32, 116.
25. Ibid., 168, 188, 203.
26. Ibid., 67, 94, 137, 194, 127.
27. Ibid., 37, 70, 108, 140, 172, 203.
28. Ibid., 31, 106.
29. I am grateful to Jennifer Harris for this observation.
30. McClatchy and Lennard, *American Writers at Home,* 7, emphasis added.
31. Ibid.
32. Ibid., 75, 210, 204. A similar message can be found in the introduction to *A Journey through Literary America;* apparently the relative poverty in which classic American authors struggled at the beginning of their careers differs sharply from the spending sprees of contemporary society: "What a pleasure beyond wealth it was for them to be able to write and . . . to read." After all, "reading is inexpensive." Hummel and Dempsey, *A Journey through Literary America,* 1. The houses and gardens we see in this book, not to mention the leisure time needed to enjoy them, are not so easy to come by, however.
33. Ibid., 127.
34. Marie Proeller Hueston, *Decorating with Books: Use Your Library to Enhance Your Décor* (New York: Hearst Books, 2006). Other examples of coffee table books specializing in bibliophilic decoration advice include Leslie Geddes-Brown's *Books Do Furnish a Room* (London: Merrell, 2009); and Damian Thompson, *Books Make a Home* (London: Ryland Peters and Small, 2011).
35. Hueston, *Decorating with Books,* 123, 30, 35, 36, 107, 119.
36. Ibid., 54, 63, 137, 133.
37. Ibid., 19. Certain photos in *Decorating with Books* show that we can even juxtapose books with kitchens, bathrooms, and pools. See the kitchen with built-in bookcases, the guest

bathroom with library, and the picture of two bookcases flanking a window that overlooks the pool (59, 118, 63). For more on Wharton (and her take on libraries and unread books), see Caroline Hellman's chapter in this volume. For my own take on Wharton and nonreading, see Ben De Bruyn, "Where to Do Things with Words: Circulating Books, Decorating Rooms and Locating Modern Reading," *Orbis Litterarum* 68, no. 6 (2013): 457–72.

38. Hueston, *Decorating with Books,* 60, 92, 73, 29, 125, 116. In the terminology of Jim Collins, we are in a "Lit-lit" setting here. For further details, see Collins, *Bring on the Books.*
39. Hueston, *Decorating with Books,* 136, 121, 56, 115, 56, 116.
40. Ibid., 91.
41. Ibid., 24, 87, 43.
42. Ibid., 12, 15, emphasis added to both.
43. If the literary movies analyzed by Collins are an expression of "cine-bibliophilia" (*Bring on the Books,* 120), library photographs in coffee table books express a related *photographic* form of bibliophilia. Note, in that respect, that one of the first photographs ever published in book form was William Henry Fox Talbot's "A Scene in a Library," included in his mid-nineteenth-century collection *The Pencil of Nature.* This photographic bibliophilia has a long history, in other words, and should be studied in more detail. H. Fox Talbot, *The Pencil of Nature* (London: Longman, Brown, Green and Longmans, 1844). I'm grateful to Jan Baetens for this reference.
44. Eudora Welty bequeathed her ancestral home to the State of Mississippi. Originally built in the 1920s, it closely resembles that way it appeared in the 1980s. Allegedly, it is "one of the most intact literary houses in America"; "its exterior, interior and furnishings" are unchanged, with "thousands of books in their original places." Robinson Jeffers's idiosyncratic and partly self-constructed Tor House in Carmel, California, has been acquired and maintained by a foundation of volunteers; it looks much as it did in the late 1950s. Herman Melville's Arrowhead was built in the late eighteenth century and underwent several alterations after Melville spent his most productive years there in the middle of the nineteenth century. Acquired by the Berkshire County Historical Society in 1975, it has since been actively restored to a state closer to Melville's period. See Eudora Welty Foundation, "The House," http://eudorawelty.org; Robinson Jeffers Tor House Foundation, "Tor House," www.torhouse.org/; Berkshire Historical Society; "Herman Melville and Arrowhead," http://berkshirehistory.org.
45. McClatchy and Lennard, *American Writers at Home,* 200; and Hueston, *Decorating with Books,* 80.
46. Hueston, *Decorating with Books,* 71.
47. Ibid., 15.
48. Ibid., 11.
49. McClatchy and Lennard, *American Writers at Home,* 196; Hueston, *Decorating with Books,* 136.
50. Hueston, *Decorating with Books,* 136.
51. McClatchy and Lennard, *American Writers at Home,* 196, Hueston, *Decorating with Books,* 136.
52. Hueston, *Decorating with Books,* 36.
53. McClatchy and Lennard, *American Writers at Home,* 160; Hueston, *Decorating with Books,* 68.
54. Hueston, *Decorating with Books,* 45.
55. McClatchy and Lennard, *American Writers at Home,* 125; Hueston, *Decorating with Books,* 138.
56. That these photos of libraries imaginatively place the reader in the position of the owner of such books is made clear if we compare them to pictures of authors in their libraries, such as the images featuring Paul Beatty (12), Lucille Clifton (24), Edwidge Danticat (28), Haki R. Madhubuti (70), and Albert Murray (85) that appear in *African American*

*Writers.* In this instance the blurred books provide a backdrop for the presentation of the author, rather than functioning as objects to be scrutinized in their own right, and hence underline the difference between author and reader. If the reader is here excluded from participation, so to speak, the chairs and books in the coffee-table books I'm examining invite the reader, as it were, to participate in the literary life and construct his or her own home accordingly.

57. Price, *Unpacking My Library,* 183, 111, 47, 128, 108.
58. Hueston, *Decorating with Books,* 64.
59. Goldstein quoted in Price, *Unpacking My Library,* 66.
60. Ibid., 7, 163, 198–99, 212, 219.
61. Nicole Krauss, *Great House* (London: Penguin Books, 2010), 8.
62. Lest we forget, many writers were not well-off and experienced financial and other forms of hardship that are diametrically opposed to the good-life fantasies I have described. Lauren Berlant might add that the good life remains brittle in our "precarious" contemporary times. For further details, see Lauren Berlant, *Cruel Optimism* (Durham: Duke University Press, 2011).
63. Daniel Harris, *Cute, Quaint, Hungry and Romantic: The Aesthetics of Consumerism* (Cambridge: Da Capo Press, 2000).
64. Ibid., 41, 42.
65. This is one example of what she calls the "commodified authentic." Elizabeth Outka, *Consuming Traditions: Modernity, Modernism and the Commodified Authentic* (Oxford: Oxford University Press, 2009), 85, 89.
66. Ibid., 72, 71, 80, 84.
67. Ibid., 69, 69, 90. Compare Anne Rigney's remarks on "memorial layering" and the "tension between . . . memorial layers" in memory sites like Walter Scott's Abbotsford. Anne Rigney, "Abbotsford: Dislocation and Cultural Remembrance," in Hendrix, *Writers' Houses,* 81.
68. See Dean MacCannell, "Staged Authenticity: Arrangements of Social Space in Tourist Settings," *American Journal of Sociology* 79, no. 3 (1973): 589–603.
69. The distinction between "objects" and "things" (and the material culture perspective more generally) is based on Bill Brown's seminal volume *A Sense of Things: The Object Matter of American Literature* (Chicago: University of Chicago Press, 2003).
70. Hueston, *Decorating with Books,* 20.
71. Price, *Unpacking My Library,* 85, 47.
72. Ibid., 103.
73. McClatchy and Lennard, *American Writers at Home,* 105; Harris, *Cute, Quaint, Hungry and Romantic,* 45.

# 10

# *The Allure of American Authors' Homes*

## Surveying Nineteenth- and Twentieth-Century Literary Guides

SUSANN BISHOP

*Surveying some of the more than one hundred guides for literary tourists produced between 1853 and 1940, Susann Bishop delves into the American interest in literary biography and literary homes. She notes that our interest in literary "coffee table" books has a long history. Some of the early guides featured etchings that rendered authors' homes from every possible vantage point; others more carefully negotiated the private lives of writers. These guides helped mightily in the development of American literary culture and may have provided a blueprint for our obsession with celebrity. Bishop's chapter and her bibliography of these guides opens a window into how Americans have made their attachment to literary places and people more than a hobby but also a long-standing industry and fascination.*

It was the belief of many mid-nineteenth-century Americans that one way in which a nation demonstrated its maturity was through the production of an original and vibrant national literature. As Longfellow wrote, "The true glory of a nation is moral and intellectual preeminence." Writers were encouraged to contribute to the project through writing on national themes; readers were invited to participate in the project through purchasing and reading these works. Doing so, it follows, wasn't simply a matter of intellectual engagement; it was a celebration of national achievement. For many devoted readers, it wasn't enough simply to read the works. They wanted to experience a closer connection to the authors they valued, the undisputed celebrities of their day. These readers also purchased or collected materials associated with them. Visiting their homes—even through the written word—was the next logical step. In this way, American literary tourism, emerging in the 1820s and 1830s, came of age with American literature itself. The result was the production of over a hundred literary guides between 1853 and 1940, all of which relate to the homes and haunts of American authors. Through illustrations, photographs, and colorful descriptions, these volumes sought to feed the public's fascination with a writer's home and environment. Serving the interests of publishers—who sought to build an audience—as much as they did writers, these literary guides played a meaningful role in establishing American literary culture, and reveal much about the writers, reading public, and publishers of the period. (For a select bibliography of guides for literary tourists, especially those early and influential works that attest to the rise and depth of the phenomenon, see the appendix at the end of this chapter.)

Harald Hendrix has noted that literary tourism has its roots in the 1340s, when Petrarch, accompanied by friends, undertook a self-described literary pilgrimage to Naples in search of sites associated with Virgil. In the nineteenth century, however, literary tourism assumed unprecedented popularity, when, increasingly, British travelers developed a taste for visiting a range of places associated with favorite authors and their writings.[1] Julian North has tied this cultural phenomenon to another: the period's rage for biography. Locating the market success of biography in its representation and publication of domestic life, North goes on to claim that "in many ways biography encouraged and sustained the practice of literary tourism." In fact, she says, "it was one of the most significant means of establishing authors as celebrities."[2]

Notably, biographies included descriptions or even engravings of writers' houses as well as extended descriptions of the communities, towns, cities, and/or other environs in which they might be found. A familiarity with the author's environment was presented as key to understanding the author. As H. N. Powers claims in *The Homes and Haunts of Our Elder Poets,* "We find in all biographies that all writers, even the greatest, are influenced by their surroundings."[3]

The circulation of images of authors' homes and re-creations of an "authentic" experience as presented in such biographies facilitated an imaginary journey that might further mobilize readers themselves to go and visit the houses in which their favorite authors lived, worked, and wrote. As a result, there was a growing interest in places associated with writers and artists on both sides of the Atlantic during the mid- to late 1800s, even among authors themselves. But of course, authors were there from the start, creating their own shrines and visiting others. For example, by the mid- to late nineteenth century, American writers Ralph Waldo Emerson, Henry Wadsworth Longfellow, and Harriet Beecher Stowe all made pilgrimages to Great Britain to visit Sir Walter Scott's Abbotsford and Robert Burns's birthplace and his favorite haunts in Scotland.

There are numerous factors that laid the groundwork for American literary tourism. The early nineteenth century led to the rise of the professional author in the United States, respected for his or (less commonly) her work, and this for the first time enabled authors to eke out a living from their writing. The rise of literacy, combined with the expansion of the publishing industry and the increase in population, meant that not only were more people reading, but also they were reading a wider variety of indigenous materials than they had previously been able to access.[4] As Margaret D. Stetz has observed, publishers and booksellers were eager to maintain a captive audience by actively promoting authors, and in the 1820s and 1830s, numerous accounts of literary journeys were produced for public consumption.[5] During the 1830s and 1840s, the increased interest in the domestic space of authors and the sites that inspired them, or to areas related to their works of fiction, spawned literary tourism in America. Visiting the houses of famous authors not only helped foster an appreciation of literature and writing but also enabled travelers to immerse themselves in the local culture while increasing their knowledge about the authors and their works.

Authors, acutely aware of readers' interests, and more than likely prompted by their publishers to increase sales, actively encouraged readers to imagine their domestic spaces or sites associated with their works as sites of consumption. William Cullen Bryant, considered by many to be the first truly American poet, helped inspire readers with his poetry about the quintessential American landscape surrounding his "Homestead" in Cummington, Massachusetts. *The Bryant Homestead-Book* (1870) was issued with "A Supplementary Word from the Author," preceded by Bryant's mounted photographic portrait as frontispiece, under which appears a facsimile holograph personal note: "Yours at the Old Homestead. / William Cullen Bryant. / —Cummington August 7th 1869—." This note not only personalized the volume but also represented Bryant's personal seal of approval. According to the publisher, Putnam, the book was "intended to honor our Veteran Poet and to gratify his hosts of friends and admirers with sketches of his home life in connection with themes from his works."[6] Another nineteenth-century author, N. P. Willis, encouraged readers to imagine him as a literary celebrity. He represented his study in ways we recognize from biography: as an imagined site of pilgrimage. According to Francis Whiting Halsey, Willis was "the first magazine writer who was tolerably well paid," and it was Willis "who took the lead in pecuniary success among authors that were next in succession to Irving and Cooper."[7] Of course, being from a family of publishers, Willis more than likely saw the financial advantage and was aware that his reputation was based in part on the relationship he built with his readers by infusing his personality into his writing. In addition, the vivid descriptions of American scenes found in poetry and prose then—as well as now—enticed readers to visit the places that had inspired the writers. As Mark Twain wrote in *Tom Sawyer Abroad,* "There ain't anything that is so interesting to look at as a place that a book has talked about."[8]

That said, the reported personality of the author—perceived or real—also played a part in attracting readers to literary sites. Poets in particular captivated Americans, whose appetite for information about them seemed insatiable. Newspapers and magazines carried monthly literary portraits and profiles; photographs and *cartes de visite* circulated, and photographic stereographs provided three-dimensional looks at celebrity authors' homes. This fascination with authors not only provided reading enjoyment but also entered into nineteenth-century parlor entertainment by way of trivia, charades, and card games such as "Authors."

Authors themselves were not unaware of themselves as commodities. Washington Irving was the first American author who benefited from the interest in literary homes. Paul Westover has argued that it was Irving who suggested how an American itinerary of British and, by analogy, American literary tourist sites might be established. By the late 1820s, Irving gained a reputation in Europe and America as a great writer. During the nineteenth century, Irving's Sunnyside in Tarrytown, New York, exemplified *the* "American Home" to the public, and images of it appeared in prints, paintings, magazines advertisements, sheet music, tourist maps, and daguerreotypes, and even on cigar boxes. Oliver Wendell Holmes remarked that Sunnyside stood "next to Mount Vernon, the best known and most cherished of all dwellings in our land."[9] Francis Whiting Halsey attributes the growth of interest and attention paid to authors' homes to Washington Irving more, perhaps, than any other person, and *The Knickerbocker Gallery* and *The Homes and Haunts of Our Elder Poets* owe much to the success of Irving's publications. According to Halsey, "before Irving went to Stratford, few were the pilgrims who sought the streets of Shakespeare's town."[10] Westover claims that by establishing classic ground in his native country and by weaving literary associations into its landscape, Irving had created a literary America—an America of interest to literary tourists.[11] Authors such as Irving and Longfellow sought to preserve American regionalism and their hometowns through their writings. Correspondingly, readers welcomed this opportunity to visit an author's environs—even if only vicariously through reading.

At once participating in and inventing this celebrity culture, American popular presses began to supply a growing number of guidebooks, periodicals, and maps focusing on literary heritage for use as travel companions for virtual or actual literary pilgrimages to satisfy nineteenth-century readers and their fascination with authors. For the Victorian-era Americans who could not travel to the literary shrines, the books provided the next best thing to being there. The "homes and haunts" guides integrated biographical and geographical information about literary personalities. In addition, by the mid-nineteenth century, publishers soon discovered that they could help attract readers and increase sales by binding their books in fashionable, appealing styles with ornate designs. Correspondingly, the guidebooks, ephemera, and other print material furthered the activities of literary tourism.

The experience of reading literary guidebooks, according to Francis Halsey, was, "one form of gratitude . . . for several delightful hours, obtained for the price of a pair of gloves, or for less, through a subscription at the library; a gratitude responding to those who, by their writings for a modest pecuniary recompense, have spread learning, developed culture, consoled sorrow, and assuaged pain."[12] Gratitude, of course, may have been one reason for reading or purchasing these books; for many readers, however, such books provided an additional form of pleasure and a source for self-improvement. Alison Booth elaborates: "Literary shrines answered to spectators' demands for a mixture of entertainment and self-improvement at the thresholds of mortality. Later in the nineteenth century, volumes of 'homes and haunts' capitalized on developments in travel, publishing, education, and leisure, serving as travel memoirs, guidebooks, and albums of literary portraiture and criticism."[13]

The 1820s and 1830s saw the publication of a number of accounts of journeys to the homes of authors such as Washington Irving and William Cullen Bryant. Many of these accounts were based on interviews with the authors and were printed in various newspapers and periodicals of the time. In 1853 G. P. Putnam took matters a step further by publishing the first American full-length book on literary homes, *Homes of American Authors* (hereafter *HAA*). The volume is a collection of author profiles written by a group of thirteen different writers devoted to the studies and descriptions of the homes and the works of representative American authors of the time. It is a wonderfully illustrated guide to the homes, habits, and towns of Irving, Emerson, Longfellow, Hawthorne, and others. According to Charles Frederick Briggs, who edited the collection of essays, the plan for the series originated with Putnam. The publisher, however, was probably inspired in part by *Homes and Haunts of the Most Eminent British Poets,* published by his London friend William

Howett.[14] George William Curtis was asked to oversee the book's preparation and composition; he declined, however, but offered instead to contribute individual sketches. Putnam himself assumed primary responsibility with help from Frederick Sanders and Charles Frederick Briggs, who at the time was editor of *Putnam's Monthly.* Scheduled for Christmas 1852, *HAA* proved to be one of the most ambitious projects Putnam embarked on that year.[15]

The authors selected were those "in whom the public were imagined to feel a sufficient degree of interest to entitle them to a place in a work like this."[16] Many of the authors included in *HAA* were those whom Putnam was already publishing (e.g., Irving, Hawthorne, Bryant), and others such as Longfellow and Emerson were writers with whom he had a friendship or acquaintance. As entrepreneurs, publishers made the decisions and accepted the risks necessary to make the book trade operate and succeed. Therefore, choice of authors was determined by whom the publisher perceived as having the greatest potential for attracting the largest audience—quite simply, which authors were selling the most books. Publishing, however, was not strictly an economic activity. Several firms, such as Putnam, Ticknor and Fields, and Lothrop, were noted for concentrating on publishing literature and poetry for the higher-minded purpose of educating, inspiring, and developing an appreciation for American literary culture.[17] So the decision about which authors to include in this and other works was made on the basis of literary tastes at the time, inspiration, canon building, and economics, among other factors.

In the case of *HAA,* the book proved not to be as good a business proposition as Putnam had hoped, as the preparation and production costs were extraordinarily high. The production of the volume was labor intensive. Not only did it involve sometimes delicate negotiations with subjects for their permission to be included, but also it called for extensive correspondence and meetings with contributors willing to write the sketches of the selected American authors and their residences.[18] Likewise, it required Putnam's oversight of the artists and engravers. The volume includes images engraved from original drawings, with the exception of two that were made from daguerreotypes. In addition to the tedious work involved, Putnam chose to employ a costly progressive color printing technology for the illustrations. The volume contains fourteen very charming color vignettes made from wood engravings and printed on thin tissue and mounted onto the book's sheets in the manner of chiaroscuro printing, whereby each color is successively printed, and the whites are unprinted portions of the image.[19] This technique, which never caught on in America, emphasized the interplay of light and dark. Daniel Francis McGrath notes that *HAA* offers "one of the most polished and complex examples of this technique in American books."[20]

Putnam, noted for being involved in developing literary culture, promoting American authorship, and producing finely illustrated books, wanted to attract and market this book to readers with varying tastes and means. As with previous endeavors, he was confident that there existed a sufficiently large and prosperous readership to justify this elaborate publication. He offered it as a gift book in at least five different full leather bindings and four different decorative cloth bindings. As evidenced by the variety of bindings, the book was obviously designed to be an object of pleasure—decorating the house of the individual and testifying to his or her taste just as the descriptions within testified to the merit of the authors.

*HAA* is additionally interesting because it was written by prominent American authors. George William Curtis, William Cullen Bryant, Caroline M. Kirkland, George Hillard, H. T. Tuckerman, and Parke Godwin wrote about Cooper, Emerson, Hawthorne, and others. Although it is not clear who wrote some of the sections (a few are still the subject of scholarly debate), Curtis proudly mentions his role in the Emerson article.[21] His boast would also seem to be about putting himself in the company of the authors included in the book.

Like Putnam and a few other mid-nineteenth-century publishers, D. Lothrop and Company concentrated on publishing literature, appealed to the literary culture of the day, and encouraged American authors. Lothrop issued more books written by Americans than any other publisher at that time.[22] In 1877 Lothrop published *Poets' Homes: Pen and Pencil Sketches of American Poets and Their Homes* by R. H. Stoddard. Though lacking color illustrations, and less impressively bound than *HAA,* the set profiles twenty-six authors, including several women. It would be impractical to give a complete list here, but among the more prominent are Henry Wadsworth Longfellow, John Greenleaf Whittier, James Russell Lowell, Bayard Taylor, Mrs. Celia Thaxter, Thomas Bailey Aldrich, Oliver Wendell Holmes, Walt Whitman, Joaquin Miller, and Elizabeth Stuart Phelps, to name a few. In 1881 D. Appleton and Company published *The Homes and Haunts of Our Elder Poets: With Portraits and Illustrations.* It was beautifully bound in green cloth with lettering and design in gold. Illustrations within include portraits, autograph verses, exteriors and interiors of homes and scenes, and portraits of Bryant, Emerson, Longfellow, Whittier, and Holmes.

Then along came Elbert Hubbard with his *Little Journeys* series, perhaps the most widely known collection of literary pilgrimages.[23] *HAA* was the source text for G. P. Putnam's Sons' second volume of Hubbard's *Little Journeys.* In fact the reissue, also brought out by Putnam's Sons, incorporates Hubbard's new piece on Whitman. The essays were printed as originally written for George Putnam's volume because, "there is a certain literary interest in having again before us the point of view of these writers of 1853, even though in certain cases their final conclusions may have been somewhat modified or their mature literary judgment may have arrived at some different form of literary expression."[24]

Clearly Hubbard's involvement with Putnam's original homes-of-authors venture demonstrated further that the audience for this kind of material was popular around the 1890s. Yet by the time of Hubbard's entrance, many of the authors Putnam had covered were dead—though their homes were still very much "alive"—thereby shifting the genre to a historical one. Of course this is also the period of time when biography comes greatly into vogue in America.[25] Likewise, G. P. Putnam's Sons elected to reprint the papers of the original contributors as a second group in a series into this newly published work, titled *Little Journeys to the Homes of American Authors.*[26]

Between 1886 and 1907 G. P. Putnam's Sons, the successors to G. P. Putnam, reprinted the "little journeys" pieces twenty-two times as the second group of Elbert Hubbard's series of *Little Journeys.* Hubbard took over publication from Putnam in 1900, and according to McKenna, "although the details of the transfer are unknown it is evident that part of the agreement was Hubbard's permission for Putnam's to continue to publish those titles already issued by them and that Hubbard would not duplicate those *Little Journeys.* Putnam's could not have been pleased to have this series pass out of its hands, since every journey had exceeded ten printings of the bound volumes, and the most popular, *Little Journeys to the Homes of Famous Women,* went to twenty thousand copies.[27] Hubbard's involvement expanded well beyond that of American authors to include the homes of famous women, eminent painters, American statesmen, and "good men and great," which covers English authors and in which Hubbard includes one George Eliot, though her portrait assures the reader that this is not one of the "good men."

Hubbard was not the only one to capitalize on the ongoing interest in American writers. Equally ambitious was Theodore F. Wolfe, whose four-volume series was published by J. B. Lippincott Company in the late 1890s. Unlike Putnam or Hubbard, Wolfe had the distinction of being a genuine literary tourist himself, boasting no professional credentials as an author or publisher. A noted physician-surgeon who served in the Army of the Potomac, Wolfe had later established a lucrative practice in New Jersey. Upon retiring, he and his wife traveled to the homes and haunts of some their favorite authors. According to Wolfe, the materials for each volume had been derived from prolonged or repeated sojourns in the localities described and from personal intercourse and correspondence with the authors mentioned or with their surviving friends and neighbors. Wolfe encouraged reading vicariously through his experiences, personal details, and impressions. Walt Whitman was quite popular and open to visits from the public—and those who sought him out in Camden, New Jersey, are referred to as "Whitmaniacs" in the chapter "A Day with the Good Gray Poet"—whom Mr. and Mrs. Wolfe were pleased to meet in his upstairs room. Wolfe later includes a section on and an image of Whitman's final resting place, his tomb in Harleigh Cemetery, located in Camden.[28] Turning to yet another favorite, Wolfe writes that the view of Poe Cottage in Fordham, New York, was made just prior to its removal.

Each of Wolfe's four volumes was complete within itself; in fact, each volume was differently titled to indicate clearly that it stood alone but could be grouped with its companions, since they were uniformly sized and displayed the same cover decorations. No volume number was assigned to any title. The buyer could purchase them separately or in any combination, choosing among "Crushed Buckram, Half-Calf, or Half Morocco" (according to the verso of the half-title page in Wolfe's *Literary Haunts and Homes* volume). There was also the option offered to purchase a larger-format set of the first two volumes, referred to as the "Edition De Luxe." These two volumes featured additional illustrations beyond the four photogravures found in each of the regular volumes, were printed on special handmade paper, were numbered, and were bound in buckram with a special gilt cover design. Many illustrations in Wolfe's series were reproduced from "new and heretofore unpublished photographs" (according to the publisher's preface).

The initial Wolfe-Lippincott volume, *A Literary Pilgrimage: Among the Haunts of Some Famous British Authors* (1895), focuses on the lives and works of writers beginning with Chaucer's time. The second volume in the series, *Literary Shrines: The Haunts of Some Famous American Authors* (1895), includes Hawthorne, Emerson, Alcott, Thoreau, Longfellow, Lowell, Whittier, Howells, Holmes, Parkman, Fuller, and others. The mere presence of the uniformly sized volume of American authors alongside its British counterpart demonstrably places the Americans on a similar plane of worthiness, although Wolfe doesn't explicitly say so in his preface. Additionally, at both front and back, the second editions of the British and American volumes reciprocally contain advertisements for the other volume.

As more volumes in Wolfe's series appeared, more American authors were presented. *Literary Haunts and Homes* (1898), the third volume in the series, features an assemblage of the stomping grounds of key American literary figures from the latter half of the 1800s, including Kipling (admittedly British but with notable American residency), as well as Mark Twain, Warner,

Howells, Poe, Bryant, Cooper, Irving, Stowe, and Whitman. Of course the accounts reflected Wolfe's very personalized self-guided tour, and for the most part presented sanitized versions suitable for family reading; for example, Poe's haunts were not fully disclosed, although Wolfe does allude to "the pathetic circumstances of his life" and "its miseries and debasements." Further insights were garnered from the connection Wolfe made with neighbors or relatives who shared some of their reminiscences and perceptions of the writers. The final book in the series, *Literary Rambles at Home and Abroad* (1901), served as a catchall volume further expanding the roster of Americans in the first five chapters, while the last five "add to the succession of popular British authors" (as the preface puts it). The two-sides-of-the-pond mix is thought-provoking.

While Putnam's book was very much of the moment, the Wolfe volumes benefited from the growth of the publishing industry in the 1850s–1890s and the corresponding filtering of literary reputations through the sieve of historical hindsight, determining which would be the lasting ones. The *Literary Shrines* volume is very New England and Transcendentalist in orientation, while its immediate successor, *Literary Haunts,* greatly expanded the field into New York.

Wolfe's series was a success, something he did not shy away from mentioning. A note in the preface of the 1898 edition of *Literary Haunts and Homes* announces that "the kindness which has been accorded to the previous books of this series—a kindness so generous that it has already called for ten editions besides an 'Edition de Luxe'—encourages the author to hope that the present volume may receive a measure of the same favor."[29] He encouraged those who had not yet purchased the earlier volumes to do so.

Authors were cognizant of the power of literary tourism, many having participated in their own such journeys. When making her literary pilgrimage in 1892 to the Brontë parsonage in Haworth, England, writer Sarah Orne Jewett astutely stated, "When you visit the home of a writer, you always find something of what made them the souls they were . . . you see their sky and their earth."[30] Accordingly, authors were aware of not only the interest the public might have in them but also the way in which such interest might increase their own reputation, sales, and opportunities. Publishers seized on this, inviting writers to participate actively in the promotion of their reputation by contributing to literary guidebooks. In 1901 James Pott and Company published the first of a three-part series, *American Authors and Their Homes: Personal Descriptions and Interviews,* edited by Francis Whiting Halsey. Authors the publisher was interested in featuring received a handwritten letter that read:

> James Pott and Co. desires a photograph of an exterior of your home or of your library for reproduction in a vol. he is [about] to publish entitled "Amer. Authors and Their Homes"—a vol. made up chiefly of matter reprinted from the N.Y. [Saturday] Rev. & restricted to 25 of the best known names [of] many writers now living. The book will have an introduction by Mr. Francis W. Halsey, editor of the Sat. Rev., & be prepared for the press by Mr. Halsey. My intent is to send a review proof to you before printing the book.[31]

Presumably authors were expected to be flattered by being considered among the "25 of the best known" living writers and to assent. Many did. The homes of Richard Stoddard, John Burroughs, Henry van Dyke, and William Dean Howells are included in this volume. At the same time, featured writers received no profit from the sale of the book or other ephemera associated with them, from the "Authors" card games to postcards. It is clear, however, that the publisher intended to profit handsomely from the volume. The verso of the title page states that the articles were printed originally in the *New York Times,* all but two of them in the *New York Times Saturday Review of Books and Art Times.*

Because of the increasing number of authors earning a living from writing, James Pott and Company decided to publish a second volume in the series. Edited and compiled by Halsey, *Authors of Our Day in Their Homes* (1902) included twenty-two additional "noteworthy writers." Mark Twain (whose photograph is on the front cover), Edwin Markham, and John Bigelow were among the authors included who were still alive at publication; only two of the featured authors, John Fiske and Charles Dudley Warner, had died "somewhat recently," according to the introduction. The articles on the writers in this volume were originally published by the *New York Times Saturday Review of Books* (in 1898, 1899, 1901, and 1902); Halsey, however, made additions and changes to the sketches.

While the first two volumes issued in the series dealt exclusively with homes of men, the last volume abruptly changed genders: *Women Authors of Our Day in Their Homes* (1903). Halsey, who again edited and compiled the sketches, writes in the preface that since the appearance of the first two volumes, "authorship has become a source of income to women," a considerable number of whom "found it the means to a comfortable livelihood." Profiles by a dozen writers feature twenty-seven authors, including Frances Hodgson Burnett, Kate Douglas Wiggin, Julia Ward Howe, and Mary Mapes Dodge, to name only a few. As in the first two books of the series, the sketches were based on interviews and visits to the authors' homes and included some biographical information and a short list of notable works.

In 1902 the Wessels Company reprinted O. M. Dunham's 1888–89 edition of *Authors at Home: Personal and Biographical Sketches of Well-Known American Writers,* edited by J. L. and J. B. Gilder. The sketches had previously appeared from time to time in *The Critic,* where, according to the "Editor's Note" in the first edition, they attracted particular attention by virtue of their authenticity as well as the names of the subjects and writers. The sketches in the 1888 edition offer an intimate view of twenty-seven authors—all living at the time of publication—and provide very specific descriptions of the furnishings of their homes and particular details of the neighborhoods in which they lived, conveying a sense of place. The 1902 edition adds Mrs. Margaret Deland, F. Marion Crawford, and Paul Leicester Ford to the list of authors. Although the 1888 edition contains no illustrations, the 1902 edition adds portraits of Walt Whitman, George William Curtis, William Dean Howells, and F. Marion Crawford. What is particularly interesting and important about both editions, we are told, is that the sketches of authors have "as their special value the fact that the writer of each article was selected for the purpose by the author himself."[32]

In 1902 L. C. Page and Company published two of E. F. Harkins's titles: *Little Pilgrimages among the Men Who Have Written Famous Books* and *Little Pilgrimages among the Women Who Have Written Famous Books.* Although the volumes focused more on biographical information than on homes and haunts, the aim of both books was to present sketches of American literary heroes. Thus the narrative touches on the places the authors frequented and presents information about their social or personal lives as well as their professional side.

While many guides claimed to be national, some focused exclusively, or almost exclusively, on writers from the Northeast. Edwin M. Bacon's 1902 *Literary Pilgrimages in New England* emphasized an awareness of the beginnings, development, and expansion of American literary efforts in New England. Bacon describes the homes and haunts of "all New England writers who have made a distinct mark on American literature" and the places about which they wrote that he and his friend Percy Denison visited during their summer vacation.[33] The book includes something about the authors' literary lives, their methods of work, and their influence on the literature of their day. In this way Bacon is participating in a kind of canon formation, or at least a form of historical literary criticism. *Literary Pilgrimages* covers several celebrated authors—such as Whittier, Longfellow, Hawthorne, Celia Thaxter, and Sarah Orne Jewett—as well as several now obscure women writers. He includes Mary Abigail Dodge (who published under the pseudonym Gail Hamilton), who was among the earliest to write in a popular vein for women's rights, and Elizabeth Oakes Smith, the first woman in America to appear as a public lecturer. Bacon also writes about Anna S. W. Stephens, a writer from Portland, Maine, who authored fifty novels. One of her novels, *Fashion and Famine,* in its day reached a circulation second only to Harriet Beecher Stowe's *Uncle Tom's Cabin,* yet how many readers are aware of her or recognize her name now? Bacon's account is a tad sentimental, and in some instances emphasizes the morality of the authors (something no one did for a man like Poe). This may be because the book was aimed at children and marketed to schools and libraries.[34]

To avoid a glut of such books on the market, sometimes the approach to constructing these literary guidebooks changed depending on the target audience. In some cases the content was more oriented toward a coffee table approach—a book to be shared in the parlor or library. The emphasis was on the architecture, aimed at house lovers, rather than solely on insights into the author's life at that house. In other instances there may have been a regional or particular geographic focus. The emphasis could diverge widely from the norm; for example, a book might describe the surrounding flora and fauna, as though directed to the naturalist. One might judge such volumes to be a bit quirky or eccentric; there was, however, a range of articles and books published at this time that focused on naturalist observations, such as William Howitt's *Book of the Seasons.*

A good example of the large coffee table type is Oliver Branson Capen's *Country Homes of Famous Americans,* published in 1905. This sumptuous volume "takes the reader into the country homes of nearly a score [eighteen] of famous men of the past" and offers "ideal examples of the most beautiful and homelike country places that have been developed in this country." In the book's introduction, Thomas Wentworth Higginson (prolific author and noted supporter of Emily Dickinson) proclaims that "this book is based upon the principle that no man's biography is at all complete without some portrayal of the house he lived in. The house, moreover, is sure to represent, in a greater or less degree, not merely the tastes and habit of his household, but the private background of his public life." The book is profusely illustrated with exterior and interior views of the homes of these "famous Americans," over half of whom were authors, with the rest being divided between mostly political and military types. Although the textual content naturally focuses on each personage selected, the book includes many photographic views of the houses, some of their contents, and a number of photos reserved for insights into the setting and grounds surrounding each house. Certainly there is a great deal of emphasis on the houses and their architectural styles beyond what many previous "literary pilgrimage" books presented. In this, photography played a strong supportive role, almost seeming to induce the viewer to build or restore any structure of his or her own along the same lines.

Dealing with a geographical region or even a particular city or area, some of these literary travel books became identified with an individual or group of writers and the world depicted in their literature. In Lilian Whitings's *Boston Days* (1903), we find a chapter on "Concord and Its Famous Authors" and a chapter on the "Golden Age of Genius and Dawn of the Twentieth Century," or even more narrowly delimited literary regions such as in Winthrop Packard's *Whittier Land* (1904). A number of books and especially pamphlets espoused the more geographic approach, defining the subject within a regional context or, more specifically, within one particular setting alone.

With his book *Literary Pilgrimages of a Naturalist,* Packard sought to present a particular perspective on the literary journey: the journey as seen through the eyes of a naturalist. The book's gilt-decorated cover richly emphasizes his approach, with a house nestled between a background of towering trees and dense shrubbery and an open foreground with pond plants. The photographs, taken by Packard himself, depict the setting of the country home, the valleys or mountains, ponds or lakes, or the rocky ridges of the inland or seacoast. Truly this is the perspective of the hiker-wanderer, the delight of the naturalist, and the book offers insights into the authors by way of these natural wonders—both large and small. Here are the homes and the areas that inspired the authors and poets whom Packard selected.

As historical documents, the guides themselves are of significant value, sometimes less for the accuracy of their information than for what they tell us about which authors were popular, or how particular authors were read, or just what it was readers wanted—or, rather, what publishers imagined their readers wanted. Some volumes are equally important because they contain engravings or descriptions of houses that no longer exist and images of interiors that few were privy to or that have been destroyed by subsequent remodeling.

While some bemoaned the fact that the rise of new technologies displaced the book's primacy, radio, perhaps ironically, became a way of introducing literary tourism and facilitating literary connections through a new medium. In 1939, NBC Blue Network developed a radio program originating in the actual homes of American poets. The producers likened the then "modern" radio pilgrimage to that of the assorted band of adventurous religious travelers described in Geoffrey Chaucer's *Canterbury Tales*—a befitting analogy since secular literary pilgrimages are connected to place in the same way that religious ones are.

Through the magic of radio, the listening audience of the *Pilgrimage of Poetry* traveled to Maine, Alabama, and California, visiting the homes of poets from the American past, as programs were broadcast weekly from these "poetic shrines" from October 15, 1939, to May 26, 1940. The anecdotal

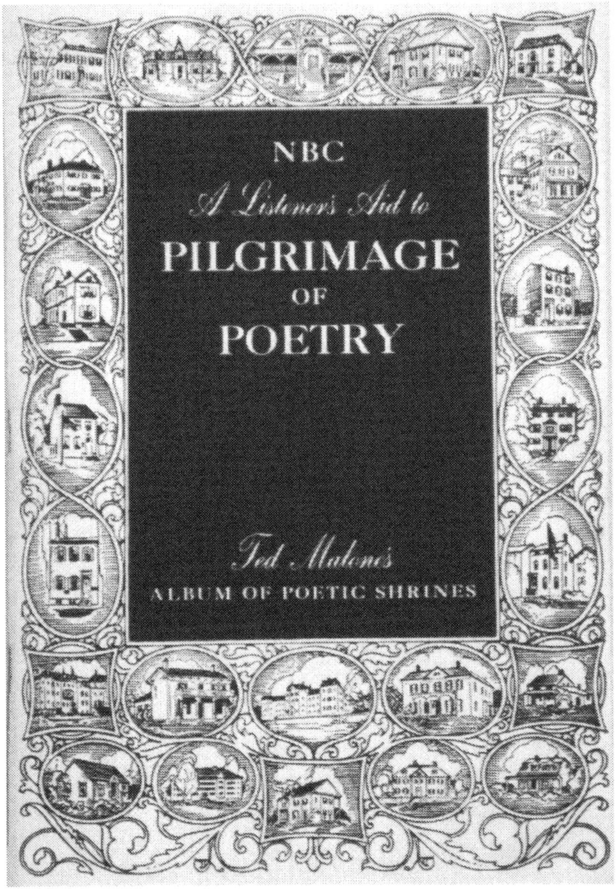


FIGURE 10.1. The guide that accompanied the NBC program *Pilgrimage of Poetry. Photo by Sherry McCamant.*

broadcasts featured the lives of thirty-two poets, including Edgar Allan Poe, Joyce Kilmer, Walt Whitman, Stephen Crane, Sara Teasdale, Ralph Waldo Emerson, and Emily Dickinson. Acknowledging the limitations of radio, as well as the curiosity of its audience, an illustrated album of "poetic shrines" (*A Listener's Aid to Pilgrimage of Poetry: Ted Malone's Album of Poetic Shrines*) was prepared for listeners as a visual aid to the broadcasts (fig. 10.1). The popularity of this program is evidenced by a note on the verso of the title page indicating that there were at least three reprints of the 1939–40 *Album of Poetic Shrines* along with a notation that reduced prices for ordering multiple copies were available on request. Furthermore, the radio program was reintroduced and continued for at least another season under the program title *American Pilgrimage* from October 13, 1940, to May 11, 1941. This time the program included visits to the homes of thirty-one of America's "greatest storytellers," such as Mark Twain, Herman Melville, Harriet Beecher Stowe, Nathaniel Hawthorne, Louisa May Alcott, Thomas Wolf, and Edith Wharton. It too had its own accompanying illustrated listener's guide, *Ted Malone's Mansions of Imagination: A Listener's Aid to American Pilgrimage.* Each listener's guide contained narrative sketches—part biographical and part descriptive—accompanied by a picture that "embodied the spirit" of the pilgrimage and the life and poetry or prose of the author.

The producers tried to translate the life and philosophy of each poet into the atmosphere of the home from which the broadcast was made. They composed the narrative—words, phrases, allusions, and quotations—for the express purpose of fueling the listening audience's interest in the author. This is demonstrated in the following excerpt from the November 3, 1940, broadcast from Herman Melville's home, Arrowhead, as printed in *Mansions of Imagination:*

> "Arrowhead" . . . wide, rambling country home high in the Berkshire Hills . . . once the old inn on the road from Lenox to Pittsfield . . . the dark pines and quiet elms . . . its massive chimney, 144 square feet . . . three great fireplaces . . . watching the flames flicker in the huge fireplace and writing his greatest masterpiece of man's eternal and terrible struggle with the white specter of destruction. . . . Melville's books were read by many and damned by more . . . The plates of *Moby Dick* were destroyed by fire in 1853 . . . after that he abandoned the struggle and wrote little more . . . Thirty years after Herman Melville was dead *Moby Dick* was recognized as one of the greatest books ever written . . . but like most crusaders he had been ahead of his time.[35]

During the November 26, 1939, program from Stephen Crane's Newark, New Jersey, home, a telling excerpt from the *Pilgrimage of Poetry* listener's guide demonstrates that then as now, literary houses were lost to the ravages of time:

> Mulberry Place in Newark, 1871 . . . a fine residential section . . . trim houses . . . bright curtained windows . . . massive doorways . . . carriages at the curb . . . a prosperous Methodist parsonage on a quiet Newark street . . .
>
> . . . Stephen Crane . . . A vivid career . . . newspaper correspondent . . . a great novel written in pain and financial distress . . . fame at twenty-four . . . and a legacy the world will not forget . . . *The Red Badge of Courage* . . .
>
> Mulberry Place in Newark . . . 1939 . . . a dreary tenement . . . windows boarded . . . empty, echoing rooms . . . dirty, disreputable . . . no trace of the happy family of long ago . . . the house with all its memories to go . . . but in its place a playground where children will romp once more . . . A

> fountain . . . in memory of Stephen Crane . . . in memory of a young life richly lived and abruptly ended.[36]

According to the listener's guide introduction, the producers hoped to convey the feeling of being present in these homes. But most vital of all, they told their audience, "We hope to demonstrate how the poetry of each author is related to your life and how a fuller understanding of poetry can give you a fuller understanding and appreciation of living."[37] This keenly captured the appeal of rubbing shoulders with the ghosts of our literary heroes and their haunts.

Just as radio didn't displace Americans' fascination with writers and their homes, neither has television or the Internet. The fascination survives to this day and manifests itself in more recent book publications, newspaper and magazine articles, literary guides and maps, and television and film journeys into the lives and homes of authors (for example, PBS's *American Masters* and *American Experience* series, or Ken Burns's *Mark Twain*), recognizing writers through national landmarks and plaques, and through local, regional, and national organizations that preserve the visible domestic portions of literary heritage. The digital age has provided new and expanded opportunities. The Internet has granted scholars and general readers the opportunity to access literary guidebooks no longer in print and otherwise unavailable to the reader, and has opened a new world of literary tourism by enabling house museums to promote themselves through websites. People can now share their personal experiences of visiting literary sites with an audience worldwide via blogs, zines, chat groups, and all manner of social media. And the development of electronic devices for reading books has sparked new innovations in literary tourism. For example, travel guides accompanying some novels allow the reader to visit sites remotely or gather information for a literary vacation. There are even tour and travel agencies that develop and promote literary tours.

Recent publications continue to offer such guides as companions for the armchair traveler as well as for readers who wish to pay homage in person to those who made great writing and great reading in America by journeying through our country's rich literary heritage. Most contain some background on the authors and tantalizing tidbits to make the visits memorable; some include reviews of their major literary works in relation to their environment, and many are lavishly illustrated with color prints as well as images reproduced from archival materials. In addition, many of the modern literary guides now include information on how to get to the landmarks and when to visit, listing hours of operation if open for public visitation. As with the older versions, contemporary publications vary in their approach and content. Some seek to be all-encompassing, such as B. J. Welborn's 2005 book *Traveling Literary America: A Complete Guide to Literary Landmarks.* Welborn includes more than two hundred homes, museums, exhibits, literary walks, memorials, monuments, and imaginative tributes in nearly all fifty states. Her book has been marketed as a "comprehensive guide to the exciting places where America's literary lions lived, wrote or set their literary masterpieces."[38] Indeed publishers remain invested in the genre. *The Oxford Illustrated Literary Guide to the Unites States,* for instance, was compiled to help travelers find places associated with the lives and works of more than fifteen hundred literary figures across the country, from "colonial times to the present."

By contrast, other works are increasingly specialized—based on a region of the country, an interest of the editor or contributor, or a monograph on a particular writer. For example, Theresa Craig's book *Edith Wharton: A House Full of Rooms; Architecture, Interiors, and Gardens* focuses on Wharton the writer as much as Wharton the designer. Craig has united Wharton's personal history with a discussion—and many photographs—of her homes, as well as the elaborate settings she created for her fictions. Even more specific is *Chrysalis: Willa Cather in Pittsburgh.* This book focuses on the young Willa Cather in a specific city during the time of the emergence of her writing career (1896–1906).[39]

The original purpose of these books on the homes and haunts of American authors and poets remains that of opening a window onto an earlier age. The books demonstrate how the canon of American literature has changed over time, just as comparing historic literary maps can do.[40] As we have come to see, the interests of the writers and publishers of these works helped to enlighten and inform their audiences even to the point of helping to shape the literary canon of successive generations. These literary guidebooks gave insight into an author's life and inspired the reader to embark on a literary pilgrimage, whether imaginary or more or less real. But on the consumer side, we have not fully accounted for how readers used these works as conduits beyond facilitating the idea of an imagined closer connection to their favorite authors. That connection, whether real or not, is delineated by the readers' perception that it was factual and certainly helped to shape their relation to the writer and their interpretation of the writer's work. As a sub-field of literary criticism, an investigation into literary tourism heightens our awareness of these works, and heightened awareness breeds further investigation.

One can safely say that these literary travel books had some impact on helping shape the American literary canon and reader interest. Nevertheless, to tease out the ramifications of that impact and how it altered the readers themselves is a line of inquiry that is certainly in need of much more cross-disciplinary research and investigation both within the field of literary tourism and indeed for those with interests in travel writing and literary biography. Still, the field of literary tourism, at least as it existed in the nineteenth and early twentieth centuries, has to come to grips with the pre-radio, pre-television, pre-computer world of authors and their audiences and the role these literary travel books played for the then emerging American middle-class readers who wanted a keyhole view into the lives of their favorite authors. Furthermore, with literary homes being severely limited in their hours, closed, restructured for other use, or worse, destroyed altogether, the importance of these places needs to be chronicled and honored. Today these original texts can be sources for the cross-disciplinary research now being conducted in the field of literary tourism and for those with interests in travel writing, literary biography, and our literary heritage.

## APPENDIX

### A Bibliography of Guides for Literary Tourists

*A select working bibliography of guides from the nineteenth century to the present.*

Anderson, William. *The World of Louisa May Alcott: A First-Time Glimpse into the Life and Times of Louisa May Alcott, Author of "Little Women."* New York: Harper Perennial, 1995.

Bacon, Edwin M. *Literary Pilgrimages in New England: To the Homes of Famous Makers of American Literature and among Their Haunts and the Scenes of Their Writings.* New York: Silver, Burdett, and Company, 1902.

Bass, Geri, and Eben Bass. *U.S. Guide to Literary Landmarks.* 2nd printing. Coraopolis, Pa.: J. Pohl Associates, 1985.

Beach, Stewart. *Lexington and Concord: In Color.* Photographs by Samuel Chamberlain. New York: Hastings House Publishers, 1976.

Beckwith, Henry L. P., Jr. *Lovecraft's Providence and Adjacent Parts.* West Kingston, R.I.: Donald M. Grant, 1979.

Below, Ida Comstock. *Eugene Field: In His Home.* New York: E. P. Dutton and Company, 1898.

Benedict, Stewart, consultant ed. *The Literary Guide to the United States.* New York: Facts on File, 1981.

Bolton, Sarah K. *Famous American Authors.* New York: Thomas V. Crowell and Company, 1905.

Bonstelle, Jessie, and Marian DeForest, comps. *Little Women Letters.* Boston: Little, Brown, and Company, 1914.

Bradbury, Malcolm, general ed. *The Atlas of Literature.* London: DeAgostini Editions, 1996.

Brooks, Van Wyck, and Otto Bettmann. *Our Literary Heritage: A Pictorial History of the Writer in America.* 3rd printing. New York: E. P. Dutton and Company, 1956.

Brown, Alan. *Literary Levees of New Orleans.* Montgomery, Ala.: Starrhill Press, 1998.

Bruccoli, Matthew J., et al., eds. *The Romantic Egoists.* New York: Charles Scribner's Sons, 1947.

Bullard, F. Lauriston. *Historic Summer Haunts from Newport to Portland.* Boston: Little, Brown, and Company, 1912.

Burke, Michelle Prater. *The Ideals Guide to Literary Places in the U.S.* Nashville: Ideals Publications, 1998.

Butler, Joseph T. *Washington Irving's Sunnyside.* Tarrytown, N.Y.: Sleepy Hollow Restorations, 1974.

Byrne, Kathleen D., and Richard C. Snyder. *Chrysalis: Willa Cather in Pittsburgh, 1896–1906.* Pittsburgh: Historical Society of Western Pennsylvania, 1980.

Capen, Oliver Bronson. *Country Homes of Famous Americans.* New York: Doubleday Page and Company, 1905.

Chamberlin, Samuel. *Longfellow's Wayside Inn: A Camera Impression.* New York: Hastings House Publishers, 1938.

Clarke, Helen Archibald, *The Poets' New England.* New York: Baker and Taylor Company, 1911.

———. *Hawthorne's Country.* Garden City, N.Y.: Doubleday, Page and Company, 1913.

Craig, Theresa. *Edith Wharton: A House Full of Rooms: Architecture, Interiors, and Gardens.* Special Photography by John Bessler. New York: Monacelli Press, 1996.

Curtis, Geo. Wm., Henry T. Tuckerman, George Washington Greene, Charles F. Briggs, George S. Hillard, William C. Bryant, G. W. Peck, Rufus W. Griswold, Parke Godwin, Edward E. Hale and Mrs. C. M. Kirkland, contributors. *Homes of American Authors: Comprising Anecdotal, Personal, and Descriptive Sketches.* New York: G. P. Putnam, 1853.

———. *Homes of American Authors: Comprising Anecdotal, Personal, and Descriptive Sketches.* New York: D. Appleton and Company, 1854.

Cutler, David. *Literary Washington: A Complete Guide to the Literary Life in the Nation's Capital.* 2nd edition. Lanham, Md.: Madison Books, 1992.

Deedy, John. *Literary Places: A Guided Pilgrimage; New York and New England.* Kansas City: Sheed, Andrews and McMeel, 1978.

Eastman, John. *Who Lived Where: A Biographical Guide to Homes and Museums.* New York: Bonanza Books, 1987.

Ehrlich, Eugene, and Gorton Carruth. *The Oxford Illustrated Literary Guide to the United States.* New York: Oxford University Press, 1982.

Eubanks, Georgann. *Literary Trails of the North Carolina Mountains: A Guidebook.* Chapel Hill: University of North Carolina Press, 2007.

Faude, Wilson H. *The Renaissance of Mark Twain's House: Handbook for Restoration.* New York: Larch-Mont, 1978.

Felsen, Gregg. *Tombstones: Seventy-Five Famous People and Their Final Resting Places.* Berkeley: Ten Speed Press, 1996.

Ferlinghetti, Lawrence, and Nancy J. Peters. *Literary San Francisco: A Pictorial History from Its Beginnings to the Present Day.* Philadelphia: Harper and Row Publishers, 1980.

French, Allen. *Old Concord.* Boston: Little, Brown, and Company, 1915.

Gilder, J. L., and J. B. Gilder, eds. *Authors at Home: Personal and Biographical Sketches of Well-Known American Writers.* New York: Cassell and Company, 1888.

Gilman, Arthur, et al. *Poets' Homes: Pen and Pencil Sketches of American Poets and Their Homes.* 2nd series. Boston: D. Lothrop and Company, 1879.

Haas, Irvin. *Historic Homes of American Authors.* Washington, D.C.: Preservation Press, 1991.

Halsey, Francis Whiting, ed. *American Authors and Their Homes: Personal Descriptions and Interviews.* New York: James Pott and Company, 1901. First in a series of three.

———, ed. *Authors of Our Day in Their Homes: Personal Descriptions and Interviews.* New York: James Pott and Company, 1902. Second in a series of three.

———, ed. *Women Authors of Our Day in Their Homes: Personal Descriptions and Interviews.* New York: James Pott and Company, 1903. Third in a series of three.

Hansen, Harry. *Longfellow's New England.* New York: Hastings House, 1972.

Harkins, E. F. *Little Pilgrimages among the Men Who Have Written Famous Books.* 1st series. Boston: L. C. Page and Company, 1902.

Harkins, E. F., and C. H. L. Johnston. *Little Pilgrimages among the Women Who Have Written Famous Books.* Boston: L. C. Page and Company, 1902.

Hatfield, Julia. *The Bryant Homestead-Book by the Idle Scholar.* New York: G. P. Putnam and Son, 1870.

Herron, Don. *The Literary World of San Francisco and Its Environs,* edited by Nancy J. Peters. San Francisco: City Lights Books, 1990.

Howe, M. A. DeWolfe, and Samuel Chamberlain. *Who Lived Here? A Baker's Dozen of Historic New England Houses and Their Occupants.* Boston: Little, Brown, and Company, 1952.

Howells, W. D. *Literary Friends and Acquaintances: A Personal Retrospect of American Authorship.* New York: Harper and Brothers Publishers, 1900.

Hubbard, Elbert, comp. Curtis, George William, Caroline H. Kirkland, Geo. S. Hillard, Chas. F. Briggs, William Cullen Bryant, Elbert Hubbard, Parke Godwin, H. T. Tuckerman, and George W. Greene, contributors. *Little Journeys to The Homes of American Authors.* New York: G. P. Putnam's Sons, 1896.

Jackson, Joseph. *Literary Landmarks of Philadelphia.* Philadelphia: David McKay Company, 1939.

Jerome, Robert D., and Herbert A. Wisbey, Jr., eds. *Mark Twain in Elmira.* Elmira, N.Y.: Mark Twain Society, 1977.

Kaplan, Justin. *Mark Twain and His World.* New York: Simon and Schuster, 1974.

Kennedy, Richard S., ed. *Literary New Orleans: Essays and Meditations.* Baton Rouge: Louisiana University Press, 1992.

Knox, Maxine, and Mary Rodriguez. *Steinbeck's Street: Cannery Row.* San Raphael, Calif.: Presidio Press, 1980.

Kraft, Stephanie. *No Castles on Main Street: American Authors and Their Homes.* New York: Rand McNally and Company, 1979.

Larson, Susan. *The Booklover's Guide to New Orleans.* With additional research by Kevin McCaffrey. Baton Rouge: Louisiana State University Press, 1999.

Leisner, Marcia. *Literary Neighborhoods of New York.* Washington, D.C.: Starrhill Press, 1989.

Levine, Miriam. *A Guide to Writers' Homes in New England.* Cambridge: Applewood Books, 1984.

Longsworth, Polly. *The World of Emily Dickinson.* New York: W. W. Norton and Company, 1990.

Lothrop, Margaret M. *The Wayside: Home of Authors.* New York: American Book Company, 1940.

Lowe, Hilary Iris. *Mark Twain's Homes and Literary Tourism.* Columbia: University of Missouri Press, 2012.

Mabie, Hamilton Wright. *Backgrounds of Literature.* New York: Outlook Company, 1903.

Malone, Ted. *NBC: A Listener's Aid to Pilgrimage of Poetry; Ted Malone's Album of Poetic Shrines.* 4th printing. New York: Columbia University Press for the National Broadcasting Company, 1940.

———. *Ted Malone's Mansions of Imagination Album: A Listener's Aid to American Pilgrimage.* New York: Columbia University Press for the National Broadcasting Company. 1940.

McClatchy, J. D. *American Writers at Home.* New York: Library of America in association with Vendome Press, 2004.

McDermott, Kevin. *Elephant House or, The Home of Edward Gorey.* San Francisco: Pomegranate Communications, 2003.

McIver, Stuart B. *Hemingway's Key West.* Sarasota: Pineapple Press, 1993.

Morrison, Kathleen. *Robert Frost: A Pictorial Chronicle.* New York: Holt, Rinehart, and Winston, 1974.

Packard, Winthrop. *Literary Pilgrimages of a Naturalist.* Boston: Small, Maynard and Company, 1911.

Pickard, Samuel T. *Whittier-Land.* Boston: Houghton Mifflin Company, 1904.

Powers, H. N., et al. *The Homes and Haunts of Our Elder Poets.* With Portraits and illustrations. New York: D. Appleton and Company, 1881.

Premoli-Droulers, Francesca. *Writers' Houses.* New York: Vendome Press, 1995.

Rideing, W. H. *The Boyhood of Living Authors.* New York: Thomas Y. Crowell and Company, 1887.

Rolfe, Lionel. *Literary L.A.* San Francisco: Chronicle Books, 1981.

Schafer, Edith Nalle. *Literary Circles of Washington.* Washington, D.C.: Starrhill Press, 1993.

Scherman, David, and Rosemarie Redlich. *Literary America: A Chronicle of American Writers from 1607–1952 with 173 Photographs of the American Scene That Inspired Them.* New York: Dodd, Mead, and Company, 1952.

Sears, Clara Endicott, comp. *Bronson Alcott's Fruitlands: With "Transcendental Wild Oats" by Louisa May Alcott.* Boston: Houghton Mifflin Company, 1915.

Sherr, Lynn, and Jurate Kazickas. *Susan B. Anthony Slept Here: A Guide to American Women's Landmarks.* New York: Times Books / Random House, 1994.

Shivers, Frank R., Jr. *Maryland Wits and Baltimore Bards: A Literary History with Notes on Washington Writers.* Baltimore: Maclay and Associates, 1985.

Sidney, Margaret. *Old Concord: Her Highways and Byways.* Revised and enlarged Edition. Boston: D. Lothrop Company, 1893.

Smith, A. G. *Historic Houses of New England Coloring Book.* New York: Dover Publications, 1993.

Stoddard, R. H., Arthur Gilman, et al. *Poets' Homes: Pen and Pencil Sketches of American Poets and Their Homes.* 2 vols. Boston: D. Lothrop and Company, 1877 (vol. 1), 1879 (vol. 2).

Stoddard, R. H., et al. *Poets' Homes: Pen and Pencil Sketches of American Poets and Their Homes.* 2 vols. in 1. Boston: D. Lothrop Company, 1879.

Stowell, Robert F. *A Thoreau Gazetteer.* Princeton: Princeton University Press, 1970.

Thum, Marcella. *Exploring Literary America.* New York: Athenaeum, 1979.

Ticknor, Caroline. *Glimpses of Authors.* Boston: Houghton Mifflin Company, 1922.

Van Hulsteyn, Peggy. *Sleeping with Literary Lions: The Booklover's Guide to Bed and Breakfasts.* Golden, Colo.: Fulcrum Publishing, 1997.

Walser, Richard. *Literary North Carolina: A Brief Historical Survey.* Raleigh, N.C.: State Department of Archives and History, 1970.

Ward, Geoffrey C., and Dayton Duncan. Preface by Ken Burns. *Mark Twain: An Illustrated Biography.* New York: Alfred A. Knopf, 2001.

Welborn, B. J. *Traveling Literary America: A Complete Guide to Literary Landmarks.* Lookout Mountain, Tenn.: Jefferson Press, 2005.

Whiting, Lilian. *Boston Days: The City of Beautiful Ideals; Concord, and Its Famous Authors; The Golden Age of Genius / Dawn of the Twentieth Century.* Boston: Little, Brown, and Company, 1903.

Wilson, Rufus Rockwell, and Otilie Erickson Wilson. *New York in Literature: The Story Told in the Landmarks of Town and Country.* Elmira, N.Y.: Primavera Press, 1947.

Wolfe, Theodore F. A. *Literary Shrines: The Haunts of Some Famous American Authors.* 2nd edition. Philadelphia: J. B. Lippincott Company, 1895.

———. *A Literary Pilgrimage: Among the Haunts of Famous British Authors* and *Literary Shrines: The Haunts of Some Famous American Authors.* 2-volume deluxe set. Philadelphia: J. B. Lippincott Company, 1896.

———. *Literary Haunts and Homes: American Authors.* Philadelphia: J. B. Lippincott Company, 1899.

———. *Literary Rambles: At Home and Abroad.* Philadelphia: J. B. Lippincott Company, 1901.

## NOTES

1. Harald Hendrix, ed., *Writers' Houses and the Making of Memories* (New York: Routledge Taylor and Francis, 2008), 15.
2. Julian North, "Literary Biography and the House of the Poet," in *Literary Tourism and Nineteenth-Century Culture,* ed. Nicola J. Watson (Houndmills: Palgrave Macmillan, 2006), 49–62.
3. H. N. Powers et al., *The Homes and Haunts of Our Elder Poets: With Portraits and Illustrations* (New York: D. Appleton and Company, 1881), 67–68.
4. Francis Whiting Halsey points out that besides the improved conditions, authors received another reward: "the personal relation he is made to feel he bears toward his readers . . . usually persons whom the author has never met." It was this relationship that led to increased reading of the biographies of authors and hence the interest the reading public had in the daily pursuits of authors, their methods of work, and their homes. Francis Whiting Halsey, ed., *American Authors and Their Homes: Personal Descriptions and Interviews* (New York: James Pott and Company, 1901), 15.
5. Margaret D. Stetz, "Selling Literary Tourism in *The Bookman,*" in Watson, *Literary Tourism and Nineteenth-Century Culture,* 119–27. *The Bookman* was a British magazine that was distributed in America as well. During the Victorian period it was one of the chief disseminators of information about literary tourism. The main consumers of this monthly periodical were publishers, owners of bookshops, editors, and authors. Among the novelty goods that *The Bookman* sold to this audience was the idea of literary tourism.
6. The Idle Scholar [Julie Hatfield], publisher's notice, *The Bryant Homestead-Book* (New York: G. P. Putnam and Son, 1870), [v] It is interesting to note that Bryant's verse helped to inspire the nineteenth-century land conservation movement. Bryant served as editor and publisher of the *New York Evening Post* for fifty years. As a passionate conservationist and horticulturalist, he used his editorials to rally support for what was to become New York's Central Park.
7. Francis Whiting Halsey, introduction to *Women Authors of Our Day and Their Homes* (New York: James Pott and Company, 1903), 6–7.
8. Mark Twain, *Tom Sawyer Abroad* (New York: Charles L. Webster and Company, 1894), 110.
9. Wayne R. Kime, *Pierre M. Irving and Washington Irving: Collaboration in Life and Letters* (Waterloo, Ont.: Wilfrid Laurier University Press, 1977), 151.
10. Halsey, preface to *Women Authors of Our Day,* viii.
11. Paul Westover, "How America 'Inherited' Literary Tourism," in Watson, *Literary Tourism and Nineteenth-Century Culture,* 191.
12. Halsey, *American Authors and Their Homes,* 16.
13. Alison Booth, "Author Country: Longfellow, the Brontës, and Anglophone Homes and Haunts," *Érudit* 48 (November 2007): 1–20.
14. Ezra Greenspan, *George Palmer Putnam: Representative American Publisher* (University Park: Pennsylvania State University Press, 2000); for Putnam's comparison of his book to Howett's in a letter soliciting Ralph Waldo Emerson to be included in the volume (G. P. Putnam to Ralph Waldo Emerson, April 7, 1852, Houghton Library, Harvard University), see 283n73.
15. Greenspan, *George Palmer Putnam,* 269; also see the corresponding endnote, 283n74.
16. George William Curtis et al., preface to *Homes of American Authors: Comprising Anecdotal, Personal, and Descriptive Sketches* (New York: G. P. Putnam, 1853), iii–iv.
17. For further information on the publishing history and contributions to American culture, see Greenspan, *George Palmer Putnam;* Michael Winship, *American Literary Publishing in the Mid-Nineteenth Century: The Business of Ticknor and Fields* (Cambridge: Cambridge University Press, 1995), 191–92; and the Wikipedia article "Daniel Lothrop," http://en.wikipedia.org.

18. Greenspan, *George Palmer Putnam,* 271.
19. Geoffrey Ashall Glaister provides a definition of chiaroscuro printing in *Glaister's Glossary of the Book,* 2nd ed. (London: George Allen and Unwin, 1979), 94: "Chiaroscuro: properly *chiaro-oscuro,* meaning light and dark, and the name for the single-colour wood engravings printed from successive blocks of wood for solid masses of lighter or darker shades. A key block for the darkest tone is printed first followed by from one to three tint blocks to add either light shades of the same colour or tones of a different colour."
20. Daniel Francis McGrath, "American Colorplate Books, 1800–1900" (Ph.D. diss., University of Michigan, 1966), 27.
21. This edition is also of importance because in the chapter on Concord's literary residents, Thoreau's Walden experiment is described one year before Thoreau published his own account, making this the first description of Thoreau at Walden published in a book. The reference, which appears on pages 247–48 of the 1853 edition of Curtis et al., *Homes of American Authors,* reads: "Thoreau lives in the berry-pastures upon a bank over Walden Pond, and in little house of his own building. One pleasant summer afternoon a small party of us helped him raise it—a bit of life as Arcadian as any at Brook Farm." According to Kevin MacDonnell, a literary rare book collector and a Mark Twain scholar, the Emerson article is credited to George William Curtis, who, interestingly enough, helped Thoreau raise his cabin along with Alcott, Channing, Emerson, and four others. Kevin MacDonnell, "Collecting Henry David Thoreau," *Firsts Magazine,* July–August and September 1999, 50.
22. It is interesting to note that in 1883, Lothrop purchased The Wayside (the only home owned by Nathaniel Hawthorne), where he entertained guests from both sides of the ocean. "Daniel Lothrop," wikipedia.org.
23. According to Paul McKenna, the *Little Journeys* were originally conceived by Hubbard's sometime partner Harry P. Taber in 1895. Hubbard was about to make a tour of Europe and thought he should write a book about it for publication upon his return. Taber suggested that he instead keep a journal of visits to homes of famous European authors. This he did, and when Hubbard got back, Taber and Hubbard unsuccessfully pitched the manuscript to commercial publishers. The duo created a mock-up of the book on printing equipment that Taber had acquired and resubmitted it. This time Putnam accepted it and contracted with Hubbard to write one "little journey" a month, which continued until 1900, when Hubbard acquired the rights to publish his little journeys on his own. Paul McKenna, *A History and Bibliography of the Roycroft Printing Shop,* 2nd ed. (Grand Island, N.Y.: Tona Graphics, 1996).
24. Publisher's note in *Little Journeys to the Homes of American Authors,* comp. Elbert Hubbard (New York: G. P. Putnam's Sons, 1896). Hubbard was also one of the contributors to the volume.
25. See Scott E. Casper, *Constructing American Lives: Biography and Culture in Nineteenth-Century America* (Chapel Hill: University of North Carolina Press, 1999), in which biography is shown to have been an important medium prior to radio and television in helping to shape an individual's public character, to define our national identity, and to give standing to American literary practices and reputations in a transatlantic world of letters.
26. McKenna, *A History and Bibliography.* In Hubbard's article on himself written for *The Cosmopolitan* (January 1902), Hubbard indicates it was he who first approached George Haven Putnam, who was "induced to issue the periodical [*Little Journeys*] at a venture for one year. . . . [T]he scheme seemed to meet with success . . . [and] the subscription reached nearly a thousand in six months" (311).
27. Ibid., 58.
28. Thomas F. Wolfe, *Literary Shrines: The Haunts of Some Famous American Authors* (Philadelphia: J. B. Lippincott Company, 1895), 201.
29. Thomas F. Wolfe, preface to *Literary Haunts and Homes: American Authors* (Philadelphia: J. B. Lippincott Company, 1899), 3.

30. Claire Whitcomb, "Sarah Orne Jewett: Discovering a Writer's Heart," *Victoria,* September 1996, 78.
31. This manuscript letter was found inside a copy of *American Authors and Their Homes* in my collection on books of the homes and haunts of American writers.
32. J. L. and J. B. Gilder, eds., "Editor's Note," in *Authors at Home: Personal and Biographical Sketches of Well-Known American Writers* (New York: A. Wessels Company, 1902).
33. Edwin Bacon, "The Scheme," in *Literary Pilgrimages in New England: To the Homes of Famous Makers of American Literature and among Their Haunts and the Scenes of Their Writings* (New York: Silver, Burdett, and Company, 1902), 2.
34. Two advertisements appearing at the end of Bacon's *Literary Pilgrimages in New England* demonstrate the publisher's reputation for educational books and purposes. The first one lists the "Leading Books for Higher Schools," also published by Silver, Burdett, and Company. The second advertisement is for *Historic Pilgrimages in New England* (1898), a companion volume to *Literary Pilgrimages,* also by Edwin Bacon, in which it is suggested that the book is "For School Libraries and Reading Circles. . . . For Supplemental Reading in higher grades it is a mine of interest and delightful instructiveness."
35. Ted Malone, *Ted Malone's Mansions of Imagination Album: A Listener's Aid to American Pilgrimage* (New York: Columbia University Press for the National Broadcasting Company, 1940), [12].
36. *A Listener's Aid to Pilgrimage of Poetry: Ted Malone's Album of Poetic Shrines* (New York: Columbia University Press for the National Broadcasting Company, 1940), [18]. Ted Malone, whose legal name was Frank Alden Russell, broadcast on all commercial networks for five decades. A leading program was *Between the Bookends,* which began in 1929. According to Malone's obituary printed in the *New York Times* (October 27, 1989), he was assigned to read poetry for fifteen minutes. He agreed but, embarrassed by the task, declined to use his own name. Another announcer called him Ted Malone, and a national personality was born.
37. Introduction, ibid., iv.
38. Publisher's note on back cover of B. J. Welborn, *Traveling Literary America: A Complete Guide to Literary Landmarks* (Lookout Mountain, Tenn.: Jefferson Press, 2005).
39. Kathleen D. Byrne and Richard C. Snyder, *Chrysalis: Willa Cather in Pittsburgh* (Pittsburgh: Historical Society of Western Pennsylvania, 1980).
40. The August 1993–January 1994 Library of Congress exhibition *Language of the Land: Journeys into Literary America* (with its accompanying exhibition catalog, now an LOC online exhibition) presented maps printed from the 1930s onward covering the major regions of the country: New England and the Northeast, Mid-Atlantic, South, Midwest, West, and West Coast. These "literary" maps—a map being the quintessential instrument for the tourist—demonstrate how the canon of American literature had changed over the years, if indeed the whole concept of literary canon can remain intact, given the attack on it in the 1980s on the grounds that many women and minority writers were excluded from the traditional formulation, and with the emergence of many a previously suppressed literary text.

# *Notes on Contributors*

Rebecca Rego Barry is the editor of *Fine Books & Collections* magazine. She earned a dual bachelor's degree in English and magazine journalism from Syracuse University, as well as a master's degree in book history from Drew University, where she then stayed on to work in the library's preservation department and university archives for several years. Her writing has appeared in *Preservation, American Libraries, Book History,* and *The Millions.*

Susann Bishop is an avid collector of literary tour guides, and the managing director of All in One Tours & Cruises. She has presented at the Northeast Modern Language Association conference on literary guides. Her article "Haunting the Hearths of the Muse" was published in the September 1997 issue of *BIBLIO,* and she and her husband co-wrote an article, "An Ongoing Spirit of Serenity: Acorn Cottage and Oak Acre Gardens," which was published in the Spring 2015 issue of *American Bungalow.*

Ben De Bruyn is associate professor of comparative literature at Maastricht University, the Netherlands. He is the author of the first book-length overview of Wolfgang Iser's reception theory (2012) and co-editor of *Literature Now: Key Terms and Methods for Literary History* (2016). He has published on reading practices and consumer culture as well as posthumanism and literature's response to environmental issues in journals such as *Oxford Literary Review, Critique,* and *Orbis Litterarum.*

Jennifer Harris is an associate professor in the Department of English Language and Literature at the University of Waterloo, Canada. She is the co-editor of the 2012 Norton critical edition of *The Coquette and The Boarding School,* as well as *The Oprah Phenomenon* (2007). Past president of the Canadian Association for American Studies, and a former Fulbright scholar, Harris has also published over two dozen essays and book chapters in venues ranging from *African American Review* and *Legacy* to *Canadian Literature.*

Erin Hazard is a lecturer in art and architectural history at Illinois Institute of Technology. She has taught at Western Washington University and the University of Illinois at Chicago. Her work has appeared in *Nineteenth Century Studies, Morrissey: Fandom, Representation, and Identities, Literary Tourism and Nineteenth-Century Culture* and *Art History.* She has been working on a book titled *The Attraction of the American Author's House.*

CAROLINE HELLMAN is an associate professor of English at City Tech, City University of New York. In 2011 she was a Fulbright scholar at the University of Antwerp. She is the author of "Domesticity and Design," in *American Women's Lives and Literature: Stowe, Alcott, Cather, and Wharton Writing Home* (2011), and *The Children of the Raven and the Whale: Visions and Revisions in American Literature* (forthcoming 2017), along with chapters and articles on other facets of American letters. She is also interested in public education policy and remediation reform.

HILARY IRIS LOWE is director of the Center for Public History and an assistant professor of history at Temple University. Her first book, *Mark Twain's Homes and Literary Tourism,* came out in 2012, and her next book examines the preservation movement in the United States, with special attention to the histories of gender and sexuality. She is also engaged in writing the administrative history of the John Fitzgerald Kennedy National Historic Site.

MICHELLE MCCLELLAN is an assistant professor in the Department of History and the Residential College at the University of Michigan–Ann Arbor. A board member of the Ultimate History Project, she is also working on a book about Laura Ingalls Wilder and the appeal Wilder has had among Americans since the 1930s. An active public historian, McClellan has worked in a house museum, curated exhibits, and supervised preservation projects. She received a B.A. from Amherst College and a Ph.D. in American history from Stanford University.

MARA SCANLON is a professor of English at the University of Mary Washington. She is co-editor of the collection *Poetry and Dialogism: Hearing Over* (2014), and her articles have been published in *College Literature; LIT: Literature, Interpretation, Theory; Bucknell Review; World Literature Today; Virginia Review of Asian Studies; Asian American Novelists; The Writer's Chronicle;* and *Approaches to Teaching H.D.'s Poetry and Prose.* Her professional work includes a collaborative multi-university National Endowment for the Humanities Grant awarded for a project in the digital humanities called "Looking for Whitman: The Poetry of Place in the Life and Work of Walt Whitman."

KLARA-STEPHANIE SZLEZÁK is a postdoctoral researcher and lecturer in American studies at the University of Passau, Germany. She received a Ph.D. in American studies from the University of Regensburg, Germany. Her first monograph, *"Canonized in History": Literary Tourism and Nineteenth-Century Writers' Houses in New England,* appeared in late 2015, as did her first co-edited essay collection, *Referentiality and the Films of Woody Allen.* In addition to visual culture studies and film studies, her conference papers, publications, and research interests are focused on literary tourism and the intersections of material culture studies, memory studies, and museum studies.

# Index